Fundamentals of Engineering (F.E.) Examination

(Previously known as Engineer-in-Training
Examination)

A Study Guide for the Licensed Professional Engineer Examination

Eugene L. Boronow, M.E.E., P.E.

ARCO PUBLISHING, INC.
New York

Published by Arco Publishing, Inc.
215 Park Avenue South, New York, N.Y. 10003

Library of Congress Cataloging-in-Publication Data

Boronow, Eugene L.
    Fundamentals of Engineering (F.E.) examination.

    "Previously known as Engineer-in-training."
    1. Engineering—Problems, exercises, etc.
2. Engineering—Examinations, questions, etc.
I. Title.
TA159.B67   1986   620'.0076   85-20162
ISBN 0-668-05721-1 (Paper Edition)

Printed in the United States of America

CONTENTS

PREFACE

This book is designed to help you bring your skills up to their very best when you take the Fundamentals of Engineering examination. This examination, which was known as the Engineer-in-Training examination, represents a significant first step toward qualifying for the Professional Engineer's License.

The early sections of this book explain the practical importance of this license, describe the rationale and the content of the Fundamentals of Engineering examination, and outline the methods by which a serious candidate can embark on a successful study program.

The main sections of this book present two typical Fundamentals of Engineering examinations in their entirety. Each examination includes a 4-hour Morning Section (which contains 140 compulsory problems), and a 4-hour Afternoon Section (which contains 100 problems, of which 70 are required). These 480 engineering problems cover each of the engineering disciplines that constitute the actual examination, with the same numerical distribution, and with a comparable level of complexity and difficulty. Complete solutions have been worked out for each problem, and are presented logically and clearly, with explanations as necessary, in order to facilitate independent study.

The author gratefully acknowledges the assistance given to him in the preparation of this book, and wishes to express his appreciation to Prof. Edward Reitz, P.E., Prof. Jacques Benveniste, P.E., Walter Boronow, P.E., William Adler, P.E., Albin Litty, William Shao, Steven Kiefer, Benjamin Boronow, and Susan Hite.

I. HOW IMPORTANT IS THE PROFESSIONAL ENGINEER'S LICENSE?

Registration and licensing has become vitally important and increasingly necessary for virtually all categories of engineers. This was not always true.

The licensing process provides a measure of assurance that an engineer who is responsible for a given project will in no way jeopardize the safety, health, or well-being of the general public. The criteria for licensing therefore attempt to measure the validity and sufficiency of an engineer's education, training, experience, judgment, analytic ability, and overall competence. At this time, roughly one-third of the approximately 1.5 million engineers who practice in the United States are registered under state laws. By such registration, the state legally acknowledges that an engineer has demonstrated an acceptable level of overall competence, and is duly qualified to practice as a professional engineer.

Many years ago, P.E. licenses were only required for a relatively small group of engineers—namely, those who were responsible for work on construction-oriented projects such as bridges, dams, sewers, tunnels, railways, highways, structures, power stations, etc. Licensing was therefore important to most civil engineers, and to only a few electrical and mechanical engineers. With the passage of time, however, the concept of public protection and public safety has steadily expanded. It now includes such engineering specialties as air and water pollution control, urban planning and development, agriculture, fire protection, industrial, manufacturing, metallurgical, nuclear, electronics, chemical, environmental control, ceramics, plastics, petroleum, mining, avionics, acoustics, and aerospace.

Most city, state, and federal government agencies now require a professional engineer's license for all its employees who perform responsible engineering duties of any kind. Furthermore, since industry is becoming increasingly liable for product design, product performance, and environmental damage, they are increasingly requiring that responsible engineers in industry must have a P.E. license. This requirement is formulated in the positive sense in order to assure the maintenance of high professional standards, and in the negative sense in order to establish a measure of legal protection with respect to technology issues that may be brought to court. Most states have enacted legislation that virtually prohibits non-licensed engineers from engaging in private practice, from providing engineering consultation, from performing engineering services, from entering into contracts, or from submitting designs, plans, or specifications for approval. Most engineering colleges now require a P.E. license for any professor or instructor who teaches engineering courses. This trend is also being adopted by institutions offering degrees in Engineering Technology and in Engineering Science.

Therefore, the P.E. license provides engineers with the following clear advantages:

1. It establishes a well-defined level of professional recognition.
2. It is the only avenue by which an engineer can work on most projects which affect public safety.
3. It is the only avenue by which most states will legitimately permit an engineer to do consulting work.
4. It affords job opportunities that are simply not available to non-licensed engineers, and that usually command higher rates of pay.
5. It connotes a sense of professionalism and prestige.

In today's environment, any engineer who chooses not to obtain the P.E. license has chosen to impose a severe handicap on his or her future professional career.

II. HOW IS THE PROFESSIONAL ENGINEER'S LICENSE CONFERRED?

The licensing of professional engineers is not accomplished on a national basis. Rather, each state or territory of the United States has the autonomous authority to confer its own Professional Engineer's License, to formulate its own eligibility qualifications, and to insist that its license be mandatory for all persons performing responsible engineering work within its territorial jurisdiction. Each state establishes its own Board of Registration which carefully administers the licensing process. Therefore, an engineer who plans to work in several states must obtain a separate license from each of these states. Fortunately, the principle of reciprocity usually applies, and most states, after careful review, will grant their own license to an applicant who has previously qualified for a license in another state.

Although the qualifications required by each state or territory are different, there is a marked degree of similarity and standardization. The precise requirements imposed by each state may be obtained from the individual sources presented in Section V on page 9. The generic requirements, in chronological order, are:

1. The satisfactory completion of a 4-year educational program in an approved branch of engineering leading to the Bachelor's degree, conferred by an institution accredited by the Accreditation Board for Engineering and Technology (ABET), previously known as the Engineering Council for Professional Development (ECPD).
2. Taking and passing the Fundamentals of Engineering examination (previously known as the Engineer-in-Training examination).
3. Performing a given number of years of increasingly responsible engineering work at satisfactory professional levels.
4. Taking and passing the Principles and Practice of Engineering examination.

Most states are reasonably flexible and permit a certain amount of substitution of valid experience for education, or vice versa. However, the Boards of Registration can be expected to review all qualifications with meticulous care before declaring a candidate eligible to take each written examination.

Most candidates take the Fundamentals of Engineering examination shortly after obtaining the Bachelor's degree in Engineering. A few candidates take this examination later in their career. Occasionally, however, an eminent engineer with more than 20 years of high-level, responsible engineering experience applies for a license, at which time some state boards may exempt such a candidate from taking the Fundamentals of Engineering examination, provided that his or her qualifications and credentials are impeccable.

In general, upon showing satisfactory evidence of acceptable education and experience, and upon demonstrating satisfactory performance in both written examinations, the candidate will then be awarded the Professional Engineer's License by the cognizant State Board of Registration.

III. WHAT IS THE ROLE OF THE NATIONAL COUNCIL OF ENGINEERING EXAMINERS?

As described in Section II, each state or territory has the authority to establish its own eligibility criteria for the Professional Engineer's License which it confers. This authority includes devising and administering its own written examinations. The question then arises as to the role of a national body such as the National Council of Engineering Examiners (NCEE).

Since most states developed eligibility criteria that were quite comparable and often identical, it became evident that a great deal of redundancy and expense was involved when each of some 55 state or territorial Boards of Registration had to devise and administer two separate examinations, each given twice a year. The concept of using standardized nationwide engineering examinations became attractive to more and more states. At the time of this writing, it is understood that all states and territories, with the sole exception of Illinois, employ the National Council of Engineering Examiners as their agency for devising and preparing the required written examinations.

However, each state or territory continues to retain its sole authority to formulate its own criteria for evaluating eligibility to take the examinations, as well as its own criteria for evaluating satisfactory performance on the examinations. For further detailed information on the role of this national agency, or on the examinations they prepare, the candidate is advised to write directly to the National Council of Engineering Examiners, P. O. Box 1686, Clemson, South Carolina, 29633-1686.

IV. ALL ABOUT THE FUNDAMENTALS OF ENGINEERING EXAMINATION

A. What Is It?

The Fundamentals of Engineering examination is the first of two 8-hour examinations that are required for the P.E. license. This first examination is designed to evaluate a candidate's basic understanding of mathematics and the physical sciences, and his or her ability to apply these fundamentals to the solution of engineering problems. This examination is the first significant step toward attaining the professional engineer's license.

B. Who Takes This Examination?

Eligibility is determined solely by each State Board of Registration. Qualifications differ from state to state, but on the whole they are reasonably comparable. The fundamental requirement is generally a Bachelor's degree in Engineering from an ABET accredited institution. Some states permit engineering seniors to take this examination just prior to graduation. A few states permit candidates with a degree in Engineering Technology or in Engineering Science to take the examination. Most states permit some measure of substitution of demonstrably valid engineering experience for engineering education. The final evaluation rests with the particular State Board of Registration whose license is sought.

One interesting sidelight on eligibility may be noted, however. Suppose a candidate's credentials are deemed insufficient by his or her home state to qualify the candidate to take the Fundamentals of Engineering examination, but a neighboring state would consider him or her to be qualified. The candidate might then apply for the P.E. license in the neighboring state, and take the examination. If he or she is able to pass the examination, and if he or she is eventually granted a license from the neighboring state, the candidate's home state would probably grant him or her a license at that time based on reciprocity. In fact, once such a person passes the Fundamentals of Engineering examination, his or her home state can be expected to give full recognition to this status.

C. Who Gives the Examination?
When and Where?

The Fundamentals of Engineering examination is given twice a year (usually in April and October) by the particular State Board whose license is being sought. Each state will designate the exact location where the examination will be held.

D. The Examination Format and
Disciplines Covered

The Fundamentals of Engineering examination is an open-book, open-handbook, open-notes examination in which a slide rule or calculator is not only permitted but actually required. The total examination consists of a 4-hour Morning Section, a lunch break, and a 4-hour Afternoon Section. All questions are posed in a multiple-choice format, requiring the candidate to designate the correct answer from among five possible choices.

The Morning Section consists of 140 questions in 13 specific categories, namely: Electrical Circuits, Statics, Dynamics, Mechanics of Materials, Fluid Mechanics, Thermodynamics, Mathematics, Chemistry, Computer Programming, Mathematical Modeling of Engineering Systems, Engineering Economics, Materials Science, and Structure of Matter. All 140 questions in this Morning Section are to be answered.

The Afternoon Section requires that a total of 70 questions be answered. The first 50 questions are compulsory, and are subdivided into four general categories, namely: Engineering Mechanics (Statics, Dynamics, and Mechanics of Materials), Mathematics, Electrical Circuits, and Engineering Economics. The remainder of the Afternoon Section requires that the candidate answer 10 questions in each of two categories, these two to be selected from among the following five categories: Computer Programming, Electronics and Electrical Machinery, Fluid Mechanics, Mechanics of Materials, and Thermodynamics/Heat Transfer.

E. How Is the Examination Scored?

The Morning Section questions comprise 50 percent of the total grade, and the Afternoon Section questions comprise the remaining 50 percent. Within each section, every question has equal weight, and only the correct answers are counted. No deduction is made for incorrect answers. The raw score so obtained is then modified by a normalizing factor that takes into account the degree of difficulty of this particular examination as it relates to previous examinations of the same type.

V. WHERE TO FILE FOR THIS EXAMINATION

Each candidate for the P.E. license is required to file an application with the appropriate State Board of Registration or Examiners for Professional Engineers. A listing of all the cognizant Boards for every state and territory in the U.S.A., including the address, the telephone number, and the name of the contact person in charge, is presented below. Up-dated listings are published periodically by the National Council of Engineering Examiners, P. O. Box 1686, Clemson, South Carolina 29633-1686.

ALABAMA: State Board of Registration for Professional Engineers and Land Surveyors, Suite 212, 750 Washington Avenue, Montgomery 36130.
Sarah E. Hines, Executive Secretary, Telephone: (205) 261-5568.

ALASKA: State Board of Registration for Architects, Engineers and Land Surveyors, Mail: Pouch D (State Office Building, 9th Floor), Juneau 99811.
Susan C. Hendrix, Licensing Examiner, Telephone: (907) 465-2540.

ARIZONA: State Board of Technical Registration, 1645 West Jefferson Street, Suite 140, Phoenix 85007.
Ronald W. Dalrymple, Executive Director, Telephone: (602) 255-4053.

ARKANSAS: State Board of Registration for Professional Engineers and Land Surveyors, Mail: P. O. Box 2541, Little Rock 72203 (Twin City Bank Building, Suite 700, North Little Rock 72114).
Kirby Smith III, Secretary-Treasurer, Telephone: (501) 371-2517.

CALIFORNIA: The Board of Registration for Professional Engineers and Land Surveyors, 1006 Fourth Street, 6th Floor, Sacramento 95814.
G. Harrison Hilt, P.E., Executive Secretary, Telephone: (916) 445-5544.

COLORADO: State Board of Registration for Professional Engineers and Professional Land Surveyors, 600-B State Services Building, 1525 Sherman Street, Denver 80203.
Susan Miller, Program Administrator, Telephone: (303) 866-2396.

CONNECTICUT: State Board of Registration for Professional Engineers and Land Surveyors, The State Office Building, Room G-3A, 165 Capitol Avenue, Hartford 06106.
John J. Moran, P.E., Administrator, Telephone: (203) 566-3386.

DELAWARE: Delaware Association of Professional Engineers, 2005 Concord Pike, Wilmington 19803.
Margaret E. Wise, Executive Secretary, Telephone: (302) 656-7311.

DISTRICT OF COLUMBIA: Board of Registration for Professional Engineers, 614 H Street, N.W., Room 910, Washington 20001.
George Abraham, P.E., Executive Secretary, Telephone: (202) 727-7454.

FLORIDA: State Board of Professional Engineers, 130 North Monroe Street, Talla-hassee 32301.
Allen "Rex" Smith, Jr., Executive Director, Telephone: (904) 488-9912.

GEORGIA: State Board of Registration for Professional Engineers and Land Sur-veyors, 166 Pryor Street, SW, Atlanta 30303.
Thomas M. Wilson, P.E., Executive Director, Telephone: (404) 656-3926.

GUAM: Territorial Board of Registration for Professional Engineers, Architects and Land Surveyors, Department of Public Works, Government of Guam, P. O. Box 2950, Agana 96910.
Carl J. C. Aguon, P.E., Chairman, Telephone: (671) 646-8643.

HAWAII: State Board of Registration for Professional Engineers, Architects, Land Surveyors and Landscape Architects, P. O. Box 3469, (1010 Richards Street), Honolulu 96801.
George M. Arine, Executive Secretary, Telephone: (808) 548-7637.

IDAHO: Board of Professional Engineers and Land Surveyors, 842 La Cassia Drive, Boise 83705.
R. W. Underkofler, P.E., Executive Secretary, Telephone: (208) 334-3860.

ILLINOIS: Department of Registration and Education, Professional Engineers' Examining Committee, 320 West Washington, 3rd Floor, Springfield 62786.
Beth Wilkin, Unit Manager, Telephone: (217) 782-0177.

INDIANA: State Board of Registration for Professional Engineers and Land Sur-veyors, Regulated Occupations and Professional Service Bureau, 1021 State Office Building, 100 North Senate Avenue, Indianapolis 46204.
Gene Snowden, Executive Director, Telephone: (317) 232-1840.

IOWA: State Board of Engineering Examiners, Capitol Complex, 1209 East Court Avenue, Des Moines 50319.
Patricia Peters, Executive Secretary, Telephone: (515) 281-5602.

KANSAS: State Board of Technical Professions, 214 West Sixth St., 2nd Floor, Topeka 66603.
Betty Rose, Executive Secretary, Telephone: (913) 296-3053.

KENTUCKY: State Board of Registration for Professional Engineers and Land Sur-veyors, Rt. 3, 96-5, (Kentucky Engineering Center), Millville Road, Frankfort 40601.
Larry S. Perkins, Executive Director, Telephone: (502) 564-2680 and 564-2681.

LOUISIANA: State Board of Registration for Professional Engineers and Land Sur-veyors, 1055 St. Charles Avenue, Suite 415, New Orleans 70130.
Paul L. Landry, P.E., Executive Secretary, Telephone: (504) 568-8450.

MAINE: State Board of Registration for Professional Engineers, State House, Station 92, Augusta 04333.
Daniel Webster, Jr., Secretary, Telephone: (207) 289-3236.

MARYLAND: State Board of Registration for Professional Engineers, 501 St. Paul Place, Room 902, Baltimore 21202.
William J. Moore, P.E., L.S., Executive Secretary, Telephone: (301) 659-6322.

MASSACHUSETTS: State Board of Registration of Professional Engineers and of Land Surveyors, Room 1512, Leverett Saltonstall Building, 100 Cambridge Street, Boston 02202.
Robert W. Hall, P.E., Secretary, Telephone: (617) 727-3055.

MICHIGAN: Board of Professional Engineers, P. O. Box 30018, (611 West Ottawa), Lansing 48909.
Jack C. Sharpe, Administrative Secretary, Telephone: (517) 373-3880.

MINNESOTA: State Board of Registration for Architects, Engineers, Land Surveyors and Landscape Architects, Room 162, Metro Square Building, St. Paul 55101.
Lowell E. Torseth, Executive Secretary, Telephone: (612) 296-2388.

MISSISSIPPI: State Board of Registration for Professional Engineers and Land Surveyors P. O. Box 3, (200 South President Street, Ste. 516), Jackson 39205.
Rosemary Brister, Executive Director, Telephone: (601) 354-7241.

MISSOURI: Board of Architects, Professional Engineers and Land Surveyors, P. O. Box 184, (3523 North Ten Mile Drive), Jefferson City 65102.
Shirley Nixon, Executive Director, Telephone: (314) 751-2334.

MONTANA: State Board of Professional Engineers and Land Surveyors, Department of Commerce, 1424 9th Avenue, Helena 59620-0407.
Joan Haubein, Administrative Secretary, Telephone: (406) 444-4285.

NEBRASKA: State Board of Examiners for Professional Engineers and Architects, P. O. Box 94751, (301 Centennial Mall, South), Lincoln 68509.
Arthur Duerschner, Arch., Executive Director, Telephone: (402) 471-2021, or 471-2407.

NEVADA: State Board of Registered Professional Engineers and Land Surveyors, 1755 East Plum Lane, Ste. 102, Reno 89502.
Elizabeth Hykes, Acting Executive Secretary, Telephone: (702) 329-1955.

NEW HAMPSHIRE: State Board of Professional Engineers, Storrs Street, Concord 03301.
Sue Ann Sargent, Executive Secretary, Telephone: (603) 271-2219.

NEW JERSEY: State Board of Professional Engineers and Land Surveyors, 1100 Raymond Boulevard, Room 317, Newark 07102.
Cathleen A. McCoy, Executive Secretary-Director, Telephone: (201) 648-2660.

NEW MEXICO: State Board of Registration for Professional Engineers and Land Surveyors, P. O. Box 4847, (Maya Building, Suite A, 440 Cerrillos Road), Santa Fe 87502.
Eva A. VanderSys, Secretary, Telephone: (505) 827-9940.

NEW YORK: State Board for Engineering and Land Surveying, The State Education Department, Cultural Education Center, Madison Avenue, Albany 12230.
Douglas C. Hasbrouk, P.E., Executive Secretary, Telephone: (518) 474-3846.

NORTH DAKOTA: State Board of Registration for Professional Engineers and Land Surveyors, P. O. Box 1357, (420 Avenue B East), Bismarck 58502.
Laverne L. Zink, P.E., Executive Secretary, Telephone: (701) 258-0786.

NORTHERN MARIANA ISLANDS: Board of Professional Licensing, P. O. Box 55 CHRB, Saipan, CM 96950.
Pedro Sasamoto, P.E.

OHIO: State Board of Registration for Professional Engineers and Surveyors, 65 South Front Street, Room 302, Columbus 43266-0314.
Joseph J. De Jonghe, P.E., Executive Secretary, Telephone: (614) 466-8948.

OKLAHOMA: State Board of Registration for Professional Engineers and Land Surveyors, Oklahoma Engineering Center, Room 120, 201 N.E. 27th Street, Oklahoma City, 73105.
Norma Unruh, Executive Secretary, Telephone: (405) 521-2874.

OREGON: State Board of Engineering Examiners, Department of Commerce, 403 Labor and Industries Building, Salem 97310.
Edward D. Graham, PLS, Executive Secretary, Telephone: (503) 378-4180.

PENNSYLVANIA: State Registration Board for Professional Engineers, Mail: P. O. Box 2649, (Transportation and Safety Building, 6th Floor, Commonwealth Avenue and Forester Street), Harrisburg 17120-2649.
J. Robert Kline, Administrative Assistant, Telephone: (717) 783-7049.

PUERTO RICO: Board of Examiners of Engineers, Architects, and Surveyors, Box 3271, (Tanca Street, 261, Comer Tetuan), San Juan 00904.
Carmen Ramirez Vega, Director, Examining Boards, Telephone: (809) 722-2121.

RHODE ISLAND: State Board of Registration for Professional Engineers and Land Surveyors, 100 North Main Street, Providence 02903.
Agnes R. Smith, Administrative Assistant, Telephone: (401) 277-2565.

SOUTH CAROLINA: State Board of Registration for Professional Engineers and Land Surveyors, P. O. Drawer 50408, 2221 Devine Street, Suite 404, Columbia 29250.
Mary M. Law, Agency Director, Telephone: (803) 758-2855.

SOUTH DAKOTA: State Commission of Engineering and Architectural Examiners, 2040 West Main Street, Suite 212, Rapid City 57702-2497.
Helen Walsh, Executive Secretary, Telephone: (605) 394-2510.

TENNESSEE: State Board of Architectural and Engineering Examiners, 546 Doctors' Building, 706 Church Street, Nashville 37219-5322.
Betty A Smith, Administrator, Telephone: (615) 741-3221.

TEXAS: State Board of Registration for Professional Engineers, Mail: P. O. Drawer 18329, (1917 1H 35 South), Austin 78760.
Kenneth J. Bartosh, P.E., Executive Director, Telephone: (512) 475-3141.

UTAH: Representative Committee for Professional Engineers and Land Surveyors, Division of Registration, Mail: P. O. Box 45802, (160 East 300 South), Salt Lake City 84145.
Robert O. Bowen, Director, Telephone: (801) 530-6628.

VERMONT: State Board of Registration for Professional Engineers, Division of Licensing and Registration, Pavilion Building, Montpelier 05602.
Marilyn Jean Davis, Executive Secretary, Telephone: (802) 828-2363.

VIRGINIA: State Board of Architects, Professional Engineers, Land Surveyors and Certified Landscape Architects, 3600 West Broad St., Seaboard Building, 5th Floor, Richmond 23230-4917.
(Ms.) Johnsie L. Williams, Assistant Director, Telephone: (804) 257-8512.

VIRGIN ISLANDS: Board for Architects, Engineers and Land Surveyors, Submarine Base, Mail: P. O. Box 476, St. Thomas 00801.
Cecil A. George, P.E., Secretary, Telephone: (809) 774-1301.

WASHINGTON: State Board of Registration for Professional Engineers and Land Surveyors, Mail: P. O. Box 9649, (3rd Floor, 1300 Quince Street), Olympia 98504.
Alan Rathbun, P.E., Executive Secretary, Telephone: (206) 753-6966.

WEST VIRGINIA: State Board of Registration for Professional Engineers, 608 Union Building, Charleston 25301.
Ann Hicks, Executive Director, Telephone: (304) 348-3554.

WISCONSIN: State Examining Board of Architects, Professional Engineers, Designers, and Land Surveyors, Mail: P. O. Box 8936, (1400 East Washington Avenue), Madison 53708.
William Dusso, Administrator, Telephone: (608) 266-1397.

WYOMING: State Board of Examining Engineers, Herschler Building, Room 4135, Cheyenne 82002.
Elva Myers, Secretary-Accountant, Telephone: (307) 777-6156.

VI. CONTENT OF THE EXAMINATION

    Typical examinations, or actual examinations from previous years, constitute an excellent starting point from which to study. Since the frontiers of science and engineering continue to expand, engineering fundamentals undergo a slow but continuous change in content and in priorities. In order to maintain validity and keep abreast of the state of the art, engineering examinations must reflect these changes, and the Fundamentals of Engineering examination is no exception. Therefore, modest year-to-year modifications should be expected.

    The following tabulation presents the major subjects which the National Council of Engineering Examiners presently deems as required for a comprehensive understanding of engineering fundamentals.

A. Morning Examination Subjects

ELECTRICAL CIRCUITS
- DC circuits
- AC circuits
- Three-phase circuits
- Capacitance and inductance
- Electric and magnetic fields

STATICS
- Vector algebra
- 2D equilibrium
- 3D equilibrium
- Concurrent force systems
- Centroid of area
- Moment of inertia
- Friction

DYNAMICS
- Kinematics
- Force, mass, and acceleration
- Impulse and momentum
- Work and energy

MECHANICS OF MATERIALS
- Stress and strain
- Tension
- Shear
- Beams
- Columns
- Torsion
- Bending

FLUID MECHANICS
- Fluid properties
- Fluid statics
- Pipe flow
- Flow measurement
- Impulse and momentum
- Similitude
- Dimensional analysis

THERMODYNAMICS
- Thermodynamic properties—enthalpy, entropy, free energy
- Thermodynamic processes
- Energy, heat, and work
- Phase changes
- First law
- Second law
- Availability-reversibility
- Cycles
- Ideal gases
- Mixtures of gases

MATHEMATICS
- Analytic geometry
- Differential calculus

Integral calculus
Differential equations
Probability and statistics
Linear algebra

CHEMISTRY
Nomenclature
Equations
Stoichiometry
Periodicity
States of matter
Metals and nonmetals
Oxidation and reduction
Acids and bases
Solutions
Kinetics
Equilibrium
Electrochemistry
Organic chemistry

COMPUTER PROGRAMMING
Number systems
Algorithms
Computer organization
Problem solving with FORTRAN and BASIC

MATHEMATICAL MODELING OF ENGINEERING SYSTEMS
Models
Feedback
Block diagrams
System functions

Laplace transforms
Steady state and transient performance
Frequency response
Step and impulse response
Stability criteria
State variable descriptions

ENGINEERING ECONOMICS
Time value of money
Annual cost
Present worth
Future value
Capitalized cost
Breakeven analysis
Valuation and depreciation

MATERIALS SCIENCE
Physical properties
Chemical properties
Electrical properties
Atomic bonding
Crystallography
Phase diagrams
Processing tests and properties
Diffusion
Corrosion

STRUCTURE OF MATTER
Nuclei
Atoms
Molecules

B. Afternoon Examination Subjects

ENGINEERING MECHANICS
Statics
   Resultants of force systems
   Equilibria of rigid bodies
   Analyses of internal forces
   Couples and moments
Dynamics
   Kinematics
      Relative motion
      Curvilinear motion
   Inertia and force
   Particles and solid bodies
   Impulse and momentum
   Work and energy

Mechanics of Materials
   Stress and strain
   Tension
   Shear
   Simple beam
   Torsion
   Bending

MATHEMATICS
Analytic geometry
Differential calculus
Integral calculus
Differential equations
Probability and statistics
Linear algebra

ELECTRICAL CIRCUITS
DC circuits
AC circuits
Three-phase circuits
Capacitance and inductance
Electric and magnetic fields
Transients

ENGINEERING ECONOMICS
Time value of money
Annual cost
Present worth
Future value
Capitalized cost
Break-even analysis
Valuation and depreciation

COMPUTER PROGRAMMING
Number systems
Algorithms
Computer organization
Problem solving with FORTRAN and BASIC

ELECTRONICS AND ELECTRICAL MACHINERY
Solid-state devices and circuits
Electrical machinery

FLUID MECHANICS
Fluid statics
Pipe flow
Compressible flow
Flow measurement

Impulse and momentum
Similitude
Hydraulics

MECHANICS OF MATERIALS
Stress and strain
Tension
Shear
Combined stress
Beams
Columns
Composite sections
Uniaxial loading
Torsion
Bending
Combined loading
Shear and moment diagrams

THERMODYNAMICS/HEAT TRANSFER
Chemical reactions
Cycles
  Thermal
  Gas power
  Vapor power
Refrigeration
Air conditioning
Combustion
Gas mixtures
Flow through nozzles, turbines, and compressors
Availability and reversibility
Heat transfer

VII. HOW TO PREPARE FOR THIS EXAMINATION

A. Establish Your Study Schedule

1. Organize regular daily study sessions of moderate duration. They will prove to be far more effective than long duration sessions once or twice a week.
2. Be ruthless in ruling out any other activities that might interfere with a study period.
3. Select a regular time for studying when you have sufficient available energy, and when you can be most effective.
4. Arrange a location and conditions for study that will minimize or entirely eliminate extraneous interruptions.
5. Start your study schedule at least six full months prior to the actual examination date.

B. Maintain Study Discipline

1. Make all of your study sessions count, even the early ones.
2. Avoid the tendency to let study material slide. Don't postpone serious study. Panicky last-minute cramming is not very effective.
3. Sign up to attend preparatory classes for the P.E. license, which are given by most engineering schools, professional organizations, and many government agencies.
4. Arrange to study for this examination together with one or two friends who are pursuing similar goals.
5. Announce loudly to family and friends your unavailability for the duration, due to your study commitment.
6. If you have been out of school for some time, you can expect your first few problem-solving sessions to be disastrous. It will be like turning a faucet on full, but watching with dismay as only a rusty trickle dribbles out. Don't panic. Don't be discouraged. Have patience. All of your skills will start coming back if you just keep working diligently.

C. Suggestions for Effective Study

1. Avoid undue stress. Keep relaxed in the knowledge that through conscientious study sessions you can improve your skills appreciably, and can be confident of performing well on the examination.
2. Keep organizing your study material, updating your old notes, and making effective new notes, so that they will be most helpful to you during the actual examination.
3. Keep, as part of your notes, clear orderly solutions of every problem that you solve. It is quite likely that you will wish to refer to one or more of your completely worked-out solutions.
4. Analyze your study performance and your success in solving problems. Identify any areas of weakness and take positive steps to correct them.
5. Balance your study time between mastering fundamentals and solving typical problems.

D. Solving Problems

1. Solve as many new problems as possible. Solving typical problems will prove to be the most effective method for improving and sharpening your skills.
2. Read the problem statement carefully before doing anything, to make sure that you do not go off on a tangent and solve a perceived problem rather than the real one.
3. Before embarking on a detailed, rigorous solution, spend a few moments establishing the numerical parameters of the problem and try for a rough approximate answer. If the available choices have a wide spread, your ball-park solution may suffice, or it may eliminate several of the choices. At the very least, your preliminary work will provide a rough check for your ultimate answer.
4. When confronted with each new problem, develop a plan—a logical, orderly approach that will lead to a valid solution—before embarking on calculations that may yield only partial and perhaps unnecessary results.

E. Taking Open-Book Examinations

1. Organize your notes into separate folders for each major subject, and subdivide your material into well-indexed subtopics. Use these notes

during your study periods so that you become thoroughly familiar with them. Since loose notes will not be allowed at the examination, you must staple them to the folder at your last study session.

2. Most candidates have no idea how much valuable time they waste once they start paging through textbooks, handbooks, or notes in search of a certain topic or a certain solution. A good, practical rule is, "If you don't know exactly where the material is located, forget it and don't bother looking for it." Decide either to do the best you can without the reference material, or else come back to the search after all other problems have been completed.

3. Although most states will allow you to bring along a complete library in a wheelbarrow, there is a practical limit to how many books or reference sources you can effectively use. Make your selective choice well before the examination date, and study within the framework of this reference material.

VIII. STRATEGIES FOR IMPROVING YOUR TEST SCORE

A. Budget Your Time

Take a watch with you and budget your time carefully. Four hours are allotted for the 140 compulsory questions given in the Morning Examination, which averages out to 1.7 minutes per morning question. Similarly, with 70 questions to be answered in the 4-hour Afternoon Examination, the average is 3.4 minutes per afternoon question. If you find yourself exceeding your time limit, it would be wise to move on to the next question and return to the longer or tougher ones as time permits.

B. Give Priorities to Preferred Subject Matter

The Morning Examination is divided into 13 separate subject areas, and the Afternoon Examination has 6 subject areas. Each subject area is well-defined, and consists of a sequential set of consecutively numbered problems.

It makes sense to start each examination by working on the subject areas with which you feel most comfortable, and by facing up to the more difficult subject areas after you are warned up and working smoothly.

Similarly, it makes sense to follow the same procedure on an individual question basis, initially answering all the questions which you can handle easily, saving the more difficult questions for a second go-around.

C. Guessing Improves Your Grade

The Morning and Afternoon examinations are weighted equally; each is worth 50 percent. Within each examination, all test questions have the same weight. The overall test grade is based on the number of correct answers; no deduction is made for wrong answers. Therefore, it pays to answer every single question, to the extent of guessing on any otherwise unanswered question. Sheer guesswork has a 20 percent chance of being correct, which is certainly better than 0 percent. However, if analysis of the problem can result in the elimination of some of the five choices prior to guessing, this percentage will be appreciably enhanced. It is wise to work as long as possible on solving problems, and save the guessing for the very last two or three minutes of the examination.

D. Take Occasional Refresher Breaks

You will find it refreshing to take an occasional half-minute break during the long and grueling 4-hour sessions. While seated, by closing your eyes and relaxing all of your tense muscles, even for a few moments, you will gain renewed energy for continuing the examination.

E. Use All Available Time

If you should finish the examination ahead of time, don't leave early and don't sit back and relax. This examination is far too important for you to indulge in such luxuries. Review your answers thoughtfully, and try to pick up any errors that you may have made. Think very carefully before effecting such changes, however, to make sure that you are not rejecting a correct answer in favor of a wrong one.

IX. FIRST PRACTICE EXAMINATION IN FUNDAMENTALS OF ENGINEERING

This practice examination was developed as a study guide for use by candidates for the P.E. license who are preparing to take the Fundamentals of Engineering examination given by the National Council of Engineering Examiners. This is a multiple-choice, open-book, open-notes examination in which a battery-operated calculator or a slide rule is permitted.

The following pages present a typical 4-hour Morning Section examination containing 140 questions (all of which must be answered) and a 4-hour Afternoon Section examination containing 100 questions (of which 70 must be answered), together with answers and completely worked out solutions for each problem.

Answer Sheet
Practice Examination 1—A.M. Part

Electrical Circuits

1 Ⓐ Ⓑ Ⓒ Ⓓ Ⓔ   5 Ⓐ Ⓑ Ⓒ Ⓓ Ⓔ   9 Ⓐ Ⓑ Ⓒ Ⓓ Ⓔ   13 Ⓐ Ⓑ Ⓒ Ⓓ Ⓔ   17 Ⓐ Ⓑ Ⓒ Ⓓ Ⓔ

2 Ⓐ Ⓑ Ⓒ Ⓓ Ⓔ   6 Ⓐ Ⓑ Ⓒ Ⓓ Ⓔ   10 Ⓐ Ⓑ Ⓒ Ⓓ Ⓔ   14 Ⓐ Ⓑ Ⓒ Ⓓ Ⓔ   18 Ⓐ Ⓑ Ⓒ Ⓓ Ⓔ

3 Ⓐ Ⓑ Ⓒ Ⓓ Ⓔ   7 Ⓐ Ⓑ Ⓒ Ⓓ Ⓔ   11 Ⓐ Ⓑ Ⓒ Ⓓ Ⓔ   15 Ⓐ Ⓑ Ⓒ Ⓓ Ⓔ

4 Ⓐ Ⓑ Ⓒ Ⓓ Ⓔ   8 Ⓐ Ⓑ Ⓒ Ⓓ Ⓔ   12 Ⓐ Ⓑ Ⓒ Ⓓ Ⓔ   16 Ⓐ Ⓑ Ⓒ Ⓓ Ⓔ

Statics

19 Ⓐ Ⓑ Ⓒ Ⓓ Ⓔ   22 Ⓐ Ⓑ Ⓒ Ⓓ Ⓔ   25 Ⓐ Ⓑ Ⓒ Ⓓ Ⓔ   28 Ⓐ Ⓑ Ⓒ Ⓓ Ⓔ   31 Ⓐ Ⓑ Ⓒ Ⓓ Ⓔ

20 Ⓐ Ⓑ Ⓒ Ⓓ Ⓔ   23 Ⓐ Ⓑ Ⓒ Ⓓ Ⓔ   26 Ⓐ Ⓑ Ⓒ Ⓓ Ⓔ   29 Ⓐ Ⓑ Ⓒ Ⓓ Ⓔ

21 Ⓐ Ⓑ Ⓒ Ⓓ Ⓔ   24 Ⓐ Ⓑ Ⓒ Ⓓ Ⓔ   27 Ⓐ Ⓑ Ⓒ Ⓓ Ⓔ   30 Ⓐ Ⓑ Ⓒ Ⓓ Ⓔ

Dynamics

32 Ⓐ Ⓑ Ⓒ Ⓓ Ⓔ   35 Ⓐ Ⓑ Ⓒ Ⓓ Ⓔ   38 Ⓐ Ⓑ Ⓒ Ⓓ Ⓔ   41 Ⓐ Ⓑ Ⓒ Ⓓ Ⓔ   44 Ⓐ Ⓑ Ⓒ Ⓓ Ⓔ

33 Ⓐ Ⓑ Ⓒ Ⓓ Ⓔ   36 Ⓐ Ⓑ Ⓒ Ⓓ Ⓔ   39 Ⓐ Ⓑ Ⓒ Ⓓ Ⓔ   42 Ⓐ Ⓑ Ⓒ Ⓓ Ⓔ

34 Ⓐ Ⓑ Ⓒ Ⓓ Ⓔ   37 Ⓐ Ⓑ Ⓒ Ⓓ Ⓔ   40 Ⓐ Ⓑ Ⓒ Ⓓ Ⓔ   43 Ⓐ Ⓑ Ⓒ Ⓓ Ⓔ

Mechanics of Materials

45 Ⓐ Ⓑ Ⓒ Ⓓ Ⓔ   48 Ⓐ Ⓑ Ⓒ Ⓓ Ⓔ   51 Ⓐ Ⓑ Ⓒ Ⓓ Ⓔ   54 Ⓐ Ⓑ Ⓒ Ⓓ Ⓔ   57 Ⓐ Ⓑ Ⓒ Ⓓ Ⓔ

46 Ⓐ Ⓑ Ⓒ Ⓓ Ⓔ   49 Ⓐ Ⓑ Ⓒ Ⓓ Ⓔ   52 Ⓐ Ⓑ Ⓒ Ⓓ Ⓔ   55 Ⓐ Ⓑ Ⓒ Ⓓ Ⓔ

47 Ⓐ Ⓑ Ⓒ Ⓓ Ⓔ   50 Ⓐ Ⓑ Ⓒ Ⓓ Ⓔ   53 Ⓐ Ⓑ Ⓒ Ⓓ Ⓔ   56 Ⓐ Ⓑ Ⓒ Ⓓ Ⓔ

Fluid Mechanics

58 Ⓐ Ⓑ Ⓒ Ⓓ Ⓔ   61 Ⓐ Ⓑ Ⓒ Ⓓ Ⓔ   64 Ⓐ Ⓑ Ⓒ Ⓓ Ⓔ   67 Ⓐ Ⓑ Ⓒ Ⓓ Ⓔ   70 Ⓐ Ⓑ Ⓒ Ⓓ Ⓔ

59 Ⓐ Ⓑ Ⓒ Ⓓ Ⓔ   62 Ⓐ Ⓑ Ⓒ Ⓓ Ⓔ   65 Ⓐ Ⓑ Ⓒ Ⓓ Ⓔ   68 Ⓐ Ⓑ Ⓒ Ⓓ Ⓔ   71 Ⓐ Ⓑ Ⓒ Ⓓ Ⓔ

60 Ⓐ Ⓑ Ⓒ Ⓓ Ⓔ   63 Ⓐ Ⓑ Ⓒ Ⓓ Ⓔ   66 Ⓐ Ⓑ Ⓒ Ⓓ Ⓔ   69 Ⓐ Ⓑ Ⓒ Ⓓ Ⓔ

Thermodynamics

72 Ⓐ Ⓑ Ⓒ Ⓓ Ⓔ   75 Ⓐ Ⓑ Ⓒ Ⓓ Ⓔ   78 Ⓐ Ⓑ Ⓒ Ⓓ Ⓔ   81 Ⓐ Ⓑ Ⓒ Ⓓ Ⓔ   84 Ⓐ Ⓑ Ⓒ Ⓓ Ⓔ

73 Ⓐ Ⓑ Ⓒ Ⓓ Ⓔ   76 Ⓐ Ⓑ Ⓒ Ⓓ Ⓔ   79 Ⓐ Ⓑ Ⓒ Ⓓ Ⓔ   82 Ⓐ Ⓑ Ⓒ Ⓓ Ⓔ   85 Ⓐ Ⓑ Ⓒ Ⓓ Ⓔ

74 Ⓐ Ⓑ Ⓒ Ⓓ Ⓔ   77 Ⓐ Ⓑ Ⓒ Ⓓ Ⓔ   80 Ⓐ Ⓑ Ⓒ Ⓓ Ⓔ   83 Ⓐ Ⓑ Ⓒ Ⓓ Ⓔ

Mathematics

86 Ⓐ Ⓑ Ⓒ Ⓓ Ⓔ   89 Ⓐ Ⓑ Ⓒ Ⓓ Ⓔ   92 Ⓐ Ⓑ Ⓒ Ⓓ Ⓔ   95 Ⓐ Ⓑ Ⓒ Ⓓ Ⓔ

87 Ⓐ Ⓑ Ⓒ Ⓓ Ⓔ   90 Ⓐ Ⓑ Ⓒ Ⓓ Ⓔ   93 Ⓐ Ⓑ Ⓒ Ⓓ Ⓔ   96 Ⓐ Ⓑ Ⓒ Ⓓ Ⓔ

88 Ⓐ Ⓑ Ⓒ Ⓓ Ⓔ   91 Ⓐ Ⓑ Ⓒ Ⓓ Ⓔ   94 Ⓐ Ⓑ Ⓒ Ⓓ Ⓔ   97 Ⓐ Ⓑ Ⓒ Ⓓ Ⓔ

Chemistry

98 Ⓐ Ⓑ Ⓒ Ⓓ Ⓔ   100 Ⓐ Ⓑ Ⓒ Ⓓ Ⓔ   102 Ⓐ Ⓑ Ⓒ Ⓓ Ⓔ   104 Ⓐ Ⓑ Ⓒ Ⓓ Ⓔ   106 Ⓐ Ⓑ Ⓒ Ⓓ Ⓔ

99 Ⓐ Ⓑ Ⓒ Ⓓ Ⓔ   101 Ⓐ Ⓑ Ⓒ Ⓓ Ⓔ   103 Ⓐ Ⓑ Ⓒ Ⓓ Ⓔ   105 Ⓐ Ⓑ Ⓒ Ⓓ Ⓔ   107 Ⓐ Ⓑ Ⓒ Ⓓ Ⓔ

Computer Programming

108 Ⓐ Ⓑ Ⓒ Ⓓ Ⓔ   110 Ⓐ Ⓑ Ⓒ Ⓓ Ⓔ   112 Ⓐ Ⓑ Ⓒ Ⓓ Ⓔ   114 Ⓐ Ⓑ Ⓒ Ⓓ Ⓔ

109 Ⓐ Ⓑ Ⓒ Ⓓ Ⓔ   111 Ⓐ Ⓑ Ⓒ Ⓓ Ⓔ   113 Ⓐ Ⓑ Ⓒ Ⓓ Ⓔ   115 Ⓐ Ⓑ Ⓒ Ⓓ Ⓔ

Mathematical Modeling of Engineering Systems

116 Ⓐ Ⓑ Ⓒ Ⓓ Ⓔ   118 Ⓐ Ⓑ Ⓒ Ⓓ Ⓔ   120 Ⓐ Ⓑ Ⓒ Ⓓ Ⓔ   122 Ⓐ Ⓑ Ⓒ Ⓓ Ⓔ

117 Ⓐ Ⓑ Ⓒ Ⓓ Ⓔ   119 Ⓐ Ⓑ Ⓒ Ⓓ Ⓔ   121 Ⓐ Ⓑ Ⓒ Ⓓ Ⓔ   123 Ⓐ Ⓑ Ⓒ Ⓓ Ⓔ

Engineering Economics

124 Ⓐ Ⓑ Ⓒ Ⓓ Ⓔ   126 Ⓐ Ⓑ Ⓒ Ⓓ Ⓔ   128 Ⓐ Ⓑ Ⓒ Ⓓ Ⓔ

125 Ⓐ Ⓑ Ⓒ Ⓓ Ⓔ   127 Ⓐ Ⓑ Ⓒ Ⓓ Ⓔ   129 Ⓐ Ⓑ Ⓒ Ⓓ Ⓔ

Materials Science

130 Ⓐ Ⓑ Ⓒ Ⓓ Ⓔ   132 Ⓐ Ⓑ Ⓒ Ⓓ Ⓔ   134 Ⓐ Ⓑ Ⓒ Ⓓ Ⓔ

131 Ⓐ Ⓑ Ⓒ Ⓓ Ⓔ   133 Ⓐ Ⓑ Ⓒ Ⓓ Ⓔ   135 Ⓐ Ⓑ Ⓒ Ⓓ Ⓔ

The Structure of Matter

136 Ⓐ Ⓑ Ⓒ Ⓓ Ⓔ   137 Ⓐ Ⓑ Ⓒ Ⓓ Ⓔ   138 Ⓐ Ⓑ Ⓒ Ⓓ Ⓔ   139 Ⓐ Ⓑ Ⓒ Ⓓ Ⓔ   140 Ⓐ Ⓑ Ⓒ Ⓓ Ⓔ

PRACTICE EXAMINATION 1
A.M. PART

Electrical Circuits

1. Two 24-volt batteries are to be connected in parallel in order to provide a total of 100 amperes to a certain load. The first battery has a no-load terminal voltage of 25.2 volts and an internal resistance of 0.04 ohms. The second battery has a no-load terminal voltage of 24.8 volts and an internal resistance of 0.02 ohms. When the circuit is connected, the current in amperes flowing through the first battery will be most nearly

   (A) 33
   (B) 40
   (C) 50
   (D) 60
   (E) 67

2. The rms voltage level of the repetitive voltage wave shape, as shown, is most nearly

   (A) 2.5
   (B) 3.3
   (C) 3.7
   (D) 4.1
   (E) 4.7

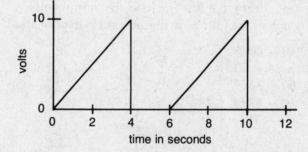

3. In the circuit shown, the numerical value of the output voltage V_0 is most nearly equal to

   (A) 48
   (B) 54
   (C) 70
   (D) 73
   (E) 120

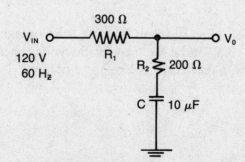

4. The speed in rpm of a 440-volt 3-phase 60-Hertz 6-pole induction motor with 5 percent slip will be most nearly

    (A) 1140
    (B) 1200
    (C) 1710
    (D) 1800
    (E) 3420

5. A 100-ohm resistor and 3 capacitors are all connected in series across a 60-volt DC source. The capacitor values are 100, 200, and 300 microfarads, respectively. After a very long time, the voltage across the 100 microfarad capacitor will be most nearly

    (A) 0
    (B) 10
    (C) 11
    (D) 30
    (E) 33

6. In the circuit shown, the switch has been in the UP position for a very long time. At time equals zero, the switch is thrown to the DOWN position. From that starting time, the output voltage V_0 is best described by which of the following mathematical expressions?

    (A) $60 - 60\varepsilon^{-0.5t}$
    (B) $-24 + 60\varepsilon^{-0.5t}$
    (C) $60 - 84\varepsilon^{-0.5t}$
    (D) $60 - 69.6\varepsilon^{-0.5t}$
    (E) $60 - 74.4\varepsilon^{-0.5t}$

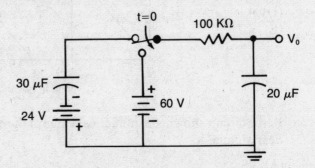

7. In the preceding problem, starting from time equals zero, the time in seconds that will be required for the voltage across the 20 microfarad capacitor to reach zero volts is most nearly

    (A) 0
    (B) 0.4
    (C) 1.6
    (D) 2
    (E) 6

8. In the circuit shown for the preceding two problems, the maximum voltage that is developed across the 100 kilohm resistor is most nearly

   (A) 36
   (B) 60
   (C) 70
   (D) 74
   (E) 84

9. A step-down autotransformer having an overall efficiency of 80% provides a 110-volt output across a 10-ohm load resistor when the input is connected to a 120-volt 60-Hertz source. The current in amperes that flows through the common winding is most nearly

   (A) 2
   (B) 6
   (C) 11
   (D) 13
   (E) 24

10. The Zener diode regulator circuit shown in the diagram converts a variable input voltage to a stable output voltage. Assume that the Zener diode requires a minimum current of 10 milliamperes. The value in ohms needed for the series resistance R_s is most nearly

    (A) 100
    (B) 200
    (C) 250
    (D) 400
    (E) 500

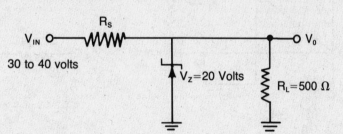

30 to 40 volts

11. In the preceding Zener voltage regulator circuit, in order to measure the current in the Zener diode branch, an ammeter is inserted whose internal resistance is 10 ohms. With this ammeter now in the circuit, as the input voltage decreases from 40 volts to 30 volts, the output voltage V_0 will

    (A) remain unchanged at 20 volts
    (B) remain constant at slightly less than 20 volts
    (C) remain constant at slightly more than 20 volts
    (D) decrease with decreasing input voltage
    (E) increase with decreasing input voltage

12. In the operational amplifier circuit as shown, the output voltage V_0 is most nearly

    (A) −6
    (B) −3
    (C) 0
    (D) +3
    (E) +6

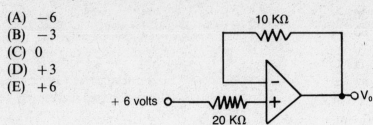

13. In the operational amplifier circuit shown, the numerical value of the output voltage V_0 is most nearly

    (A) −9
    (B) −5
    (C) −1
    (D) +9
    (E) +13

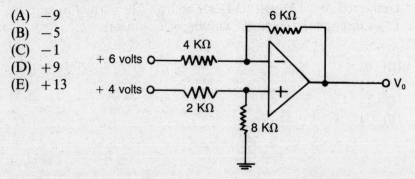

14. The indicated voltage wave shape is applied to the input of the operational amplifier circuit. The capacitor was initially uncharged. At the end of exactly 7 seconds, the output voltage V_0 will be most nearly

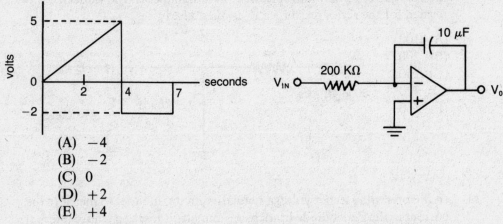

    (A) −4
    (B) −2
    (C) 0
    (D) +2
    (E) +4

15. An industrial plant draws an average current of 600 amperes daily from a three-phase 440-volt 60-Hertz line, at a power factor of 0.75 lagging. If an ideal rotary condenser is used to improve this power factor to 0.92 lagging, the new value of average daily current in amperes will be most nearly

    (A) 450

(B) 480
(C) 490
(D) 550
(E) 650

16. In the feedback system shown, the numerical value for G that will cause the output voltage level at C to equal 110% of the reference input voltage R is most nearly

(A) 2
(B) 4
(C) 5
(D) 8
(E) 92

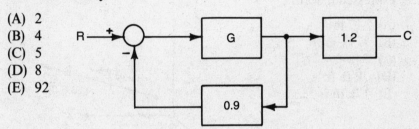

17. A feedback control system has an open loop gain (GH) in Laplace notation equal to $\dfrac{1}{s + 0.25}$. If the applied input is a steady-state sinusoidal voltage at an angular velocity ω of 2.0 radians/second, the magnitude in decibels of the system's open loop gain is most nearly

(A) −6
(B) −3
(C) +3
(D) +6
(E) +18

18. A 3-phase 3-wire 440-volt 60-Hertz source supplies a 120-kilowatt load through a 500-foot length of cable containing three conductors of 250,000 circular mils each. The load is inductive with a power factor of 0.8. The voltage drop in each conductor, measured from one end to the other, is most nearly

(A) 2.4
(B) 3.3
(C) 4.1
(D) 5.6
(E) 7.1

Statics

19. Which of the following is true of all coplanar force systems?

(A) All of the forces meet at a single point.

(B) All of the forces in the system are parallel.
(C) All of the moments, except those about axes perpendicular to the plane, are zero.
(D) All of the forces occur in couple-pairs.
(E) All of the above.

20. What is $\vec{r} \times \vec{F}$ about point 0 for the system shown? (All distances are expressed in feet.)

(A) -7 lb-ft
(B) $-7\vec{k}$ lb-ft
(C) 7 lb-ft
(D) $7\vec{k}$ lb-ft
(E) $17\vec{k}$ lb-ft

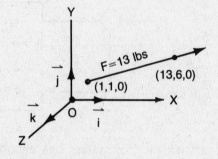

21. The right-hand reaction of the beam shown is

(A) 0^K
(B) 6^K
(C) 8^K
(D) 10^K
(E) 12^K

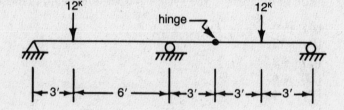

22. If F_1 has a magnitude of 14.14 lbs and F_2 has a magnitude of 15.0 lbs, the magnitude of F_3, in order to maintain equilibrium, is

(A) 0
(B) 0.86 lbs
(C) 5 lbs
(D) 10 lbs
(E) 11.2 lbs

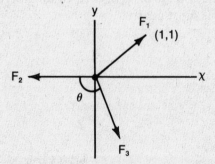

23. Problems #23 and #24 concern the cross-sectional area of a solid with a 2-inch diameter hole as shown. The distance of the centroid $\overline{Y}$ above the base for this cross-section, expressed in inches, is most nearly

(A) 2.4
(B) 2.7
(C) 3.0
(D) 3.2
(E) 3.4

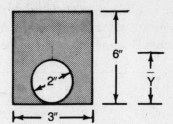

24. The moment of inertia of the cross-section shown in problem #23, about the base line, expressed in inches^4, is most nearly

   (A) 53
   (B) 55
   (C) 212
   (D) 216
   (E) 219

25. What is the minimum weight required for equilibrium if the coefficient of sliding friction for both the pulley (action angle = 90°) and the horizontal surface is $\mu = 0.2$?

   (A) 20 lbs
   (B) 73 lbs
   (C) 100 lbs
   (D) 185 lbs
   (E) 365 lbs

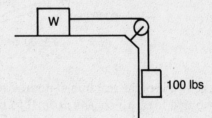

26. Determine the force in member $U_2 L_2$ in the truss shown in the diagram.

   (A) 0
   (B) 5^K
   (C) 10^K
   (D) 20^K
   (E) none of the above

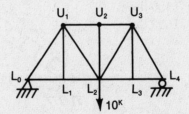

27. What is the maximum height y at which the 60-pound horizontal force may be applied without causing the block to move?

   (A) 2.0 ft
   (B) 3.0 ft
   (C) 3.3 ft
   (D) 6.0 ft
   (E) none of the above

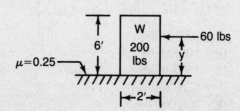

28. Three massive rolls of paper, each weighing 1000 pounds and having the same diameter, are stacked as shown. Assuming that all surfaces are frictionless, what bracing force F will be required in order to prevent motion?

(A) 289 lbs
(B) 500 lbs
(C) 577 lbs
(D) 866 lbs
(E) 1000 lbs

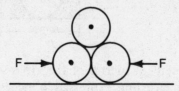

29. Each of two chain links weighs 2000 lbs and the horizontal force applied at the end of the chain is 1500 lbs. With the top link supported as shown, the equilibrium angle α of the first link is most nearly

(A) 0°
(B) 27°
(C) 45°
(D) 56°
(E) 75°

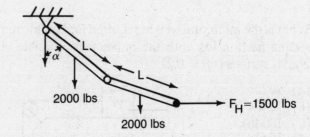

30. The magnitude of the reaction at point C for the structure shown, having a distributed load which acts normal to member AC, is most nearly

(A) 0
(B) 650 lbs
(C) 900 lbs
(D) 1300 lbs
(E) 1600 lbs

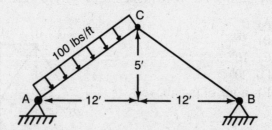

31. A train of 50 cars, each weighing 100,000 pounds, moves at a uniform speed up a 1% grade. What is the required draw bar pull at the head end of the train, assuming no friction?

(A) 25,000 lbs
(B) 50,000 lbs
(C) 100,000 lbs
(D) 125,000 lbs
(E) 200,000 lbs

Dynamics

32. A ball is thrown at an angle α with the horizontal. If its speed at the highest point of its trajectory is 10 ft/sec, the radius of curvature of the trajectory at that point is most nearly

    (A) 0.32 ft.
    (B) 3.11 ft.
    (C) 3.22 ft.
    (D) 31.1 ft.
    (E) cannot be determined without knowing the angle α

33. A truck weighing 20,000 pounds moves up a 7% slope. Neglecting all friction, the power required of its engine, so that it can maintain a 35 mph speed, is most nearly

    (A) 130 HP
    (B) 152 HP
    (C) 173 HP
    (D) 330 HP
    (E) 362 HP

34. Assuming frictionless impact and a coefficient of restitution equal to 0.8, the angle θ_2 in the sketch is most nearly

    (A) 32.6°
    (B) 38.7°
    (C) 45.0°
    (D) 51.3°
    (E) 57.4°

35. A body weighing 20 pounds is constrained to move without friction along a horizontal line. It is at rest at time equals zero. If it is subjected to a force F which varies as shown in the sketch, the maximum velocity it will attain, expressed in feet/second, is most nearly

    (A) 1.0
    (B) 2.0
    (C) 8.1
    (D) 16.1
    (E) 32.2

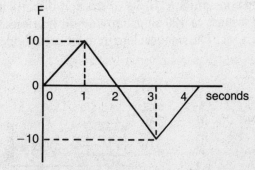

36. A pendulum consisting of a small body M attached to a string makes an angle of 30° with the vertical at the extremity of its swing. At that position the acceleration of M in feet/sec/sec is most nearly

    (A) 16.1
    (B) 32.2
    (C) 37.2
    (D) 55.8
    (E) 64.4

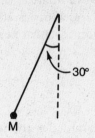

37. A truck moving with a velocity of 50 mph on a level road carries crates which are not secured to its floor. The coefficient of friction between crates and floor is 0.60. If the truck stops by decelerating uniformly, the minimum time in seconds required to come to a complete halt without having the crates slide is most nearly

    (A) 2.4
    (B) 2.6
    (C) 3.8
    (D) 4.2
    (E) 5.2

38. A body of mass M moves on a frictionless horizontal plane about a fixed point 0 to which it is attached by a massless spring having a spring constant of K. The trajectory is an ellipse having axes of 12 inches and 8 inches. If the velocity at the end of the major axis is 12 ft/sec, the velocity in feet/second at the end of the minor axis is most nearly

    (A) 8
    (B) 10
    (C) 12
    (D) 18
    (E) indeterminate without knowing K or M

39. A spring of negligible mass, having an undeformed length of 8 inches and a spring constant k = 10,800 lb/inch, is directly in the path of an object having a mass of 100 slugs moving on frictionless rails with a velocity v_0 = 6 ft/sec. The smallest length in inches attained by the spring is most nearly

    (A) 2
    (B) 3
    (C) 4
    (D) 5
    (E) 6

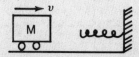

40. A man having a motorboat capable of a speed of 16 ft/sec wishes to cross a stream in the shortest possible time. If the stream is flowing west at a velocity of 8 ft/sec, he should keep the bow of the boat pointed in the direction of

(A) N 30° W
(B) N 60° W
(C) North
(D) N 30° E
(E) N 60° E

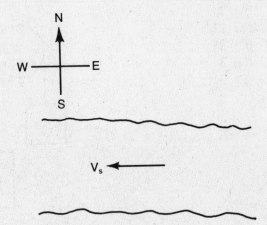

41. The velocity of a satellite in a circular orbit of radius r about the earth is proportional to

(A) r
(B) r^2
(C) $1/r$
(D) $1/r^2$
(E) $1/\sqrt{r}$

42. A homogeneous, slender, 2-meter-long bar of mass m is hinged at one end and is released from a rest position that is nearly vertical. As the bar falls, the velocity of its tip as the longitudinal axis passes through a horizontal position, expressed in meters per second, is most nearly

(A) 9.3
(B) 10.3
(C) 12.3
(D) 13.9
(E) 16.1

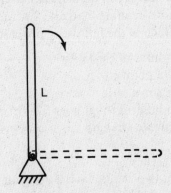

43. Two bodies, weighing 2 pounds and 4 pounds, respectively, are connected by an inextensible flexible cable that wraps around a frictionless pulley which may be assumed to have zero mass. The tension in the cable, expressed in pounds, is most nearly

    (A) 2
    (B) $2\frac{1}{3}$
    (C) $2\frac{2}{3}$
    (D) 3
    (E) $3\frac{1}{3}$

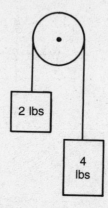

44. A truck weighing 20,000 pounds moves down a 7% slope with a velocity of 35 mph. If its brakes are applied so that a frictional force of 16,000 pounds is exerted, the distance needed for the truck to stop is most nearly

    (A) 26 ft
    (B) 36 ft
    (C) 46 ft
    (D) 56 ft
    (E) 66 ft

Mechanics of Materials

45. A tensile test is run on a specimen in a universal testing machine with a continuous-reading load dial and an extensometer attached to the specimen. Which of the following properties cannot be measured by the test?

    (A) Modulus of elasticity
    (B) Yield point
    (C) Poisson's ratio
    (D) Modulus of toughness
    (E) Ultimate strength

46. Consider two shafts, each having an outer radius of r_0. One of the shafts is hollow and has an inner radius r_1 equal to one-half of r_0. The ratio of the elastic torsional capacity of the hollow shaft to that of the solid shaft is most nearly

    (A) 0.33

(B) 0.50
(C) 0.67
(D) 0.94
(E) 1.00

47. An axially loaded cylindrical bar that is one inch in diameter is welded
     on the bias at an angle of 45 degrees as shown. If the axial load is 20,000
     pounds, the shear stress along the weld is most nearly

(A) 0 psi
(B) 10,000 psi
(C) 12,700 psi
(D) 20,000 psi
(E) 25,500 psi

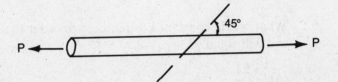

48. A 30-inch long, 1-inch square aluminum bar, $E = 10(10)^6$ psi, is loaded
     axially by a 20,000 pound force. The strain energy stored, expressed in
     inch-pounds, is most nearly

(A) 20
(B) 120
(C) 600
(D) 720
(E) 1200

49. The moment-area method is a technique for determining

(A) elastic deflections in a beam
(B) fracture mechanics
(C) plastic deformations in torsion
(D) direction of principal planes
(E) strain energy in a system

50. For the beam shown, the correct expression for the EIy elastic curve
     from $0 \leq x \leq \frac{L}{2}$ is equal to

(A) $\dfrac{Px^3}{12} - \dfrac{PLx}{16} - \dfrac{P(x - \frac{L}{2})^2}{6}$

(B) $\dfrac{Px^3}{12} - \dfrac{PLx^2}{16}$

(C) $\dfrac{Px^3}{12} - \dfrac{PL^2x}{16}$

(D) $\dfrac{Px^3}{12} - \dfrac{P}{L}\dfrac{x^4}{24} - \dfrac{PL^2x}{24}$

(E) $\dfrac{Px}{6} - \dfrac{PLx^2}{8}$

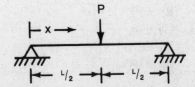

51. A steel bar, characterized by $E = 30 \times 10^3$ Ksi, $v = 0.3$, $\alpha = 6 \times 10^{-6}$ inches/inch/°F, is fully restrained in the longitudinal axial direction. The lateral strain (perpendicular to the axial strain) for a temperature rise of 100°F is

(A) 18μ
(B) 180μ
(C) 360μ
(D) 600μ
(E) 1800μ

52. What spring constant k is required in order that the reaction at the left end will equal $\frac{P}{4}$?

(A) $\dfrac{3\,EI}{4\,L^3}$

(B) $\dfrac{EI}{L^3}$

(C) $\dfrac{6EI}{L^3}$

(D) $\dfrac{12EI}{L^3}$

(E) $\dfrac{48EI}{5L^3}$

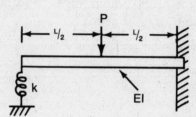

53. The neutral axis for fully plastic bending on the section shown is located at $\bar{y}$ equal to

(A) 0
(B) 1"
(C) 2"
(D) 3.2"
(E) 4"

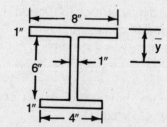

54. The maximum shear stress, expressed in pounds per square inch, in a one-inch diameter shaft which is transmitting 5.0 horsepower at 600 rpm is most nearly

(A) 220
(B) 450
(C) 670
(D) 2670
(E) 5340

55. A steel shaft 30 inches long and 2 inches in diameter is subjected to a torque of 60,000 inch-pounds. If G is assumed to be $12(10)^6$ psi, the angular rotation in degrees at the end of the shaft is most nearly

    (A) 0.06
    (B) 0.10
    (C) 0.57
    (D) 5.7
    (E) 45

56. Which of the following is *not* a theory of failure?

    (A) The maximum normal stress theory.
    (B) The maximum strain energy theory.
    (C) The maximum shear stress theory.
    (D) The stress deviation theory.
    (E) The Euler–Bernoulli theory.

57. The kern of a section refers to that cross-sectional core of a symmetric column in which the placement of an eccentric compressive load will not result in tensile stresses. For a circular column of diameter d, the kern of the section is

    (A) $\pm\dfrac{d}{12}$

    (B) $\pm\dfrac{d}{8}$

    (C) $\pm\dfrac{d}{6}$

    (D) $\pm\dfrac{d}{2}$

    (E) $\pm\infty$ (infinity)

Fluid Mechanics

58. Approximately how high will water at 60°F rise in a vertical glass tube whose top is open to the atmosphere and whose inner diameter is 0.012 inches? (Assume that the angle of contact β is zero and that surface tension σ is 0.005 lb/ft.)

    (A) 0.04 ft.
    (B) 0.08 ft.
    (C) 0.16 ft.
    (D) 0.32 ft.
    (E) 0.64 ft.

59. What is the pressure at the base of a one-square-foot bar of uniform cross-section weighing one ton and floating vertically in water of density 62.4 lb/ft³ at sea level?

(A) 13.9 psia
(B) 23.9 psia
(C) 32 feet of water
(D) 42.5 psia
(E) 62.4 psf

60. What is the "critical pressure ratio" for a compressible fluid of k = 1.6 to reach sonic velocity?

(A) 0.497
(B) 0.528
(C) 1.894
(D) 2.0
(E) ∞

The system illustrated below applies to problems #61 through #65, inclusive.

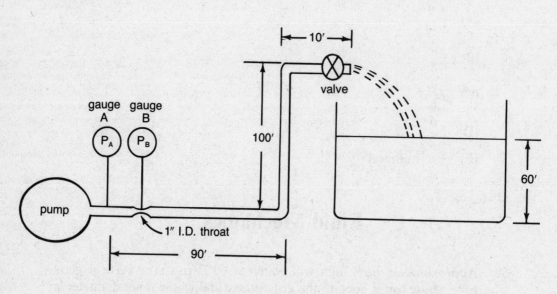

Water at 60°F is pumped into a reservoir through a 2-inch I.D. pipe. The exit velocity is 10 feet/second and the pump is at sea level. Assume the following constants:

Valves: K = 10
90° Bends: K = 1 (each)
Venturi: K = 0.05 based on throat conditions
Friction: f = 0.022

61. What is the Reynolds number in the straight duct?

    (A) 27,380
    (B) 136,900
    (C) 273,800
    (D) 1,643,000
    (E) 4,408,000

62. In the system shown, the frictional pressure loss expressed in psi due to the 200-foot total length of pipe is most nearly

    (A) 1.5
    (B) 1.8
    (C) 3.5
    (D) 17.8
    (E) 21.0

63. The pressure loss across the venturi, expressed in psi, is most nearly

    (A) 0.034
    (B) 0.067
    (C) 0.14
    (D) 0.27
    (E) 0.54

64. The pressure reading in psig on gauge A is most nearly

    (A) 43.3
    (B) 61.1
    (C) 61.6
    (D) 69.7
    (E) 70.4

65. Neglecting the losses between A and B, the pressure reading in psig on gauge B is most nearly

    (A) 50.86
    (B) 50.99
    (C) 51.53
    (D) 58.94
    (E) 59.61

66. What is the hydraulic radius, in feet, of a rectangular open channel ten feet wide when the water flow depth is two feet?

    (A) 1.0

(B) 1.4
(C) 1.7
(D) 2.0
(E) 6.0

67. What is the critical depth, in feet, in a rectangular channel that is ten feet wide when the flow rate is 350 cubic feet/second?

(A) 0.84
(B) 1.68
(C) 3.36
(D) 6.17
(E) 10.7

68. When inertial and gravitational forces predominate, similarity between a model and prototype can be achieved by matching the

(A) kinematic forces
(B) Reynolds number
(C) Cauchy number
(D) Froude number
(E) Weber number

69. Which of the following instruments is not normally used to measure flow?

(A) Venturi meter
(B) Orifice meter
(C) Pitot-static tube
(D) Anemometer
(E) Bourdon gage

70. If sonic velocity is attained at the throat of a convergent-divergent nozzle, the downstream flow in the nozzle:

(A) will always be supersonic
(B) will always include a shock wave
(C) may be supersonic and subsonic
(D) may have a total pressure higher than that of the throat
(E) cannot be influenced by disturbances upstream of the throat

71. What input horsepower is required for a pump with an 80% efficiency, inlet pressure of 10 psia, outlet pressure of 20 psig, and a flow of 5 cfs of water? (Assume sea level conditions.)

(A) 0.292 HP

(B) 10.4 HP
(C) 14.0 HP
(D) 15.0 HP
(E) 17.5 HP

Thermodynamics

72. Humid air at a temperature of 100°F and a pressure of 14.7 psia has a dew point of 80°F. The partial pressure of the air in psia is most nearly

   (A) 0.51
   (B) 0.95
   (C) 13.8
   (D) 14.2
   (E) 14.7

73. One pound mole of oxygen gas is compressed isentropically from a volume of 100 cubic feet at 70°F to a pressure of 100 psia. What is the final temperature of the gas in degrees Fahrenheit?

   (A) 163
   (B) 185
   (C) 210
   (D) 224
   (E) 231

74. Two hundred pounds of beef at 80°F are to be frozen and maintained at a temperature of 0°F. Beef freezes at 26°F with a latent heat of fusion of 123 Btu/lb. Assume specific heats of 0.9 Btu/lb/°F above freezing and 0.45 Btu/lb/°F below freezing. What is the total heat in Btu's that must be removed from the meat?

   (A) 15,000
   (B) 20,000
   (C) 25,000
   (D) 30,000
   (E) 37,000

75. What is the maximum efficiency of a Carnot cycle operating between temperatures of 980°F and 500°F?

   (A) 33%
   (B) 50%

(C) 67%
(D) 75%
(E) 100%

76. Ten pounds of helium at a constant pressure of 20 psia are heated for two hours at a constant rate of 100 Btu/hour. The helium volume is allowed to increase in a frictionless manner from 700 cubic feet to 1000 cubic feet. How much work is done?

(A) 0 ft-lb/hr
(B) 550 Btu
(C) 1110 Btu
(D) 43,200 ft-lb/hr
(E) 86,400 ft-lb/hr

77. For the conditions of problem #76, what is the change in internal energy?

(A) 750 Btu decrease
(B) 750 Btu increase
(C) 910 Btu decrease
(D) 910 Btu increase
(E) 1310 Btu decrease

78. Air is compressed in a frictionless manner with no transfer of heat from a condition of 70°F and 14.7 psia to 1000 psia. What is the resulting air temperature in degrees Fahrenheit?

(A) 70
(B) 234
(C) 990
(D) 1310
(E) 10,340

79. A Brayton cycle operates under the following temperature conditions:
    (a) Heat added during the constant pressure process, from 500°R to 792°R.
    (b) Heat rejected during the constant pressure process, from 379°R to 600°R.
    Its cycle efficiency is most nearly

(A) 17%
(B) 24%
(C) 28%
(D) 37%
(E) 52%

80. Ten pounds per second of air are extracted from the compressor of a jet engine and collected into a 5-inch (inside diameter) duct at a pressure of 300 psia and an enthalpy of 396 Btu/lb (1600°R). The air flows through a 100-foot-long duct losing 30 psi due to friction and having a 27 Btu/lb reduction in enthalpy for a final temperature of 1500°R. What is the total energy of the air at the initial conditions?

    (A) 380 Btu/lb
    (B) 386 Btu/lb
    (C) 390 Btu/lb
    (D) 396 Btu/lb
    (E) 400 Btu/lb

81. How much heat is lost (or gained) in the 100-foot-long duct of problem #80?

    (A) 0 Btu/lb
    (B) 24 Btu/lb gain
    (C) 24 Btu/lb loss
    (D) 27 Btu/lb gain
    (E) 27 Btu/lb loss

82. A pressure regulator, set at 50 psia, is added to the system of problem #80 near the engine. Assuming no friction, the enthalpy downstream of the regulator is most nearly

    (A) 66 Btu/lb
    (B) 162 Btu/lb
    (C) 396 Btu/lb
    (D) 487 Btu/lb
    (E) 532 Btu/lb

83. The air taken from the engine in problem #80 is used to ventilate and cool the cabin of the aircraft. Prior to being expanded through a cooling turbine, the air is cooled by a fuel-air heat exchanger. All of the heat extracted from the air goes into the fuel, raising its heating value (in Btu/lb of fuel). As a result of the heat transfer process, the available energy

    (A) decreases
    (B) increases
    (C) remains constant
    (D) depends on the type of heat exchanger
    (E) depends on the efficiency of the combustion process

84. Based on the Second Law of Thermodynamics, what is the maximum efficiency possible for an engine using 80°F sea water for a source and 35°F sea water as a sink?

    (A) 4%
    (B) 8%
    (C) 12%
    (D) 18%
    (E) 25%

85. The change in entropy, expressed in Btu's per degree Rankine, when 50 Btu's are added to 10 pounds of water at a constant temperature of 70°F, is most nearly

    (A) 0.0094
    (B) 0.028
    (C) 0.094
    (D) 0.28
    (E) 0.94

Mathematics

86. Which of the following equations represents an exponential curve passing through the points $(0, -6)$ and $(\infty, +4)$?

    (A) $y = -6 + 4\varepsilon^{-ax}$
    (B) $y = 6 - 4\varepsilon^{-ax}$
    (C) $y = 4 + 10\varepsilon^{-ax}$
    (D) $y = 4 - 6\varepsilon^{-ax}$
    (E) $y = 4 - 10\varepsilon^{-ax}$

87. The slope of the exponential curve described in problem #86, at the point where this curve crosses the y-axis, is

    (A) zero
    (B) 6a
    (C) -6a
    (D) 10a
    (E) -10a

88. If the exponential curve in problem #86 crosses the x-axis at x equals two, the numerical value of the "a" in the exponent would be most nearly equal to

    (A) 0.39

(B) 0.46
(C) 0.50
(D) 0.57
(E) 0.68

89. Evaluate the determinant shown.

$$y = \begin{vmatrix} 3 & 1 & -1 \\ 4 & -2 & 0 \\ 2 & 1 & 4 \end{vmatrix}$$

(A) -48
(B) -32
(C) -8
(D) 8
(E) 48

90. In a normal or Gaussian distribution, the percentage of data points that lie within plus or minus one-half of one standard deviation is most nearly

(A) 17%
(B) 19%
(C) 34%
(D) 38%
(E) 68%

91. The mathematical expression $y = 10\varepsilon^{-600t}\sin 2\pi(100)t$ starts at time equals zero. When the phase angle reaches 30 degrees, the instantaneous value of this expression will be most nearly

(A) 2
(B) 3
(C) 4
(D) 5
(E) 8

92. The center of the geometric figure described by $16x^2 - 160x + 9y^2 + 36y + 292 = 0$ is at the point

(A) $(-5, 2)$
(B) $(3, 4)$
(C) $(4, 3)$
(D) $(5, -2)$
(E) $(25, 4)$

93. If 10 coins are flipped into the air, the probability that they will land showing 5 heads and 5 tails is most nearly

    (A) 0.25
    (B) 0.30
    (C) 0.35
    (D) 0.40
    (E) 0.50

94. If Cartesian coordinates are used, a straight line drawn through the points $(2, 9)$ and $(5, -3)$ will intercept the y-axis at value

    (A) -20
    (B) -17
    (C) 0
    (D) 17
    (E) 20

95. Poisson distribution is based primarily upon

    (A) Taylor series
    (B) Maclaurin series
    (C) Fourier series
    (D) Laplace transforms
    (E) binomial expansion

96. The equation $x^2 - y^2 = 1$ defines a rectangular hyperbola in which the coordinates of any point (x, y) are equal to

    (A) $\sinh \mu$ and $\cosh \mu$, respectively
    (B) $\cosh \mu$ and $\sinh \mu$, respectively
    (C) the distances to the near and to the far focal points, respectively
    (D) the difference and the sum, respectively, of the distances to the two foci
    (E) the sum and the difference, respectively, of the distances to the two foci

97. Which of the following is the general solution to the differential equation shown below?

$$\frac{d^2 y}{dx^2} - 3\frac{dy}{dx} + 2y = 0$$

    (A) $\varepsilon^{-2x} - 3\varepsilon^{-x} + 2$
    (B) $C_1 \varepsilon^{-x} + C_2 \varepsilon^{-2x}$
    (C) $C_1 \varepsilon^{x} + C_2 \varepsilon^{2x}$
    (D) $C_1 \varepsilon^{-jwx} + C_2 \varepsilon^{-j2wx}$
    (E) $C_1 \sin x + C_2 \cos x$

Chemistry

98. Elements known as the rare earths include which one of the following?

    (A) Ag
    (B) Ta
    (C) Au
    (D) U
    (E) La

99. The symbol $R{-}\overset{O}{{-}}OH$ represents

    (A) acid
    (B) alcohol
    (C) aldehyde
    (D) ketone
    (E) hydrocarbon

100. The symbol for the bicarbonate ion is

    (A) $(CO_3)_2^=$
    (B) $CO_3^=$
    (C) CO_3^{++}
    (D) HCO_3^-
    (E) Na_2CO_3

101. The symbol HO⟨◯⟩OH represents

    (A) orthophenol
    (B) metaphenol
    (C) paraphenol
    (D) resorcinol
    (E) cresol

102. If the hydrogen ion concentration of a certain solution is $1(10)^{-6}$ gm/cc, the pH is most nearly

    (A) 3
    (B) 5
    (C) 7
    (D) 9
    (E) -5

103. The average reading error of a standard 50 ml burette is most nearly

    (A) 0.0002 ml
    (B) 0.002 ml
    (C) 0.02 ml
    (D) 0.2 ml
    (E) 2 ml

104. A monobasic acid is 0.4% ionized when its concentration is 0.3 molar. Its ionization constant is most nearly

    (A) 1.2×10^{-3}
    (B) 4.8×10^{-3}
    (C) 1.6×10^{-5}
    (D) 1.6×10^{-6}
    (E) 4.8×10^{-6}

105. The pH of the acid solution defined in problem #104 is most nearly

    (A) 1.2
    (B) 2.9
    (C) 4.8
    (D) 6
    (E) 8.3

106. A product stream contains calcium nitrate impurity. The calcium is to be removed by precipitation with soda ash. The amount by weight of soda ash that will be required per 1000 pounds of calcium nitrate is most nearly

    (A) 350 lbs
    (B) 500 lbs
    (C) 650 lbs
    (D) 850 lbs
    (E) 1040 lbs

107. If one square foot of filter area is required to filter 10 pounds per hour of precipitated calcium carbonate, how much filter area in square feet is required for a flow rate of 1000 pounds per hour of calcium nitrate, in order to clarify the slurry developed in problem #106?

    (A) 35
    (B) 61
    (C) 70
    (D) 100
    (E) 610

Computer Programming

108. In the following "FOR" loop portion of a BASIC program, what will be the highest value of X for which the function "FNV1" is evaluated?

    10 FOR X = 1.5 to 50 STEP 1
    20 PRINT X, FNV1(X)
    30 NEXT X

    (A) 49.0
    (B) 49.5
    (C) 50.0
    (D) 50.5
    (E) 51.0

109. Which of the following is the binary equivalent of the decimal number 77?

    (A) 0111111
    (B) 1001101
    (C) 1101001
    (D) 1000110
    (E) 1011001

110. What is the octal equivalent of hexadecimal 129?

    (A) 451
    (B) 431
    (C) 455
    (D) 473
    (E) 427

111. Which of the following is the decimal equivalent of the two's complement number, 01010010?

    (A) −46
    (B) −173
    (C) 82
    (D) 46
    (E) 174

112. Which of the following is a correct FORTRAN statement?

    (A)   A = B × A + C
    (B) 100 IF (A = 5) GOTO 100
    (C)   Y = X↑2 + 5

(D)   A + B + C + D/2

(E)   DO 100 J = 1,100, −5

113. Which of the following logical expressions is *true*, given: A = 25, B = 10, C = 100?

  (A) (.NOT.(A**2.GE.B).AND.(B−C/A+4.EQ.B))
  (B) (B*A.LT.C.OR..NOT.A*4.NE.C)
  (C) (A.LT.B.OR.C+5.EQ.B+2*C−A/0.1.AND.B.LT.C)
  (D) (A.LT.B.AND.C.GE.B.OR.A**0.5.EQ.B)
  (E) none of the above

114. What is the sum of $(657)_8 + (325)_8$ expressed in base eight?

  (A) 1204
  (B) 982
  (C) 824
  (D) 1074
  (E) 1426

115. Which of the following is *not* a legal FORTRAN variable name?

  (A) REAL
  (B) TWO WRD
  (C) A512B
  (D) XDIST
  (E) 2PI

Mathematical Modeling of Engineering Systems

The system illustrated below applies to problems #116 through #123, inclusive. Assume a steady-state sinusoidal input voltage at R, unless otherwise indicated.

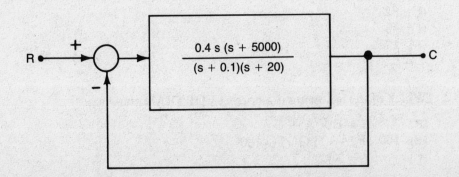

116. The bandwidth of the negative feedback system shown, expressed in terms of radians/second, is most nearly

    (A) 0.1 to 20
    (B) 0.1 to 5000
    (C) 1 to 20
    (D) 1 to 5000
    (E) 20 to 5000

117. At mid-band frequencies, the forward gain of this system has an overall amplitude in decibels most nearly equal to

    (A) 0.4
    (B) 8
    (C) 20
    (D) 40
    (E) 60

118. The transfer function of this overall system, at mid-band frequencies, has an amplitude in decibels most nearly equal to

    (A) 0
    (B) 0.4
    (C) 1
    (D) 40
    (E) 60

119. The Bode amplitude plot of the open-loop gain verifies that the unity gain crossover point occurs at an angular velocity, measured in radians/second, that is most nearly

    (A) 0.1
    (B) 20
    (C) 1000
    (D) 2000
    (E) 5000

120. The Bode amplitude plot of the open-loop gain shows that a phase angle of zero degrees will be obtained in this system at an angular velocity in radians/second of most nearly

    (A) 0.001
    (B) 0.1
    (C) 3
    (D) 20
    (E) 5000

121. In the Bode plot of the given system, as the angular velocity (measured in radians/second) increases, the maximum slope (measured in decibels per decade) at which the open-loop gain falls off from its mid-band level is most nearly

    (A) 6
    (B) 10
    (C) 12
    (D) 20
    (E) 40

122. The phase margin of this system, expressed in degrees, is most nearly

    (A) 45
    (B) 68
    (C) 90
    (D) 112
    (E) 135

123. If, at time equals zero, a 12-volt DC source were to be applied as a step function input to this system, the error signal would rise instantaneously to an *initial value* of DC voltage that would be most nearly

    (A) 0
    (B) 3
    (C) 6
    (D) 9
    (E) 12

Engineering Economics

124. If $5000 is invested at a 12% interest rate compounded semi-annually, its worth 30 years hence will be most nearly

    (A) $150,000
    (B) $165,000
    (C) $290,000
    (D) $315,000
    (E) $449,000

125. A person borrows $9000 for 5 years to purchase an automobile. If the interest rate is 15% and if the payback is to be made annually on an equal-amount basis, how much does the person have to pay each year?

    (A) $1593
    (B) $1720

(C) $1794
(D) $2497
(E) $2685

126. How much was a piece of property worth ten years ago if it is now worth $20,000 and if the interest rate is assumed to be 10%?

(A) $6440
(B) $7710
(C) $12,418
(D) $18,000
(E) $20,370

127. A bond will fall due in eight years and yields $10,000. If we are in a position to earn 8% on our money, how much is the bond worth to us today?

(A) $5403
(B) $7500
(C) $10,800
(D) $16,400
(E) $18,509

The following description applies to problems #128 and #129.

A company is considering purchasing a machine that has a list price of $13,000. The applied sales tax rate is 8%. The installation costs $750 and transportation costs $210. Assume that the machine's service life is 5 years and that it has no salvage value.

128. If the "sum-of-the-digits" method is used, the value of the machine at the *beginning* of the second year will be

(A) $4333
(B) $5000
(C) $8667
(D) $9333
(E) $10,000

129. If the "sum-of-the-digits" method is used, the value of the machine at the *end* of the second year will be most nearly

(A) $3500
(B) $4000
(C) $4700
(D) $5200
(E) $5500

Materials Science

130. Corrosion of iron can be inhibited with a more electronegative coating, while an electropositive coating tends to accelerate corrosion. Which of the following is more electropositive than iron?

    (A) Zinc
    (B) Aluminum
    (C) Magnesium
    (D) Sodium
    (E) Mill scale

131. A trial mix indicates that a $1 : 1\frac{1}{2} : 3$ mixture by volume of cement, sand, and gravel produces satisfactory concrete with 5 gallons of water per cubic-foot-bag of cement. Properties of the raw materials are:

	Voids	Bulk Density
Cement	51.3%	94 lb/ft^3
Sand	36.0%	120 lb/ft^3
Gravel	33.0%	105 lb/ft^3

    The volume of this concrete mix expressed in cubic feet per bag of cement is most nearly

    (A) 1.2
    (B) 3.5
    (C) 4.1
    (D) 5.5
    (E) 6.2

Problems #132 through #135 inclusive, refer to the phase diagram shown in the adjacent sketch. The compositions and the temperatures cited are approximate.

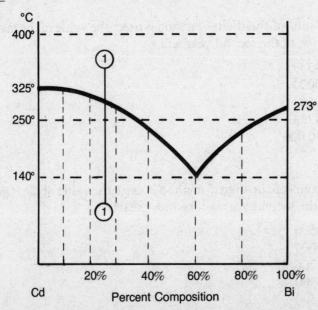

132.   Alloy ① is completely melted and is then cooled from 350°C to approximately 100°C. Which of the following statements is correct?

    (A) This alloy contains 25% Bi. The Cd starts to solidify at 280°C.
    (B) This alloy contains 25% Cd. The Cd starts to solidify at 280°C.
    (C) This alloy contains 25% Bi. Eutectic starts to solidify at 280°C.
    (D) This alloy contains 25% Cd. Eutectic starts to solidify at 280°C.
    (E) None of the above are correct.

133.   At 250°C, alloy ① consists of

    (A) 30% solid and 70% melt. The solid is pure Cd. The melt is 35% Bi.
    (B) 70% solid and 30% melt. The solid is pure Cd. The melt is 35% Bi.
    (C) 30% solid and 70% melt. The solid is a eutectic containing 60% Bi.
    (D) 70% solid and 30% melt. The solid is a eutectic containing 60% Bi.
    (E) A solution of pure Cd in a eutectic containing 60% Bi.

134.   At 100°C, alloy ① consists of

    (A) A solid solution of Cd in Bi.
    (B) Solid Cd and solid eutectic containing 60% Bi.
    (C) Solid Cd and solid eutectic containing 75% Bi.
    (D) Solid Bi and solid eutectic containing 40% Cd.
    (E) Solid Cd and liquid eutectic.

135.   Which of the following sketches best represents the cooling curve (temperature vs. time) of alloy ①?

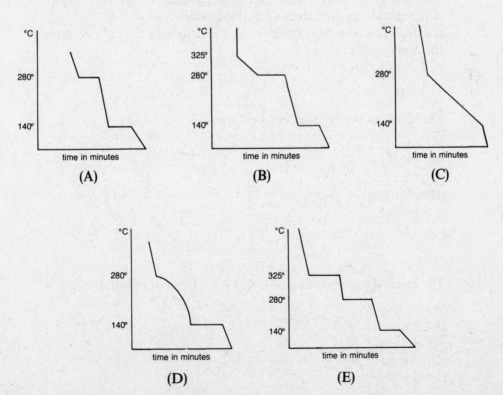

The Structure of Matter

136. The number of protons in an atomic nucleus is equal to

  (A) the atomic number
  (B) the atomic weight
  (C) the atomic number plus the atomic weight
  (D) the atomic weight minus the atomic number
  (E) none of the above

137. A violet color obtained in a flame test indicates the presence of

  (A) sodium
  (B) potassium
  (C) mercury
  (D) barium
  (E) chlorine

138. The nucleus of a fluoride ion contains

  (A) one more electron than the fluorine atom
  (B) one more neutron than the fluorine atom
  (C) one more proton than the fluorine atom
  (D) the same number of protons and neutrons as the fluorine atom
  (E) none of the above

139. The uranium decay chain ends with stable

  (A) radium
  (B) thorium
  (C) lead
  (D) plutonium
  (E) helium

140. The approximate quantity of U-238 for 1 curie of radioactivity is

  (A) 3 μg
  (B) 3 mg
  (C) 3 g
  (D) 3 Kg
  (E) 3 tonnes

Answer Key
Practice Examination 1—A.M. Part

Electrical Circuits

1.	B	7.	B	13.	C
2.	E	8.	D	14.	B
3.	C	9.	A	15.	C
4.	A	10.	B	16.	C
5.	E	11.	D	17.	A
6.	E	12.	E	18.	C

Statics

19.	C	24.	C	28.	A
20.	B	25.	E	29.	B
21.	B	26.	A	30.	C
22.	E	27.	E	31.	B
23.	E				

Dynamics

32.	B	37.	C	41.	E
33.	A	38.	D	42.	D
34.	B	39.	E	43.	C
35.	D	40.	C	44.	D
36.	A				

Mechanics of Materials

45.	C	50.	C	54.	D
46.	D	51.	B	55.	D
47.	C	52.	D	56.	E
48.	C	53.	C	57.	B
49.	A				

Fluid Mechanics

58.	D	63.	E	67.	C
59.	C	64.	D	68.	D
60.	A	65.	E	69.	E
61.	B	66.	B	70.	C
62.	D			71.	E

Thermodynamics

72.	D	77.	C	81.	E
73.	A	78.	D	82.	C
74.	E	79.	B	83.	A
75.	A	80.	D	84.	B
76.	C			85.	C

Mathematics

86.	E	90.	D	94.	D
87.	D	91.	B	95.	E
88.	B	92.	D	96.	B
89.	A	93.	A	97.	C

Chemistry

98.	E	102.	A	105.	B
99.	A	103.	C	106.	C
100.	D	104.	E	107.	B
101.	D				

Computer Programming

108.	B	111.	C	114.	A
109.	B	112.	E	115.	E
110.	A	113.	B		

Mathematical Modeling of Engineering Systems

116.	A	119.	D	122.	D
117.	D	120.	C	123.	D
118.	A	121.	D		

Engineering Economics

124.	B	126.	B	128.	C
125.	E	127.	A	129.	D

Materials Science

130.	E	132.	A	134.	B
131.	C	133.	A	135.	D

The Structure of Matter

136. A	138. D	140. E
137. B	139. C	

SOLUTIONS
PRACTICE EXAMINATION 1
A.M. PART

Electrical Circuits

1. *Answer:* (B)

   Solution: Under load-sharing conditions, the terminal voltages of both batteries must be equal. Therefore, $V_1 - i_1 R_1 = V_2 - i_2 R_2$

   But $i_2 = 100 - i_1$

   Therefore, $25.2 - 0.04i_1 = 24.8 - 0.02(100 - i_1)$

   $i_1 = 40$ amperes

2. *Answer:* (E)

   Solution: $\text{rms} = \sqrt{\dfrac{1}{t}\int_0^t v^2\,dt} = \sqrt{\dfrac{1}{6}\left[\int_0^4 \left(\dfrac{10t}{4}\right)^2 dt + \int_4^6 (0)^2\,dt\right]}$

   $\text{rms} = \sqrt{\dfrac{1}{6}\left(\dfrac{100}{16}\right)\dfrac{t^3}{3}\Big|_0^4} = \sqrt{\dfrac{1}{6}\left(\dfrac{100}{16}\right)\dfrac{64}{3}} = \sqrt{\dfrac{200}{9}}$

   $\text{rms} = 4.71$ volts

3. *Answer:* (C)

   Solution: The total impedance equals $R_1 + R_2 + \dfrac{1}{j\omega C}$

   $Z_{\text{TOT}} = 300 + 200 + \dfrac{1}{j(2\pi fC)}$

   $Z_{\text{TOT}} = 300 + 200 - j\dfrac{100{,}000}{377}$

   $Z_{\text{TOT}} = 300 + 200 - j\,265.26$

   $Z_{\text{TOT}} = \sqrt{(500)^2 + (265.26)^2}$

   $Z_{\text{TOT}} = 566.0\,\Omega$

   $\therefore I = \dfrac{120}{566.0} = 0.212$ amperes

   $V_0 = I\sqrt{(R_2)^2 + (Xc)^2}$

   $V_0 = 0.212\sqrt{200^2 + (265.26)^2}$

   $V_0 = 0.212(332.21)$

   $V_0 = 70.4$ volts

4. *Answer:* (A)

   Solution: Synchronous speed in rpm $= 120\dfrac{f}{p} = \dfrac{120(60)}{6} = 1200$ rpm

   At 5% slip, rpm $= 0.95(1200) = 1140$ rpm

5. *Answer:* (E)

   Solution: Since $v_c = \frac{1}{c}\int i\,dt$, the voltage across each capacitor is inversely proportional to the capacitance, and the integral of the current is the same constant "K" for each capacitor.

   $$v_{100\mu F} + v_{200\mu F} + v_{300\mu F} = 60 \text{ volts}$$

   $$\frac{K}{100} + \frac{K}{200} + \frac{K}{300} = 60$$

   $$\frac{6K}{600} + \frac{3K}{600} + \frac{2K}{600} = \frac{60(600)}{600}$$

   $$K = \frac{36,000}{11}$$

   $$v_{100\mu F} = \frac{K}{100} = \frac{36,000}{1100} = 32.7 \text{ volts}$$

6. *Answer:* (E)

   Solution: While the switch is in the UP position, both capacitors are in series. The voltage across each capacitor is inversely proportional to capacitance, $v_c = \frac{1}{c}\int i\,dt$. Therefore, at time equals zero the voltage across the $20\mu F$ capacitor is -14.4 volts. This voltage then increases exponentially from an initial value of -14.4 volts to a final value of $+60$ volts. The full amplitude of the exponential rise is 74.4 volts, and the equation is therefore $v_0 = 60 - 74.4\varepsilon^{-0.5t}$.

   Notes: Let $K = \int i\,dt$

   $$\text{then: } \frac{K}{30} + \frac{K}{20} = 24 \text{ volts}$$

   $$K = \frac{14,400}{50}$$

   $$\text{and} \quad V_{20\mu F} = \frac{14,400}{50} \div 20$$

   $$= 14.4 \text{ volts}$$

   The reciprocal of the Time Constant $= \dfrac{1}{RC}$

   $$\frac{1}{RC} = \frac{1}{(100 \times 1000)(0.00002)}$$

   $$= 0.5$$

7. *Answer:* (B)

   Solution: $0 = 60 - 74.4\varepsilon^{-0.5t}$

   $$\ln\frac{60}{74.4} = -0.2151 = -0.5t$$

   $$t = 430 \text{ milliseconds}$$

8. *Answer:* (D)

    Solution: The polarity of the initial 14.4 volts across the capacitor is such that it adds to the 64 volts from the battery. Therefore, the full 74.4 volts is applied across the resistor the instant after the switch is thrown.

9. *Answer:* (A)

    Solution: The secondary current is 11 amperes, and the power delivered to the load is $I^2R = 1210$ watts. The power drawn by the primary is 1210 watts $\div 0.80 = 1512.5$ watts. The primary current is therefore 12.6 amperes. Since the primary and secondary currents are in opposition, the net current through the common winding is $12.6 - 11 = 1.6$ amperes.

10. *Answer:* (B)

    Solution: $i_s = i_L + i_z = 40\text{ma} + 10\text{ma} = 50\text{ma}$

    $$R_s = \frac{(30 - 20) \text{ volts}}{50\text{ma}} = 200 \text{ ohms}$$

    Note that if 40 volts had been used for determining R_s instead of 30 volts, the resulting circuit would then fall out of regulation whenever the input voltage drops below 40 volts.

11. *Answer:* (D)

    Solution: As the input voltage decreases from 40 to 30 volts, the current through the Zener diode will decrease, the voltage drop through the ammeter's resistance will decrease, and therefore the output voltage level will decrease. However, this level will always exceed the original Zener voltage output level.

12. *Answer:* (E)

    Solution: Since the applied voltage is connected to the non-inverting input, and since the feedback goes to the inverting input, the circuit becomes a voltage follower and the output is maintained at $+6$ volts no matter what the resistance values may be.

13. *Answer:* (C)

    Solution: Using superposition, the output may be determined as the composite sum of the two partial outputs obtained by considering only one input at a time while grounding the other.

    $$V_{01} \text{ (partial due to the } +6 \text{ volt input)} = -6\left(\frac{6K\Omega}{4K\Omega}\right) = -9 \text{ volts}$$

    V_{02} (partial due to the $+4$ volt input)

    $$= 4\left(\frac{8K\Omega}{8K\Omega + 2K\Omega}\right)\left(\frac{6K\Omega + 4K\Omega}{4K\Omega}\right)$$

    $$= +8 \text{ volts}$$

    The composite sum is therefore $-9 + 8 = -1$ volt

14. *Answer:* (B)

    Solution: The output of the op amp integrator is:

$$V_0 = -\frac{1}{RC}\int_0^t V_{IN}\,dt$$

The output resulting from the ramp input is:

$$V_{OR} = -\frac{1}{2}\int_0^4 \frac{5t}{4}\,dt = -\frac{5}{8}\left[\frac{t^2}{2}\right]_0^4 = -\frac{5}{16}(16) = -5 \text{ volts}$$

The output from the constant -2 volt input is:

$$V_{OC} = -\frac{1}{2}\int_4^7 -2\,dt = +1[t]_4^7 = 3 \text{ volts}$$

Combining both outputs:

$$V_{OR} + V_{OC} = -5 + 3 = -2 \text{ volts}$$

15. *Answer:* (C)
    Solution: The current at unity power factor would be $I_{1.0} = 600\cos\theta_1 = 600(0.75) = 450$ amps.
    Therefore, the current that would flow at 0.92 power factor is $I_{0.92} = \dfrac{450}{\cos\theta_2} = \dfrac{450}{0.92} = 489$ amps.

16. *Answer:* (C)
    Solution: $C = 1.2\left[\dfrac{G}{1+GH}\right]R$

    also: $C = 1.10R$

    $$\therefore 1.10R = \frac{1.2GR}{1+0.9G}$$

    $$1.10(1+0.9G) = 1.2G$$

    $$1.1 + 0.99G = 1.2G$$

    $$G = \frac{1.1}{0.21} = 5.24$$

17. *Answer:* (A)
    Solution: $GH(s) = \dfrac{1}{s+0.25}$, $\quad GH(j\omega) = \dfrac{1}{0.25 + j\omega} = \dfrac{4}{1+j4\omega}$

    At $\omega = 2.0$ radians/sec,

    $$dB = 20\log\frac{4}{\sqrt{1^2 + 8^2}} = -6.09 \text{ dB}$$

18. *Answer:* (C)
    Solution: The line current may be found from:

    $$P_{TOT} = \sqrt{3}\, VI\cos\theta$$

    $$120{,}000 = \sqrt{3}(440)(I)(0.8)$$

    $$\therefore I = 196.8 \text{ amperes}$$

    $$R = \frac{10.4(500)}{250{,}000} = 0.0208 \text{ ohms per conductor}$$

    $$IR = 4.09 \text{ volts}$$

Statics

19. *Answer:* **(C)**

    Solution: Since all forces act in the same plane, they can have moments only about axes perpendicular to that plane.

20. *Answer:* **(B)**

    Solution: $\vec{r} \times \vec{F} = (1\vec{i} + 1\vec{j} + 0\vec{k}) \times (12\vec{i} + 5\vec{j} + 0\vec{k}) = \begin{vmatrix} 1 & 1 & 0 \\ 12 & 5 & 0 \\ \vec{i} & \vec{j} & \vec{k} \end{vmatrix} = -7\vec{k}$ lb-ft

    Since $\vec{r} \times \vec{F}$ is a cross-product and therefore a vector quantity, answers involving magnitudes only are incorrect.

21. *Answer:* **(B)**

    Solution: Since the sum of the moments about a hinge is zero, either to the right or to the left of the hinge, the result is $R(6) - 12^K(3) = 0$, from which $R = 6^K$

22. *Answer:* **(E)**

    Solution: For equilibrium, $\Sigma Fx = \Sigma Fy = 0$. Considering horizontal components,

    $$F_{1x} + F_{2x} + F_{3x} = 0$$

    $$14.14\left(\frac{1}{\sqrt{2}}\right) - 15 + F_{3x} = 0 \quad \therefore F_{3x} = 5 \text{ lbs}$$

    Considering vertical components,

    $$F_{1y} + F_{2y} + F_{3y} = 0$$

    $$14.14\left(\frac{1}{\sqrt{2}}\right) + 0 + F_{3y} = 0 \quad \therefore F_{3y} = -10 \text{ lbs}$$

    $$F_3 = \sqrt{(F_{3x})^2 + (F_{3y})^2} = \sqrt{(5)^2 + (10)^2} = 11.2 \text{ lbs}$$

23. *Answer:* **(E)**

    Solution: $\bar{Y} = \dfrac{\Sigma Ay}{\Sigma A} = \dfrac{6 \times 3 \times 3 - \pi(1)^2 \times 1}{6 \times 3 - \pi(1)^2} = 3.42 \text{ inches}$

24. *Answer:* **(C)**

    Solution: $I_{x-x} = \Sigma Icg + \Sigma Ad^2$

    $$= \left(\frac{1}{12}bh^3 - \frac{\pi r^4}{4}\right) + \left(bh\left(\frac{h}{2}\right)^2 - \pi(r)^2(r)\right)$$

    $$= \left(\frac{1}{12}(3)(6)^3 - \frac{\pi(1)^4}{4}\right) + \left(\frac{1}{4}(3)(6)^3 - \pi(1)^3\right) = 212 \text{ in}^4$$

25. *Answer:* (E)

    Solution: Due to friction of the pulley:

    $$T = 100e^{-\mu\beta}$$

    $$T = 100e^{-0.2\frac{\pi}{2}}$$

    $$T = 73.04 \text{ lbs}$$

    Due to friction on the horizontal surface:

    $$0.2W = 73.04$$

    $$W = 365 \text{ lbs}$$

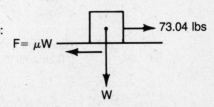

26. *Answer:* (A)

    Solution: Since joint U_2 is unloaded, and U_2L_2 is perpendicular to U_1U_2 and U_2U_3, no force can be transferred to member U_2L_2, hence the load in that member is zero.

27. *Answer:* (E)

    Solution: $F_H = W(\mu) = 200(0.25) = 50$ pounds

    Since the applied horizontal force exceeds this value, the block will move at any height at which the force is applied.

28. *Answer:* (A)

    Solution: An equilateral triangle is formed by connecting the centers, such that $F_v = W/2$. Since $\tan\theta = F_v/F_H$, and since $\theta = 60$ degrees,

    $$F_H = \frac{W}{2\tan 60°} = \frac{1000}{2\sqrt{3}} = 289 \text{ pounds}$$

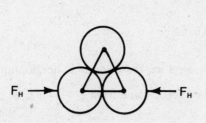

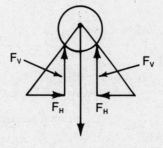

29. *Answer:* (B)

    Solution: $\Sigma M_0 = 0$

    $$1500(L\cos\alpha) - 2000(L\sin\alpha) - 2000\left(\frac{L}{2}\sin\alpha\right) = 0$$

    $$1500(L\cos\alpha) - 3000(L\sin\alpha) = 0$$

    $$\frac{\sin\alpha}{\cos\alpha} = \tan\alpha = \frac{1500\,L}{3000\,L} = 0.5$$

    $$\alpha = 26.6°$$

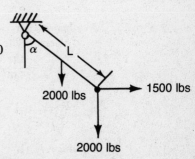

30. *Answer:* (C)

    Solution: The summation of the moments about point A equals zero.

$$\Sigma M_A = 100(13)\left(\frac{13}{2}\right) - \frac{5}{13}(R)(12) - \frac{12}{13}(R)(5) = 0$$

$$R = \frac{100(13)^3}{2(60)(2)} = 915 \text{ lbs}$$

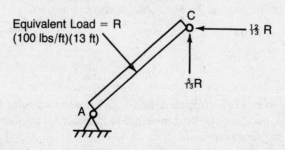

31. *Answer:* (B)

    Solution: $F = W\sin(\tan^{-1} 0.01)$

$$F = 100{,}000(50)\sin 0.5729°$$

$$F = 49{,}998 \text{ lbs}$$

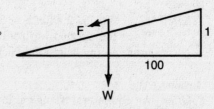

Dynamics

32. *Answer:* (B)

    Solution: At the highest point in the trajectory the velocity is horizontal; the normal acceleration is therefore vertical and from $\dfrac{mv^2}{\rho} = mg$, we have

$$\rho = \frac{v^2}{g} = \frac{10^2}{32.2} = 3.106 \text{ ft.}$$

33. *Answer:* (A)

    Solution: The power required is equal to $-\mathbf{F}\cdot\mathbf{V}$. Since friction is neglected, only the weight need be considered. The angle between W and V is $90° + \tan^{-1} 0.07 = 94.004°$ and thus

$$-\mathbf{F}\cdot\mathbf{V} = \frac{-1}{550} \times 20{,}000 \times \frac{35 \times 5280}{3600}\cos 94.004° = 130 \text{ HP}$$

34. *Answer:* (B)

    Solution: Since impact is frictionless, $V_{1y} = V_{2y}$

           Also $V_{2x} = 0.80\, V_{1x}$

           Therefore $\tan\theta_2 = 0.80\tan\theta_1 = 0.80$

           Thus $\theta_2 = 38.659°$

35. *Answer:* (D)

    Solution: From impulse and momentum relationships, $mv_2 - mv_1 = \int_0^t F\,dt$

    Since $mv_1 = 0$, mv_2 will become maximum at $t = 2$ sec (largest area)

    $$\left(\frac{20}{32.2}\right)V_{max} = 10 \times \frac{2}{2}$$

    or $V_{max} = 16.1$ ft/sec

36. *Answer:* (A)

    Solution: At the end of the swing the velocity is zero, and the normal acceleration is zero. For the tangential acceleration, $a_t = \dfrac{Mg\cos 60°}{M} = g\cos 60°$

    $= 16.1$ ft/sec^2.

37. *Answer:* (C)

    Solution: To avoid sliding, the acceleration must be limited so that

    $$\frac{T}{N} = \frac{ma}{mg} \leq 0.6 \quad\text{or}\quad a_{max} = 0.6 \times 32.2 = 19.37 \text{ ft/sec}^2$$

    Now $V = \dfrac{50 \times 5280}{3600} = 73.333$ ft/sec

    $$\therefore t = \frac{73.333}{19.32} = 3.795 \text{ sec}$$

38. *Answer:* (D)

    Solution: Since weight and normal reaction cancel (no vertical motion), the only remaining force is the spring force which always passes through the fixed point 0. Thus the angular momentum is constant and $m(\vec{v}_1 \cdot \vec{r}_1) =$

    $m(\vec{v}_2 \cdot \vec{r}_2)$ or $v_2 = v_1\dfrac{r_1}{r_2} = 12 \times \dfrac{6}{4} = 18$ ft/sec.

39. *Answer:* (E)

    Solution: When the spring length is a minimum, $v = 0$. From conservation of energy,

    $$\frac{mv^2}{2} = \frac{k\Delta l^2}{2} \quad\text{or}\quad \Delta l = \sqrt{\frac{100 \times 6^2}{10,800 \times 12}} \times 12 = 2 \text{ inches.}$$

    Thus $l_{min} = 8 - 2 = 6$ inches

40. *Answer:* (C)

    Solution: For the quickest crossing, the north component of the resultant velocity $\vec{V}_{RN}$ should be a maximum. Hence the bow should point due north at all times. Note that the downstream drift will cause the resulting path to be non-minimum.

    NOTE: If the boat were to maintain a heading of N 30° E, the westward velocity component of the stream would be canceled out, and the resulting crossing would trace the shortest possible route, but since the northward component of velocity would only be 13.86 feet/second, the actual crossing would be slower.

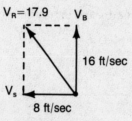

Optimum Solution

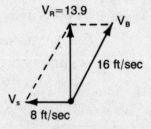

Incorrect Solution

41. *Answer:* (E)

    Solution: From $m\dfrac{v^2}{r} = \dfrac{GMm}{r^2}$ we have $v^2 = \dfrac{GM}{r}$ or $v = \dfrac{K}{\sqrt{r}}$

42. *Answer:* (D)

    Solution: From conservation of energy, $T_1 + V_1 = T_2 + V_2$

    or $0 + \dfrac{L}{2}mg = \dfrac{L}{2}I\omega^2 + 0$

    But $I = \dfrac{mL^2}{3}$ and $\omega = \dfrac{V_{tip}}{L}$

    $\therefore \dfrac{L}{2}mg = \dfrac{1}{2}\dfrac{mL^2}{3}\dfrac{V^2}{L^2}$

    or $v = \sqrt{3Lg} = \sqrt{3 \times 2 \times 32.2} = 13.90$ meters/second

43. *Answer:* (C)

    Solution: Let "a" be the linear acceleration; then we have $I\alpha = M$ and

    $\alpha = \dfrac{a}{r}$

    or $\left[\dfrac{4}{g}r^2 + \dfrac{2}{g}r^2\right]\dfrac{a}{r} = 4r - 2r$

    or $a = \dfrac{2}{6}g = \dfrac{g}{3}$

    Consider the motion of the 4-pound body. Then

    $4 - T = \dfrac{4}{g}(a)$ or $4 - T = \dfrac{4}{g}\left(\dfrac{g}{3}\right)$

    or $T = 4 - \dfrac{4}{3} = 2\dfrac{2}{3}$ lb

44. *Answer:* (D)

   Solution: Let the variable s be the stopping distance. Then from the work energy principle,

   $$\frac{1}{2}\left[\frac{20,000}{32.2}\right]\left[\frac{(35)(5280)}{3600}\right]^2 + [s \sin \alpha]20,000 = 16,000s$$

   Now $\alpha = \tan^{-1} 0.07 = 4.004°$, and $\sin \alpha = 0.06982$
   Solving for s, s = 56.03 ft

Mechanics of Materials

45. *Answer:* (C)

   Solution: Poisson's ratio measures lateral strain. Since an extensometer measures only longitudinal deformation, Poisson's ratio cannot be determined by the test.

46. *Answer:* (D)

   Solution: $T = \dfrac{\tau J}{r}$ for both shafts. If, however, the outer radius r_0 and the shear stress τ are the same, then

   $$\frac{T_{hollow}}{T_{solid}} = \frac{J_{hollow}}{J_{solid}} = \frac{R_0^4 - R_i^4}{R_0^4} = \frac{1 - (\frac{1}{2})^4}{1} = \frac{15}{16} = 0.9375$$

47. *Answer:* (C)

   Solution: $\sigma_1 = \dfrac{P}{A} = \dfrac{20,000}{\frac{\pi}{4}(1)^2} = 25,465$ psi

   Using state of stress at a point, where σ_1 = maximum normal stress and σ_2 is minimum,

   $$\tau_{max} = \tau_{45} = \sqrt{\frac{(\sigma_1 - \sigma_2)^2}{4} + 0} = \frac{25,465}{2} = 12,732 \text{ psi}$$

48. *Answer:* (C)

   Solution: $\mu = \dfrac{1}{2}\dfrac{\sigma^2}{E} = \dfrac{(20,000)^2}{2(10)(10)^6} = 20$ in-lbs/in^3

   $U = \mu V = 20(1)(30) = 600$ in-lbs

49. *Answer:* (A)

   Solution: The moment-area method is a means for integrating the moment expressions in order to obtain the slopes and deflection of beams through the elastic relation $EIy'' = M$.

50. *Answer:* (C)

   Solution: Since the left reaction is $\dfrac{P}{2}$, $M(x)$ is equal to $\dfrac{Px}{2}$ for values of x such that

   $0 \le x \le \dfrac{L}{2}$.

   Integrating twice, $EIy'' = \dfrac{Px}{2}$

   $$EIy' = \dfrac{P}{4}x^2 + C_1$$

   $$EIy = \dfrac{P}{12}x^3 + C_1 x + C_2$$

   Using boundary conditions, $EIy(0) = EIy'\left(\dfrac{L}{2}\right) = 0$

   $$\therefore C_2 = 0 \quad \text{and} \quad C_1 = -\dfrac{PL^2}{16}$$

   $$EIy = \dfrac{Px^3}{12} - \dfrac{PL^2 x}{16} + 0$$

51. *Answer:* (B)

   Solution: $\varepsilon_{\text{lateral}} = v\varepsilon_{\text{axial}}$

   $$\varepsilon_{\text{axial}} = -\alpha(\Delta T) = -6(100)\mu = \dfrac{\sigma}{E} = \dfrac{\sigma}{30K \times 10^3}$$

   $\sigma = -18 \text{ Ksi}$

   $$\varepsilon_{\text{lateral}} = \dfrac{-0.3(-18)}{30 \times 10^3} = 180\mu$$

52. *Answer:* (D)

   Solution: End deflection, $\delta = \dfrac{5PL^3}{48EI} - \dfrac{PL^3}{4 \times 3 \, EI} = \dfrac{PL^3}{48EI}$

   $$F = k\delta \text{ and } k = \dfrac{F}{\delta} = \dfrac{\dfrac{P}{4}}{\dfrac{PL^3}{48EI}} = \dfrac{12EI}{L^3}$$

53. *Answer:* (C)

   Solution: For fully plastic loading, the area above the neutral axis must equal the
   area below the neutral axis. Hence:

   $$(8)(1) + (\bar{y} - 1)(1) = (4)(1) + (7 - \bar{y})(1)$$

   $$2\bar{y} = 11 - 7$$

   $$\bar{y} = 2 \text{ inches}$$

54. *Answer:* (D)

    Solution: $HP = \dfrac{(T)(w)}{550}$ $\therefore T = \dfrac{550(5)(12)}{2\pi(600)/60} = 525$ inch/pounds

$$\tau = \frac{T(r)}{J} = \frac{525(0.5)}{\dfrac{\pi}{2}\left(\dfrac{1}{2}\right)^4} = 2674 \text{ psi}$$

55. *Answer:* (D)

    Solution: $\theta = \dfrac{TL}{JG} = \dfrac{60{,}000(30)}{\dfrac{\pi(1)^4}{2}(12)(10)^6} = 0.1$ radians

$$\theta = \frac{0.1(180)}{\pi} = 5.7 \text{ degrees}$$

56. *Answer:* (E)

    Solution: The Euler-Bernoulli theory is the means of defining elastic stresses in a prismatic beam. It is valid only up to the elastic limit and hence is not a failure theory.

57. *Answer:* (B)

    Solution: $\sigma = \dfrac{P}{A} - \dfrac{Pec}{I} = 0$

$$\frac{4P}{\pi d^2} - \frac{64\,Pe}{\pi d^4}\left(\frac{d}{2}\right) = 0$$

(in any direction)

$$e = \pm\frac{d}{8}$$

Fluid Mechanics

58. *Answer:* (D)

    Solution: $h = \dfrac{4\sigma \cos \beta}{\gamma d}$

$$h = \frac{(4)(0.005)(1)}{(62.4)\left(\dfrac{.012}{12}\right)} = 0.321 \text{ feet}$$

59. *Answer:* (C)

    Solution: $F = \gamma h A$

$$\therefore h = \frac{F}{\gamma A} = \frac{2000}{62.4(1)} = 32.05 \text{ feet}$$

60. *Answer:* (A)

    Solution: Critical pressure ratio $= \left(\dfrac{p_2}{p_1}\right)_c = \left[\dfrac{2}{k+1}\right]^{\frac{k}{k-1}}$

    $$\text{ratio} = \left(\dfrac{2}{1.6+1}\right)^{\frac{1.6}{0.6}} = 0.497$$

61. *Answer:* (B)

    Solution: $N_R = \dfrac{\rho V d}{\mu}$ where μ, the dynamic viscosity, is equal to $2.359(10)^{-5}$ lb-sec/ft^2

    $$N_R = \dfrac{62.4(10)(2/12)}{32.2(2.359)(10)^{-5}} = 136{,}900$$

62. *Answer:* (D)

    Solution: The pressure loss $\Delta P = f\dfrac{L\rho V^2}{d(2g)}$

    $$\Delta P = (0.022)\left(\dfrac{200}{2/12}\right)\left(\dfrac{62.4(10)^2}{2(32.2)}\right)\left(\dfrac{1}{144}\right) = 17.76 \text{ psi}$$

63. *Answer:* (E)

    Solution: $\Delta P = K q_t = \dfrac{K\rho V_t^2}{2}$

    $$\Delta P = (0.05)\left(\dfrac{62.4}{32.2}\right)\left(\dfrac{40^2}{2}\right)\left(\dfrac{1}{144}\right) = 0.538 \text{ psi}$$

64. *Answer:* (D)

    Solution: The static pressure at the exit equals zero psig. The summation of the pressure losses, using the method shown in solutions #62 and #63, is:

Pipe frictional loss	17.76 psig
Venturi loss	0.54
One valve and two bends	8.08
100 feet of head	43.33
Total pressure loss	69.71 psig

    Since the velocity at A is the same as the velocity at the exit, the velocity terms drop out, and the static pressure at A is the total pressure drop of 69.7 psig.

65. *Answer:* (E)

    Solution: The static pressure at B may be found by $P_B = P_A + q_A - q_T$
    where: P_A from solution #64 is 69.71 psig

    $$q_A = \dfrac{1}{2}\rho V^2 = \dfrac{62.4(10)^2}{2(32.2)(144)} = 0.673 \text{ psig}$$

    $$q_T = \dfrac{1}{2}\rho V^2 = \dfrac{62.4(40)^2}{2(32.2)(144)} = 10.77 \text{ psig}$$

    $\therefore P_B = 69.71 + 0.67 - 10.77 = 59.61 \text{ psig}$

66. *Answer:* (B)

    Solution: $R_H = \dfrac{\text{Flow Area}}{\text{Wetted perimeter}} = \dfrac{2(10)}{2 + 2 + 10} = 1.43$ feet

67. *Answer:* (C)

    Solution: Critical depth $= y_c = \sqrt[3]{\dfrac{q^2}{g}}$

    $$y_c = \sqrt[3]{\dfrac{(350/10)^2}{32.2}} = 3.36 \text{ feet}$$

68. *Answer:* (D)

    Solution: The Froude number is the ratio of inertial and gravitational forces.

69. *Answer:* (E)

    Solution: A Bourdon gage is primarily a pressure measuring device rather than a flow rate measuring device.

70. *Answer:* (C)

    Solution: May include a normal shock with a portion of the flow supersonic (upstream of the shock) and a portion subsonic (downstream of the shock).

71. *Answer:* (E)

    Solution: $HP = \dfrac{Q\gamma\Delta P}{\eta 550}$

    $$HP = \dfrac{(5)(62.4)(34.7 - 10)}{(0.80)(550)} = 17.5 \text{ HP}$$

Thermodynamics

72. *Answer:* (D)

    Solution: From the steam tables, the partial pressure of saturated water vapor at a dew-point temperature of 80°F is 0.5069 psia. From Dalton's Law, the partial pressure of air P_A is $P_A = 14.7 - 0.5069 = 14.19$ psia.

73. *Answer:* (A)

    Solution: The initial pressure is obtained from the perfect gas equation of state:

    $$p_1 = \frac{mRT}{v} = \frac{32 \text{ lb}_m \; 48.24 \dfrac{\text{ft-lb}_4}{\text{lb}_m \text{°R}} \; 530\text{°R}}{100 \text{ ft}^3}$$

    $$p_1 = 8181.5 \text{ psfa} = 56.816 \text{ psia}$$

The final temperature is obtained from the isentropic equation:

$$T_2 = T_1(p_2/p_1)^{\frac{\gamma-1}{\gamma}}$$

$$T_2 = 530(100/56.816)^{\frac{1.4-1}{1.4}}$$

$$T_2 = 622.9°R = 162.9°F$$

74. *Answer:* (E)

   Solution: Cooling the beef from 80°F to 26°F,

   $$Q = WC_P\Delta T = (200)(0.9 \text{ Btu/lb/°F})(80 - 26) = 9720 \text{ Btu}$$

   Freezing at 26°F,

   $$Q = WL = 200(123 \text{ Btu/lb}) = 24,600 \text{ Btu}$$

   Cooling the beef from 26°F to 0°F,

   $$Q = (200 \text{ lb})(0.45 \text{ Btu/lb/°F})(26 - 0) = 2340 \text{ Btu}$$

   Total Heat Removed = 9720 + 24,600 + 2340 = 36,660 Btu

75. *Answer:* (A)

   Solution: The efficiency of a Carnot cycle is:

   $$\eta = \frac{T_1 - T_2}{T_1} \quad \text{where temperature is expressed in degrees Rankine.}$$

   $$\eta = \frac{1440 - 960}{1440}$$

   $$\eta = 37.3\%$$

76. *Answer:* (C)

   Solution: For a frictionless process $W = \int p\,dV$, or for constant pressure:

   $$W = p(V_2 - V_1) = (20)(144)(1000 - 700)$$

   $$W = 864,000 \text{ ft-lb}$$

   $$W = 1110.54 \text{ Btu}$$

77. *Answer:* (C)

   Solution: From the First Law $Q = \Delta E + W$
   From problem #76, $W = 1110.54$ Btu
   $Q = 100$ Btu/hr $\times 2 = 200$ Btu.
   Both W and Q are positive, since the work is done by the system and the heat is added to the system.
   $\Delta E = Q - W = 200 - 1110.54$
   $\Delta E = -910.54$ Btu

78. *Answer:* (D)

   Solution: In an isentropic process $\gamma = 1.4$,

   $$\frac{T_2}{T_1} = \left[\frac{P_2}{P_1}\right]^{\frac{\gamma-1}{\gamma}}, \text{ where temperature is expressed in degrees Rankine,}$$

$$T_2 = 530 \left[\frac{1000}{14.7}\right]^{\frac{1.4-1}{1.4}} = 1770°R$$

$$T_2 = 1310°F$$

79. *Answer:* (B)

   Solution: Brayton Cycle Efficiency $= \eta = 1 - \frac{T_d}{T_a}$

   where T_a = Initial temperature when heat is added (500°R)
   T_d = Final temperature after heat is rejected (379°R)

   $$\eta = 1 - \frac{379}{500} = 24.2\%$$

80. *Answer:* (D)

   Solution: The density at the initial condition is:

   $$\rho = \frac{p}{RT} = 0.5061 \text{ lb/ft}^3$$

   $$V = \frac{w}{\rho A} = \frac{10 \text{ lb/sec}}{0.5061 \text{ lb/ft}^3 \frac{\pi}{4}\left(\frac{5}{12}\right)^2} = 144.9 \text{ fps}$$

   $$\frac{V^2}{2g_0} = \frac{(144.9)^2}{2(32.2)} = 326\frac{\text{ft-lb}}{\text{lb}} = 0.419 \text{ Btu/lb}$$

   $$h + \frac{v^2}{2g_0} = 396.42 \text{ Btu/lb}$$

81. *Answer:* (E)

   Solution: Using a solution similar to that for problem #80, the final energy is:

   $$\rho = \frac{300 - 30}{R(1500)} = 0.48585 \text{ lb/ft}^3$$

   $$V = \frac{10}{0.486\frac{\pi}{4}\left(\frac{5}{12}\right)^2} = 150.95 \text{ fps}$$

   $$\frac{V^2}{2g_0} = 0.455 \text{ Btu/lb}$$

   By the conservation of energy

   $$h_1 + \frac{V_1^2}{2g_0} + Q = h_2 + \frac{V_2^2}{2g_0}$$

   $$Q = -27 + 0.455 - 0.419 = -27.0$$

   $$Q = -26.964 \text{ Btu/lb (heat lost)}$$

82. *Answer:* (C)

   Solution: A pressure regulator reduces pressure by throttling the flow. Hence
   $h_1 = h_2 = 396 \text{ Btu/lb}.$

83. *Answer:* (A)

   Solution: The available energy decreases in any heat transfer process (Second Law) because a temperature difference must exist between the air and fuel.

84. *Answer:* (B)

   Solution: The maximum efficiency (η_{max}) is:

   $$\eta_{max} = \frac{T_2 - T_1}{T_2}$$

   $$\eta_{max} = \frac{540 - 495}{540}$$

   $$\eta_{max} = 8.33\%$$

85. *Answer:* (C)

   Solution: Change in entropy $\Delta S = \int \frac{dQ}{T}$

   Since $T = $ constant, $\Delta S = \frac{\Delta Q}{T} = \frac{50}{530}$

   $\Delta S = 0.09434$ Btu/°R

   NOTE: Change in entropy is defined for a reversible process.

Mathematics

86. *Answer:* (E)

   Solution: $y = 4 - 10\varepsilon^{-ax}$

   When $x = 0$, $y = 4 - 10(1) = -6$

   When $x = \infty$, $y = 4 - 10(0) = 4$

87. *Answer:* (D)

   Solution: By taking the derivative with respect to x, and evaluating that expression at x equals zero,

   $$\frac{d}{dx}[4 - 10\varepsilon^{-ax}] = 0 - 10\varepsilon^{-ax}[-a]_{x=0} = 10a$$

88. *Answer:* (B)

   Solution: The exponential equation from problem #86, $y = 4 - 10\varepsilon^{-ax}$ must now be valid at $(2, 0)$. Substituting this point and solving for a,

   $$0 = 4 - 10\varepsilon^{-2a}$$

   $$-4 = -10\varepsilon^{-2a}$$

   $$\varepsilon^{-2a} = 0.4$$

   $$-2a \ln \varepsilon = \ln 0.4 = -0.9163$$

   $$\therefore a = 0.4582$$

89. *Answer:* (A)

    Solution: $y = 3(-2)(4) + 0 + (-1)(4)(1) - (-1)(-2)(2) - 0 - 4(4)(1)$

    $y = -24 + 0 + -4 - 4 - 0 - 16$

    $y = -48$

90. *Answer:* (D)

    Solution: Statistical tables indicate that 19% of all data points in a normal distribution lie between zero and a 0.50 standard deviation. Due to symmetry, therefore, this percentage is doubled when plus or minus tolerances are considered. (The 34% and 68% values which bracket this answer reflect the well-known percentages for one standard deviation and for plus or minus one standard deviation, respectively.)

91. *Answer:* (B)

    Solution: $\dfrac{30°}{360°} = \dfrac{1}{12}$ cycle. For $\sin 2\pi(100)t$, $w = 2\pi(100)$ and $f = 100$ cps.

    At 100 cps, $t = \dfrac{1}{12}(0.01)$ seconds

    $y = 10\varepsilon^{\frac{-600(0.01)}{12}} \sin 30°$

    $y = 10[0.60653][0.5]$

    $y = 3.033$

92. *Answer:* (D)

    Solution: $16x^2 - 160x + 9y^2 + 36y + 292 = 0$

    $16[x^2 - 10x + 25] + 9[y^2 + 4y + 4] = 144$

    $16(x - 5)^2 + 9(y + 2)^2 = 144$

    $\dfrac{(x - 5)^2}{9} + \dfrac{(y + 2)^2}{16} = 1$

    This is the classical equation of an ellipse with a center at $(5, -2)$.

93. *Answer:* (A)

    Solution: Applying the binomial expansion theorem,

    $$(H + T)^{10} = H^{10} + 10\,H^9T + 45\,H^8T^2 + 120\,H^7T^3 + 210\,H^6T^4$$
    $$+ 252\,H^5T^5 + 210\,H^4T^6 + 120\,H^3T^7 + 45\,H^2T^8$$
    $$+ 10\,HT^9 + T^{10}$$

    Since the sum of all the coefficients is $(2)^{10} = 1024$, the probability of 5 heads and 5 tails, as described by the sixth term in the expansion, is $252/1024 = 0.246$.

94. *Answer:* (D)

   Solution: First, find the slope m,

   $$m = \frac{y_2 - y_1}{x_2 - x_1} = \frac{-3 - 9}{5 - 2} = \frac{-12}{3} = -4$$

   Next, substitute the values of either point into the general equation,

   $$y = mx + b$$

   Using the point (2, 9)

   $$9 = -4(2) + b$$

   $$b = 17$$

   The equation is therefore $y = -4x + 17$, and the y-intercept = 17

95. *Answer:* (E)

96. *Answer:* (B)

   Solution: As shown in the accompanying diagram, the hyperbolic functions cosh μ and sinh μ define the coordinates of the hyperbola in much the same way as cos θ and sin θ define the horizontal and vertical projections of a unit circle.

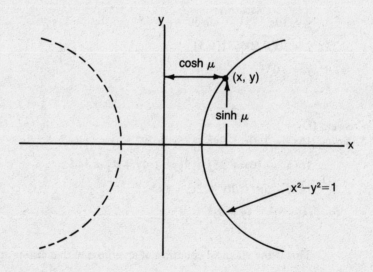

97. *Answer:* (C)

   Solution: $\dfrac{d^2y}{dx^2} - 3\dfrac{dy}{dx} + 2y = 0$

   This is a second order differential equation with constant coefficients.

   Auxiliary equation $m^2 - 3m + 2 = 0$

   $$(m - 1)(m - 2) = 0$$

   $$m = 1, \quad m = 2$$

   The roots are real and distinct, $y = C_1\varepsilon^x + C_2\varepsilon^{2x}$

Chemistry

98. *Answer:* (E)

99. *Answer:* (A)

100. *Answer:* (D)

101. *Answer:* (D)

102. *Answer:* (A)
   Solution: H^+ conc $= 1 \times 10^{-6}$ mol/cc

   $$= 1 \times 10^{-3} \text{ mol/l}$$

   $$pH = \log \frac{1}{(H)} = \log \frac{1}{10^{-3}} = \log 10^3 = 3$$

103. *Answer:* (C)

104. *Answer:* (E)
   Solution: $HA \rightarrow H^+ + A^-$

   $$\frac{[H^+][A^-]}{[HA]} = K = \text{ionization constant}$$

   $[HA] = 0.3$ molar $= 0.3$ mols/l.

   For both H^+ and A^-, 0.4% ionized $= 0.0012$ mols/l.

   $$K = \frac{[0.0012]^2}{0.3} = 4.8 \times 10^{-6}$$

105. *Answer:* (B)
   Solution: $[H^+] = 1.2 \times 10^{-3}$ mols/l.

   $$pH = \log \frac{1}{1.2 \times 10^{-3}} = 2.919$$

106. *Answer:* (C)
   Solution:
   $$\overset{1000}{Ca(NO_3)_2} + Na_2CO_3 \rightarrow \overset{x}{CaCO_3}\downarrow + 2\,NaNO_3$$
   $$\underset{164}{} \quad \underset{106}{} \quad \underset{100}{}$$

   $$x = \frac{1000}{164} \times 106 = 645 \text{ lbs soda ash/1000 lbs calcium nitrate}$$

107. *Answer:* (B)
   Solution: Since calcium carbonate has a molecular weight of 100, and the calcium nitrate has a weight of 164, the flow rate of the calcium carbonate is:

   $$\text{Flow rate} = \frac{100}{164} \times 1000 = 609.8 \text{ pounds/hour}$$

   Filter Area $= 610 \div 10$ pounds/hour $= 61$ square feet

Computer Programming

108. *Answer:* (B)
     Solution: The number 49.5 represents the largest value of x that does not exceed 50.

109. *Answer:* (B)
     Solution: Successive division by 2 develops the binary equivalent, the least significant digit first.

$$77/2 = 38, R = 1$$
$$38/2 = 19, R = 0$$
$$19/2 = 9, R = 1$$
$$9/2 = 4, R = 1$$
$$4/2 = 2, R = 0$$
$$2/2 = 1, R = 0$$
$$1/2 = 0, R = 1$$

$$(1001101)_2 = (77)_{10}$$

110. *Answer:* (A)
     Solution: In the process of converting from hex to binary, each hex digit is four binary digits. Also, each octal digit is three binary digits.

$$(129)_{16} = (0001\ 0010\ 1001)_2$$

$$(000\ 100\ 101\ 001)_2 = (0451)_8$$

111. *Answer:* (C)
     Solution: Since the leftmost bit in the 2's complement number is a 0, the number is positive.

$$(1010010)_2 =$$

$$(1*64 + 0*32 + 1*16 + 0*8 + 0*4 + 1*2 + 0*1)_{10} = (82)_{10}$$

112. *Answer:* (E)
     Solution: (A) The FORTRAN multiplication operator is *, not x.
     (B) The FORTRAN equivalence operator is .EQ., not =.
     (C) The FORTRAN exponentiation operator is **, not ↑.
     (D) This is a FORTRAN expression, not a statement.
     (E) This is correct.

113. *Answer:* (B)
     Solution: (A) NOT((625 > 10) AND (10 = 10)) ⇒ (NOT TRUE) AND TRUE
     ⇒ FALSE
     (B) (250 < 100) OR NOT (100 < > 100) ⇒ FALSE OR (NOT FALSE)
     ⇒ TRUE
     (C) (25 < 10) OR (105 = 110) AND (10 < 100)
     ⇒ FALSE OR (FALSE AND TRUE)
     ⇒ FALSE
     (D) (25 < 10) AND (100 > = 10) OR (5 = 10)
     ⇒ (FALSE AND TRUE) OR FALSE
     ⇒ FALSE

114. *Answer:* (A)
   Solution:

   $$\begin{array}{cccc} 1 & 1 & & \\ 6 & 5 & 7 & 657 \\ +3 & 2 & 5 & +325 \\ \hline (12)_8 & (10)_8 & (14)_8 & 1204_8 \end{array}$$

   so

115. *Answer:* (E)
   Solution: FORTRAN variable names must consist of one to six alphanumeric characters, the first of which must be a letter (spaces are ignored). The first character of (E) is 2, which is not a letter.

Mathematical Modeling of Engineering Systems

116. *Answer:* (A)
   Solution: The open loop gain of the unity feedback system shown, expressed in Laplace notation, is

   $$GH(s) = \frac{0.4s(s + 5000)}{(s + 0.1)(s + 20)}$$

   This open loop gain, expressed in terms of steady-state sinusoidal signals, is

   $$GH(jw) = \frac{0.4jw(jw + 5000)}{(jw + 0.1)(jw + 20)} = \frac{1000jw(1 + j.0002w)}{(1 + j10w)(1 + j.05w)}$$

   Based on this expression, the Bode amplitude plot in decibels is therefore:

   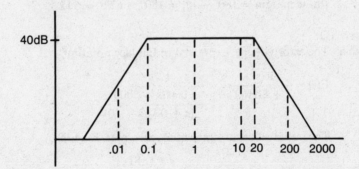

117. *Answer:* (D)
   Solution: (Shown in solution #116.) Note that the line segment with the positive slope corresponds to the 1000 jw factor. This line would have reached 60 dB at w equal to 1 radian/second, except for the denominator factor of (1 + j10w) which created the corner at w equal to 0.1 radians/second. Hence, the mid-band gain is 40 dB (not 60 dB).

118. *Answer:* (A)
   Solution: In this unity feedback system, since the mid-band value of forward gain is 100, the output will be approximately 99 percent of the input. dB $= 20 \log 0.99 = -0.09$ dB

Alternatively, a valid approximation may be obtained by using unity as the overall gain, from which dB = 20 log 1 = 0 dB.

119. *Answer:* (D)
   Solution: Shown in the Bode plot included in the solution to problem #116.

120. *Answer:* (C)
   Solution: Shown in the Bode plot included in the solution to problem #116.

121. *Answer:* (D)
   Solution: Unit slope is −20 dB per decade, or −6 dB per octave. See Bode plot in solution #116.

122. *Answer:* (D)
   Solution: Gain crossover occurs at an angular velocity of 2000 radians/second, as verified by the Bode plot. The total phase angle at this frequency equals the summation of the individual phase angles.

FACTOR	PHASE ANGLE	RESULTANT
1000 jw	$\theta = +90°$	$+90°$
$1 + j.0002w$	$\theta = \tan^{-1} .0002(2000)$	$+21.8°$
$\dfrac{1}{1 + j10w}$	$\theta = -\tan^{-1} 10(2000)$	$-90.0°$
$\dfrac{1}{1 + j.05w}$	$\theta = \tan^{-1} .05(2000)$	$-89.4°$
		$\theta_{TOTAL} = -67.6°$

Phase margin = $180° - |\theta| = 180° - 67.6° = 112.4°$

123. *Answer:* (D)
   Solution: The error voltage, expressed in Laplace notation, is

$$E(s) = \frac{R(s)}{1 + GH(s)} = \frac{12/s}{1 + \dfrac{0.4s(s + 5000)}{(s + 0.1)(s + 20)}}$$

The initial value, at time equals zero plus, is $s\,E(s)|_{s=\infty}$

$$sE(s)|_{s=\infty} = \frac{s(12/s)}{1 + \dfrac{0.4s(s + 5000)}{(s + 0.1)(s + 20)}} \cdot \frac{\dfrac{1}{s^2}}{\dfrac{1}{s^2}}\Bigg|_{s=\infty}$$

$$= \frac{12}{1 + \dfrac{0.4s\left(\dfrac{s}{s} + \dfrac{5000}{s}\right)}{\left(\dfrac{s}{s} + \dfrac{0.1}{s}\right)\left(\dfrac{s}{s} + \dfrac{20}{s}\right)}}\Bigg|_{s=\infty}$$

$$\text{I.V.} = \frac{12}{1 + \dfrac{0.4(1 + 0)}{(1 + 0)(1 + 0)}} = \frac{12}{1.4} = 8.57 \text{ volts}$$

Engineering Economics

124. *Answer:* (B)

  Solution: $F = P\left(F/P, \dfrac{12\%}{2}, 30 \times 2\right)$

  $F = \$5000(F/P, 6\%, 60)$

  $F = 5000(32.9876)$

  $F = \$164,938$

125. *Answer:* (E)

  Solution: $A = P(A/P, 15\%, 5)$

  $A = 9000(0.2983)$

  $A = \$2684.70$

126. *Answer:* (B)

  Solution: $P = \$20,000(P/F, 10\%, 10)$

  $P = 20,000(0.3855)$

  $P = \$7710$

127. *Answer:* (A)

  Solution: $P = \$10,000(P/F, 8\%, 8)$

  $P = 10,000(0.5403)$

  $P = \$5403$

128. *Answer:* (C)

  Solution: Initial value = $13,000

  $\Sigma = 1 + 2 + 3 + 4 + 5 = 15$

  Depr. factor $= \frac{5}{15} = \frac{1}{3}$

  Depr (end of 1st year) $= 13,000(\frac{1}{3}) = \$4,333$

  Value (beginning of 2nd year) = Value (end of 1st year)

  Value $= 13,000 - 4333 = \$8667$

129. *Answer:* (D)

  Solution: Depr. factor $= \frac{4}{15}$

  Depr (end of second year) $= 13,000(\frac{4}{15}) = \$3467$

  Value (at end of second year) $= 8667 - 3467 = \$5200$

Materials Science

130. *Answer:* (E)

131. *Answer:* (C)

  Solution: Tabulating net volumes,

1 bag of cement = $(1 - 0.513) = 0.487$ cubic feet

$1\frac{1}{2}$ cubic feet of sand = $1.5(1 - 0.36) = 0.96$ cubic feet

3 cubic feet of gravel = $3(1 - 0.33) = 2.01$ cubic feet

5 gallons of water = $5(0.134 \text{ ft}^3/\text{gal}) = 0.67$ cubic feet

TOTAL = 4.127 cubic feet

132. *Answer:* (A)

133. *Answer:* (A)

134. *Answer:* (B)

135. *Answer:* (D)

The Structure of Matter

136. *Answer:* (A)

137. *Answer:* (B)

138. *Answer:* (D)

139. *Answer:* (C)

140. *Answer:* (E)

Solution: Half-life = $T = 4.5 (10)^9$ years

$T = 4.5(10)^9(3.154)(10)^7 = 0.1419(10)^{18}$ seconds

$\lambda = \dfrac{0.693}{T} = 4.88(10)^{-18}$

Disintegrations/second = $4.88(10)^{-18}\left(\dfrac{W}{238}\right)(6.02)(10)^{23}$

$= 1.14(10)^4 W$

Since, by definition, 1 curie = $3.7(10)^{10}$ disintegrations/second,

$W = \dfrac{3.7(10)^{10}}{1.14(10)^4} = 3.2(10)^6$ gm ≈ 3 tonnes

Answer Sheet
Practice Examination 1—P.M. Part

Engineering Mechanics

1 (A) (B) (C) (D) (E)   4 (A) (B) (C) (D) (E)   7 (A) (B) (C) (D) (E)   10 (A) (B) (C) (D) (E)   13 (A) (B) (C) (D) (E)

2 (A) (B) (C) (D) (E)   5 (A) (B) (C) (D) (E)   8 (A) (B) (C) (D) (E)   11 (A) (B) (C) (D) (E)   14 (A) (B) (C) (D) (E)

3 (A) (B) (C) (D) (E)   6 (A) (B) (C) (D) (E)   9 (A) (B) (C) (D) (E)   12 (A) (B) (C) (D) (E)   15 (A) (B) (C) (D) (E)

Mathematics

16 (A) (B) (C) (D) (E)   19 (A) (B) (C) (D) (E)   22 (A) (B) (C) (D) (E)   25 (A) (B) (C) (D) (E)   28 (A) (B) (C) (D) (E)

17 (A) (B) (C) (D) (E)   20 (A) (B) (C) (D) (E)   23 (A) (B) (C) (D) (E)   26 (A) (B) (C) (D) (E)   29 (A) (B) (C) (D) (E)

18 (A) (B) (C) (D) (E)   21 (A) (B) (C) (D) (E)   24 (A) (B) (C) (D) (E)   27 (A) (B) (C) (D) (E)   30 (A) (B) (C) (D) (E)

Electrical Circuits

31 (A) (B) (C) (D) (E)   33 (A) (B) (C) (D) (E)   35 (A) (B) (C) (D) (E)   37 (A) (B) (C) (D) (E)   39 (A) (B) (C) (D) (E)

32 (A) (B) (C) (D) (E)   34 (A) (B) (C) (D) (E)   36 (A) (B) (C) (D) (E)   38 (A) (B) (C) (D) (E)   40 (A) (B) (C) (D) (E)

Engineering Economics

41 (A) (B) (C) (D) (E)   43 (A) (B) (C) (D) (E)   45 (A) (B) (C) (D) (E)   47 (A) (B) (C) (D) (E)   49 (A) (B) (C) (D) (E)

42 (A) (B) (C) (D) (E)   44 (A) (B) (C) (D) (E)   46 (A) (B) (C) (D) (E)   48 (A) (B) (C) (D) (E)   50 (A) (B) (C) (D) (E)

Computer Programming

51 (A) (B) (C) (D) (E)   53 (A) (B) (C) (D) (E)   55 (A) (B) (C) (D) (E)   57 (A) (B) (C) (D) (E)   59 (A) (B) (C) (D) (E)

52 (A) (B) (C) (D) (E)   54 (A) (B) (C) (D) (E)   56 (A) (B) (C) (D) (E)   58 (A) (B) (C) (D) (E)   60 (A) (B) (C) (D) (E)

Electronics and Electrical Machinery

61 (A) (B) (C) (D) (E)   63 (A) (B) (C) (D) (E)   65 (A) (B) (C) (D) (E)   67 (A) (B) (C) (D) (E)   69 (A) (B) (C) (D) (E)

62 (A) (B) (C) (D) (E)   64 (A) (B) (C) (D) (E)   66 (A) (B) (C) (D) (E)   68 (A) (B) (C) (D) (E)   70 (A) (B) (C) (D) (E)

Fluid Mechanics

71 Ⓐ Ⓑ Ⓒ Ⓓ Ⓔ   73 Ⓐ Ⓑ Ⓒ Ⓓ Ⓔ   75 Ⓐ Ⓑ Ⓒ Ⓓ Ⓔ   77 Ⓐ Ⓑ Ⓒ Ⓓ Ⓔ   79 Ⓐ Ⓑ Ⓒ Ⓓ Ⓔ

72 Ⓐ Ⓑ Ⓒ Ⓓ Ⓔ   74 Ⓐ Ⓑ Ⓒ Ⓓ Ⓔ   76 Ⓐ Ⓑ Ⓒ Ⓓ Ⓔ   78 Ⓐ Ⓑ Ⓒ Ⓓ Ⓔ   80 Ⓐ Ⓑ Ⓒ Ⓓ Ⓔ

Mechanics of Materials

81 Ⓐ Ⓑ Ⓒ Ⓓ Ⓔ   83 Ⓐ Ⓑ Ⓒ Ⓓ Ⓔ   85 Ⓐ Ⓑ Ⓒ Ⓓ Ⓔ   87 Ⓐ Ⓑ Ⓒ Ⓓ Ⓔ   89 Ⓐ Ⓑ Ⓒ Ⓓ Ⓔ

82 Ⓐ Ⓑ Ⓒ Ⓓ Ⓔ   84 Ⓐ Ⓑ Ⓒ Ⓓ Ⓔ   86 Ⓐ Ⓑ Ⓒ Ⓓ Ⓔ   88 Ⓐ Ⓑ Ⓒ Ⓓ Ⓔ   90 Ⓐ Ⓑ Ⓒ Ⓓ Ⓔ

Thermodynamics/Heat Transfer

91 Ⓐ Ⓑ Ⓒ Ⓓ Ⓔ   93 Ⓐ Ⓑ Ⓒ Ⓓ Ⓔ   95 Ⓐ Ⓑ Ⓒ Ⓓ Ⓔ   97 Ⓐ Ⓑ Ⓒ Ⓓ Ⓔ   99 Ⓐ Ⓑ Ⓒ Ⓓ Ⓔ

92 Ⓐ Ⓑ Ⓒ Ⓓ Ⓔ   94 Ⓐ Ⓑ Ⓒ Ⓓ Ⓔ   96 Ⓐ Ⓑ Ⓒ Ⓓ Ⓔ   98 Ⓐ Ⓑ Ⓒ Ⓓ Ⓔ   100 Ⓐ Ⓑ Ⓒ Ⓓ Ⓔ

PRACTICE EXAMINATION 1
P.M. PART

Engineering Mechanics

The diagram shown below applies to questions #1 through #7, inclusive.

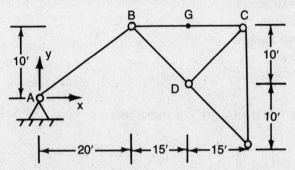

The Cartesian coordinate system for x and y is measured from point A. In problems #1 through #3, a vertical downward force of 6^K is applied to member BC at point G.

1. The center of concurrence for the external forces applied to this structure is located at which of the following pairs of x and y coordinates?

    (A) 20, 10
    (B) 35, 0
    (C) 35, 17.5
    (D) 50, 10
    (E) 50, 25

2. The reaction at support A has a magnitude most nearly equal to

    (A) 2.9^K
    (B) 3.7^K
    (C) 4.6^K
    (D) 5.4^K
    (E) 6^K

3. The reaction at support E has a magnitude most nearly equal to

    (A) 2.9^K
    (B) 3.7^K
    (C) 4.6^K
    (D) 5.4^K
    (E) 6^K

In problems #4 through #7 inclusive, assume the following:

The reaction components at A are $A_{horiz} = 4^K \rightarrow$ and $A_{vert} = 2^K \uparrow$; the reaction components at E are $E_{horiz} = 3^K \leftarrow$ and $E_{vert} = 4^K \uparrow$. All external loads are applied to member BC. An external force (not necessarily vertical) is applied at point G.

4. The bar force in member DE is most nearly

    (A) 3.6^K compression
    (B) 3.6^K tension
    (C) 4^K compression
    (D) 4^K tension
    (E) 5.4^K compression

5. The bar force in member CE is most nearly

    (A) 0
    (B) 2^K
    (C) 4^K
    (D) 6^K
    (E) 8^K

6. The bar force in member CD is most nearly

    (A) 0
    (B) 2^K
    (C) 4^K
    (D) 6^K
    (E) 8^K

7. The magnitude of the resultant external force applied at point G is most nearly

    (A) 2.0^K
    (B) 4.4^K
    (C) 6.1^K
    (D) 7.1^K
    (E) 10.8^K

The diagram below and the following description apply to problems #8 through #11, inclusive.

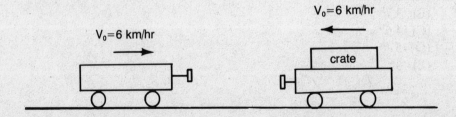

Consider two identical railroad cars, each having a mass of 20,000 kg and each moving on frictionless tracks towards the other with a velocity of 6 km/hr. The car on the left is empty, while the car on the right has a crate of mass 25,000 kg resting on the car floor. The coefficient of friction between crate and floor is 0.5. The coefficient of restitution for impact between the two cars is e, and the time duration of impact is considered extremely small.

8. The velocities of the two cars immediately following impact are not affected by the presence of the crate because

    (A) of Newton's first law of motion
    (B) of conservation of energy
    (C) of Newton's third law of motion
    (D) the force exerted on the crate is negligible
    (E) the impulse on the crate is negligible

9. If e = 0.9, the loss of energy during impact is most nearly

    (A) 0
    (B) 5555 joules
    (C) 5555 watts
    (D) 10,555 joules
    (E) 10,555 watts

10. Assume that the coefficient of restitution is such that, at the moment immediately following impact, the instantaneous velocities of each of the cars is 4.8 km/hr (away from each other). The final velocity of the car on the right will then be most nearly

    (A) 2.4 km/hr to the left
    (B) 1.2 km/hr to the left
    (C) 1.2 km/hr to the right
    (D) 2.4 km/hr to the right
    (E) none of the above

11. After the impact conditions described in problem #10, the distance in meters through which the crate will slide, relative to the car on the right, is most nearly

    (A) 0.11
    (B) 0.21
    (C) 0.31
    (D) 0.36
    (E) 0.41

The diagram below and the following description apply to problems #12 through #15, inclusive.

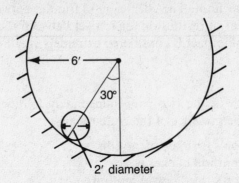

A solid cylinder, 2 feet in diameter and weighing 100 pounds, is in contact with the inner surface of a hollow cylinder with a 6-ft radius. The solid cylinder is released from rest in the position shown in the sketch. The contact is assumed to be smooth in problems #12 and #14; in problems #13 and #15, sufficient friction is assumed so that the cylinder rolls without slipping.

12. Assuming smooth contact, the initial value of the reaction, in pounds, is most nearly

(A) 50
(B) 67
(C) 75
(D) 87
(E) 100

13. The minimum value of the coefficient of friction needed to prevent slipping in the initial position is most nearly

(A) 0.05
(B) 0.10
(C) 0.19
(D) 0.35
(E) 0.96

14. Assuming smooth contact, the value of the reaction, in pounds, as the cylinder crosses the vertical plane is most nearly

(A) 87
(B) 100
(C) 112
(D) 127
(E) 143

15. Assuming that the cylinder rolls without slipping, the value of the normal reaction, in pounds, as the cylinder crosses the vertical plane is most nearly

    (A) 45
    (B) 72
    (C) 100
    (D) 112
    (E) 118

Mathematics

16. The Laplace expression $F(s) = \dfrac{12s + 6}{s(s + 1)(s + 2)}$ corresponds to which one of the following functions in the time domain?

    (A) $f(t) = 3 + \varepsilon^{-6t} - \varepsilon^{-9t}$
    (B) $f(t) = 12t\varepsilon^{-t} + 6\varepsilon^{-2t}$
    (C) $f(t) = 3 - 6\varepsilon^{-t} + 9\varepsilon^{-2t}$
    (D) $f(t) = 3t + 6t^2 - 9t^3$
    (E) $f(t) = 3 + 6\varepsilon^{-t} - 9\varepsilon^{-2t}$

17. The numerical value of the shaded area under the curve, as shown in the diagram, is most nearly

    (A) 1.5
    (B) 5
    (C) 6.5
    (D) 8.0
    (E) 11.5

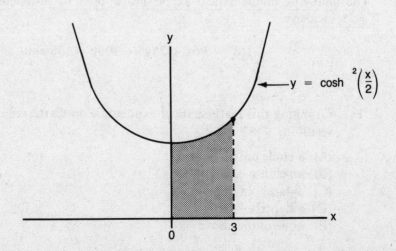

$$y = \cosh^2\left(\frac{x}{2}\right)$$

18. The equation $x^5 - x^4 - 10x^3 - 34x^2 - 56x - 20 = 0$ has a positive real root. When this root is expressed correctly to 3 significant digits, the sum of these three digits is

   (A) 15
   (B) 16
   (C) 17
   (D) 18
   (E) 19

19. The numerical value of the definite integral $\int_0^1 x\varepsilon^{2x}\, dx$ is most nearly

   (A) 2.1
   (B) 2.5
   (C) 3.1
   (D) 3.6
   (E) 4.5

20. An industrialist has on hand 1200 linear feet of fence, with which he plans to enclose a rectangular parking lot on a riverfront property adjacent to a large plant. If no fence is to be used on the side along the river, the maximum area that he can enclose, expressed in square feet, is most nearly

   (A) 100,000
   (B) 120,000
   (C) 160,000
   (D) 180,000
   (E) 230,000

The following mathematical expression applies to problems #21 through #25, inclusive.

$$16x^2 - 96x + 25y^2 + 100y - 156 = 0$$

21. Graphing this mathematical expression on Cartesian coordinates will result in

   (A) a circle only
   (B) an ellipse only
   (C) a parabola only
   (D) a hyperbola only
   (E) none of the above

22. The center of the curve discussed in problem #21 is located at

    (A) (0,0)
    (B) (−3,2)
    (C) (3,−2)
    (D) (5,4)
    (E) (4,5)

23. The major axis of the curve discussed in problem #21 is

    (A) horizontal
    (B) vertical
    (C) diagonal with a less-than-unity positive slope
    (D) diagonal with a unity-or-greater positive slope
    (E) diagonal with a negative slope

24. The ratio of the length of the major axis to the length of the minor axis of the curve discussed in problem #21 is most nearly

    (A) 1.00
    (B) 1.25
    (C) 1.50
    (D) 1.75
    (E) 2.00

25. One of the foci of the curve discussed in problem #21 is located at

    (A) (3,0)
    (B) (3,−2)
    (C) (3,2)
    (D) (6,0)
    (E) (6,−2)

26. Given the differential equation $5\dfrac{di}{dt} + 200i - 24 = 0$, which is valid for positive values of time, starting from time equals zero. The initial value of i is 0.6 when t = 0. The numerical value for i when time is exactly 50 milliseconds is most nearly

    (A) 0.12
    (B) 0.15
    (C) 0.18
    (D) 0.24
    (E) 0.48

27. In the diagram shown, the area of the shaded portion that lies between the sine wave and the triangle is most nearly

(A) 5.0
(B) 6.4
(C) 7.5
(D) 8.6
(E) 10.0

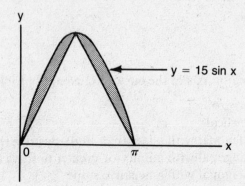

$y = 15 \sin x$

28. The definite integral $\displaystyle\int_{1.5}^{3.0} \frac{dx}{\sqrt{36 - 4x^2}}$ is equal to

(A) π
(B) $\pi/2$
(C) $\pi/4$
(D) $\pi/6$
(E) $\pi/12$

29. The third term of the Maclaurin series expansion of $\varepsilon^x(\sin x + \cos x)$ is

(A) x^2
(B) $\dfrac{x^2}{2!}$
(C) $2x^2$
(D) $\dfrac{x^3}{3}$
(E) $\dfrac{x^3}{3!}$

30. Find the solution to the second order differential equation $\dfrac{d^2y}{dx^2} + 9y = 0$

(A) $C_1\varepsilon^{3i} + C_2\varepsilon^{-3i}$
(B) $C_1\varepsilon^{3x} + C_2\varepsilon^{-3x}$
(C) $C_1\sin^3 x + C_2\cos^3 x$
(D) $C_1\sin 3x + C_2\cos 3x$
(E) $C_1\sin x + C_2\cos 3x$

Electrical Circuits

The following description applies to questions #31 through #38, inclusive.

A single-phase transformer whose overall efficiency is 80% consists of a primary winding having 600 turns and two independent secondary windings. Secondary #1 has 400 turns and is connected to a 20-ohm resistive load. Secondary #2 has 300 turns and is connected to a series combination of a 10-ohm resistor and a 0.03-henry inductor. The primary winding is connected to a 120-volt 60-Hertz source.

31. The current in amperes that will be drawn by the primary winding is most nearly

    (A) 4.2
    (B) 4.7
    (C) 5.2
    (D) 5.9
    (E) 10

32. In the transformer described previously, the total impedance in ohms as seen by the voltage source is most nearly

    (A) 23
    (B) 28
    (C) 30
    (D) 35
    (E) 44

33. In the transformer described previously, the phase angle between the applied voltage and the current drawn by the primary is most nearly

    (A) 17°
    (B) 21°
    (C) 41°
    (D) 49°
    (E) 69°

34. In the transformer previously described, a capacitor is to be connected across secondary #2 in order to correct the power factor to unity. The capacitance in microfarads that is needed will be most nearly

    (A) 130
    (B) 160

(C) 200
(D) 235
(E) 260

35. In the transformer previously described, when a shunt capacitor across secondary #2 has successfully corrected the power factor to unity, the total current in amperes that will then be drawn by the primary will be most nearly

(A) 4
(B) 5
(C) 6
(D) 8
(E) 10

36. In the transformer previously described, a capacitor is to be connected across secondary #2 that will change the overall power factor to be leading rather than lagging. The capacitance in microfarads that will cause the overall transformer to have a power factor of 0.95 leading, as seen by the source of applied voltage, is most nearly

(A) 15
(B) 125
(C) 200
(D) 275
(E) 350

37. Referring to problem #36, when the overall power factor of this transformer is changed to 0.95 leading, the current in amperes that will be drawn by the primary will be most nearly

(A) 4.3
(B) 4.7
(C) 5.2
(D) 5.5
(E) 6.0

38. For the transformer described for problem #31, a decision has been made to place a capacitor across secondary #1 rather than across secondary #2. What value of capacitance in microfarads will be required in order to achieve an overall power factor of unity, as seen from the source of voltage that is applied to the primary?

(A) 25
(B) 50

(C) 75
(D) 100
(E) 125

39. In the circuit shown, the switch is thrown downward at time equals zero. It had previously been in the UP position for a very long time. The mathematical expression for the current i_L through the inductor, in the direction shown, starting from time equals zero, is: $i_L = 0.4 - 2.4\varepsilon^{-at}$. The correct numerical values for V_1 and V_2 are

(A) $V_1 = 12$, $V_2 = 240$
(B) $V_1 = 40$, $V_2 = 60$
(C) $V_1 = 40$, $V_2 = 72$
(D) $V_1 = 60$, $V_2 = 40$
(E) $V_1 = 72$, $V_2 = 40$

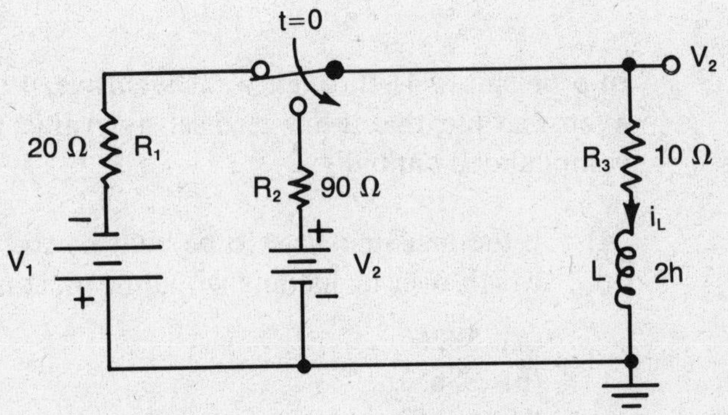

40. Referring to problem #39, the time constant τ in seconds applicable to the mathematical expression for the current flow is

(A) 0.02
(B) 0.067
(C) 13.2
(D) 15
(E) 50

Engineering Economics

The following paragraph and table apply to problems #41 through #50, inclusive.

In order to improve productivity, a company is planning to replace an out-of-date production-line machine with a new one. The company is capable of building this machine on its own, but renting or purchasing the machine is also possible. The following chart shows the itemized costs for each alternative:

BUILD	RENT	PURCHASE
A. *Initial Costs* Labor $18,000 Material $30,000 Power $1500	A. *Initial Costs* None	A. *Initial Costs* Purchase $60,000 Shipping $500
B. *Annual Operating Costs* Labor $12,000 Maintenance $1000 Power $500	B. *Annual Operating Costs* Labor $12,000 Maintenance 0 Power $500 Rental $15,000	B. *Annual Operating Costs* Labor $12,000 Maintenance $1000 Power $500

In problems #41 through #50, inclusive, it is assumed that the machine has a ten-year life, that it has zero salvage value, and that the interest rate is 15% compounded annually.

41. If the machine were to be built by the company, its equivalent annual worth over its lifetime would be most nearly

    (A) $8260
    (B) $8650
    (C) $9150
    (D) $9565
    (E) $9865

42. If the company decides to build this machine, what is its depreciation after 5 years based on the straight-line method?

    (A) $19,870
    (B) $22,400
    (C) $24,000
    (D) $24,750
    (E) $25,450

43. What is the depreciation of the company-built machine after 5 years, based on the sum-of-the-digits method?

    (A) $33,800
    (B) $34,500
    (C) $36,000
    (D) $37,200
    (E) $38,800

44. In the event that the company should decide to purchase the next replacement machine, the sinking fund amount would be most nearly

    (A) $2980

(B) $3050
(C) $3120
(D) $3200
(E) $3450

45. Which of the following statements regarding a comparison of the three alternatives, based on overall cost factors alone, is correct?

    (A) Building is the least costly, followed by renting and then purchasing.
    (B) Building is the least costly, followed by purchasing and then renting.
    (C) Purchasing is the least costly, followed by building and then renting.
    (D) Purchasing is the least costly, followed by renting and then building.
    (E) Renting is the least costly.

46. The company decides to build this machine, but subsequently encounters greater expenses than were anticipated. The maximum excess initial cost that could be absorbed without causing the building decision to be more costly than a rental decision is most nearly

    (A) $10,290
    (B) $12,350
    (C) $15,200
    (D) $18,920
    (E) $20,750

47. Assume that a present shortage of funds compels the company to choose the rental machine, but that a sinking fund is established that will permit the company to start to build its own machine 5 years hence. The required amount that must be set aside annually for this purpose is most nearly

    (A) $6750
    (B) $6900
    (C) $7340
    (D) $7550
    (E) $7750

48. Assuming a constant rate of inflation of 5% that affects all costs, the new sinking fund amount that must be set aside for the conditions of problem #47 will be most nearly

    (A) $6650
    (B) $8100

(C) $8800
(D) $9370
(E) $9520

49. The company has just decided to initiate a sinking fund (based on a zero inflation rate) for purchasing the next new machine 10 years hence. Assume, however, that the purchase price and shipping costs of the new machine will increase annually at a 5% inflation rate, but that the sinking fund amount *cannot* be increased correspondingly. For how many years beyond the normal 10-year life of the machine must the company wait before the sinking fund proceeds are roughly sufficient for the purchase of the new machine? (Express your answer correctly to the nearest year.)

(A) 2
(B) 3
(C) 4
(D) 5
(E) 6

50. In choosing between two alternative investments, one alternative is considered preferable if the

(A) labor cost is less than the interest rate
(B) rate of profit is greater than the power cost
(C) rate of profit is greater than the interest rate
(D) labor cost is less than the power cost
(E) labor cost is greater than the power cost

Computer Programming

The following BASIC program is used to reformat a listing, and applies to problems #51 through #59, inclusive.

```
 10 ON ERROR GOTO 170
 20 OPEN OLD "FILE1" AS 1
 30 OPEN NEW "FILE2" AS 2
 40 INPUT LINE #1,S$
 50 IF S$="" GOTO 40
 60 LT=LEN(S$)
 70 X=INSTR(1,S$," ")-1
 80 A$=LEFT$(S$,X)
 90 B$=RIGHT$(S$,LT-X)
100 IF LT>78 GOTO 200
```

```
110 IF LT>78 THEN C$=" ":GOTO 140
120 N=79-LT
130 C$=STRING$(" ",N)
140 Z$=A$+C$+B$
150 PRINT LINE #2,Z$
160 GOTO 40
170 IF ERR < >8 THEN ON ERROR GOTO 0
180 CLOSE 1,2
190 EXIT
200 IF INSTR(1,B$," ")< >1 GOTO 110
210 B$=MID$(B$,2):LT=LT-1:GOTO 200
```

51. How is the end-of-file condition handled?

   (A) The program terminates automatically when no more data are available.
   (B) The program looks for an end-of-file code in the file.
   (C) An end-of-file condition causes an error code of "8", which allows the program to reach lines 180 and 190.
   (D) The program terminates automatically after reading 80 lines.
   (E) None of the above.

52. What action ensues if a line read in from FILE1 is blank?

   (A) An error code is generated which causes program termination.
   (B) A blank line is written to FILE2.
   (C) The program writes out the preceding line once again.
   (D) The program tries to read in the next line from FILE1.
   (E) A string of 40 blank spaces is written to FILE2.

53. Which line in the program locates the first occurrence of a blank space in the string, S$?

   (A) 50
   (B) 70
   (C) 110
   (D) 130
   (E) 200

54. What action ensues when the first blank space is located in an input line?

   (A) The string "A$" is assigned the value of the input string (S$) from the first character position to the character position preceding the first space.
   (B) The characters of the input line, including character one up to the character preceding the first space, are removed.

(C) The blank space is replaced with the string "ACB".

(D) The program ignores that line and attempts to read in another.

(E) An error code is generated which results in program termination.

55. What are the components of each line written out to FILE2?

(A) Portions of three consecutive lines from FILE1.

(B) The portion of the input line preceding the first space, followed by a variable number of spaces, followed by some or all of the input line after the first space.

(C) A series of the character strings, "ACB".

(D) The right half of the input line, followed by its left half.

(E) The input line, with every space replaced by two or more spaces.

56. For what condition does line 200 cause the program to branch to line 110?

(A) Branch if B$ contains less than or more than one blank space.

(B) Branch if B$ contains exactly one blank space.

(C) Branch if the value of B$ is one blank space.

(D) Branch if the value of B$ is not one blank space.

(E) Branch if the first character in B$ is not a blank space.

57. What function is performed by the first part of the multiple statement in line 210?

(A) The string, B$, is reduced to its central two characters.

(B) The first two and last two characters of B$ are removed.

(C) The central two characters of B$ are removed.

(D) The first character of B$ is removed.

(E) The last character of B$ is removed.

58. Which line of the program contains the statement that produces a string of blank spaces?

(A) 70

(B) 110

(C) 130

(D) 150

(E) 200

59. The number of characters assigned to the string, B$, by the RIGHT$ function in line 90 is equal to:

(A) The number of characters in S$ to the left of the first blank space.

(B) The number of characters in S$ to the right of the first blank space.

(C) One more than the number of characters to the right of the first blank space in S$.

(D) One less than the number of characters to the right of the first blank space in S$.

(E) One less than the number of characters to the left of the first blank space in S$.

60. Which of the following FORTRAN expressions is equal to 35? A = 25, B = 10, C = 100, D = 4

(A) $A + B * D / C * (A - B ** (B - D * 2) + C)$
(B) $A + B * D / (C * A) - B ** B - (D * 2 + C)$
(C) $(A + B) * D / (C * A) - (B ** (B - D * 2)) + C$
(D) $A + B * D / C * A - B ** (B - D * 2) + C$
(E) $A + B * D / (C * A - B) ** (B - D * 2) + C$

Electronics and Electrical Machinery

The diagram shown below applies to problems #61 through #64, inclusive.

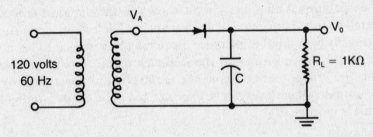

61. The half-wave rectifier shown in the diagram uses a step-down input transformer having a 4 : 1 turns ratio. The capacitance in microfarads that will be required for a 2-volt peak-to-peak ripple in the output voltage is most nearly

(A) 170
(B) 250
(C) 340
(D) 500
(E) 680

62. Refer to the half-wave rectifier in problem #61. The wave shape of the current flowing in the transformer secondary consists of

(A) a DC level with some ripple
(B) a sine wave

(C) alternate positive half-cycles

(D) continuous positive half-cycles

(E) short duration pulses

63. Refer to the half-wave rectifier in problem #61. The time interval in milliseconds during which the diode is conducting is most nearly

(A) 0.83

(B) 1.6

(C) 2.8

(D) 4.1

(E) 8.3

64. The peak current in milliamperes that flows through the diode, in the half-wave rectifier of problem #61, is most nearly

(A) 80

(B) 200

(C) 400

(D) 800

(E) 1600

65. The operational amplifier circuit shown in the diagram uses an integrated circuit "chip" having an extremely high forward gain A, and an extremely high input impedance. Both may be assumed to be infinite. If the two input resistors and the feedback resistor are all implemented with $\pm 5\%$ tolerance components, the maximum percentage by which the output voltage level can be expected to fall below its nominally ideal value is most nearly

(A) 5%

(B) 10%

(C) 19%

(D) 38%

(E) 70%

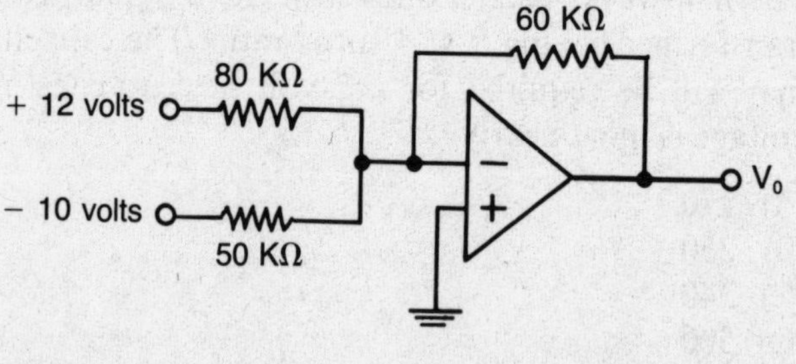

66. Refer to the operational amplifier in problem #65. If the 80 kilohm and the 60 kilohm resistors are ideally accurate, what percentage tolerance must be specified for the 50 kilohm resistor in order that the output voltage level will never drop more than 10% from its nominally ideal value?

(A) 0.6%

(B) 1.3%
(C) 2.6%
(D) 5.2%
(E) 10.4%

67. A 5 KVA, 110/220-volt, 60-Hertz transformer is operated at full load and a power factor of 0.80 lagging. With the high side open, the open circuit test with 220 volts applied produces a current of 2.0 amperes and 280 watts. With the low side shorted, the short circuit test produces rated current at 180 volts and 400 watts. The percentage efficiency under full load conditions is most nearly

(A) 80%
(B) 83%
(C) 86%
(D) 89%
(E) 92%

68. Refer to the transformer in problem #67. The percentage efficiency under half load conditions and a power factor of 0.80 lagging is most nearly

(A) 82%
(B) 84%
(C) 86%
(D) 88%
(E) 90%

69. One end of an 800-foot-long feeder connects to a 3-phase, 210-volt, 60 Hertz delta-connected source, and the other end provides 208 volts to a local distribution panel. At this panel, a balanced load is connected which draws 15 kilowatts at a power factor of 0.8 lagging. The circular mil area required for each of the three copper conductors in this feeder, such that the drop in line voltage from the source will not exceed the indicated two volts, is most nearly

(A) 215,000
(B) 300,000
(C) 375,000
(D) 470,000
(E) 650,000

70. A 320-volt peak-to-peak sinusoidal voltage is applied to an incandescent lamp rated at 500 watts and 120 volts. This particular lamp has a positive temperature coefficient of resistivity such that the ratio of resistance at any applied voltage V to the resistance at a reference voltage V_R equals

$$\frac{R_V}{R_{V_R}} = \varepsilon^{\frac{1.2(V-V_R)}{V_R}}.$$

The actual power in watts dissipated in this lamp is most nearly

(A) 450
(B) 475
(C) 485
(D) 500
(E) 615

Fluid Mechanics

The following diagram refers to problems #71 through #74, inclusive.

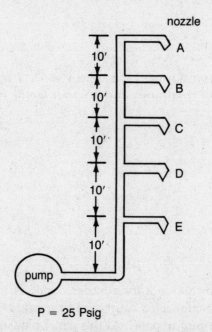

In this configuration, water is provided to a five-story building at a total pressure of 25 psig. Each story is 10′ high. One shower nozzle is placed at the ceiling level of each story, as shown.

71. If each of the five shower nozzles has 0.05 sq. in. of open area, what is the maximum flow in gallons per minute through nozzle A? (Assume no frictional losses.)

(A) 0

(B) 2.7
(C) 3.5
(D) 6.6
(E) 9.5

72. What is the maximum flow in gallons per minute through nozzle E?

(A) 0
(B) 2.7
(C) 6.6
(D) 8.6
(E) 9.5

73. If the individual flow rates through nozzles A through E are given as 3 gpm, 5 gpm, 7 gpm, 8 gpm, and 9 gpm, respectively, and if the supply pipe immediately downstream of the pump is 1/2 inch I.D., what is the static pressure at the pump outlet? (Assume no frictional losses.)

(A) 0 psig
(B) 3.3 psig
(C) 6.6 psig
(D) 25 psig
(E) 40 psia

74. There is a total of 12 feet of 3/4-inch I.D. pipe between the pump and the take-off for nozzle E. The pipe supplying nozzle E is a 90-degree take-off from the vertical run, and senses only static pressure at the tee. What is the pressure at E in psig under the total flow conditions specified in problem #73? (Assume f equals 0.02.)

(A) 3.1
(B) 6.7
(C) 11.0
(D) 20.7
(E) 25.0

The diagram and description below apply to problems #75 through #77, inclusive.

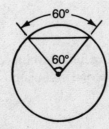

Water flows through a 2'-diameter drain pipe to a level such that a 60° arc at the top of the pipe is not wetted (as indicated in the diagram). The slope of the pipe is 1' per 10,000', and the roughness coefficient is 0.015.

75. The hydraulic radius in feet is most nearly

    (A) 0.50
    (B) 0.58
    (C) 0.67
    (D) 1.0
    (E) 2.0

76. The flow of water through this drain pipe, expressed in cubic feet per second, is most nearly

    (A) 1.7
    (B) 1.9
    (C) 2.1
    (D) 2.4
    (E) 2.6

77. If the duct were flowing full, the resulting flow of water through this drain pipe, expressed in cubic feet per second, would be most nearly

    (A) 2.1
    (B) 2.3
    (C) 2.6
    (D) 2.9
    (E) 3.1

78. Oil flows through a six-inch diameter pipe at a rate of 150 gallons per minute. Its viscosity is 0.001 pound-seconds per square foot, and its specific gravity is 0.8. Under these conditions, the Reynolds Number N_R is most nearly

    (A) 1600
    (B) 2000
    (C) 2100
    (D) 99,000
    (E) 124,000

79. In problem #78, assuming fully developed flow, the centerline velocity V_c expressed in feet per second will be most nearly

    (A) 2.2
    (B) 2.8
    (C) 3.4

(D) 4.2

(E) 102

80. In problem #78, if the friction factor f is 0.01, the shear stress at the wall, expressed in pounds per square foot, will be most nearly

(A) 0.0045

(B) 0.0056

(C) 0.0070

(D) 0.0225

(E) 0.0450

Mechanics of Materials

The following diagrams apply to problems #81 through #90, inclusive:

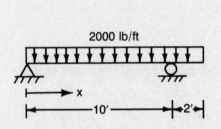

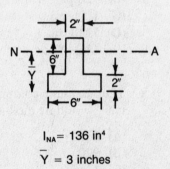

$I_{NA} = 136$ in^4

$\bar{Y} = 3$ inches

The beam illustrated above is supported as shown, and is loaded uniformly at 2000 pounds per foot. The cross-section of the beam is shown at the right with the section properties $\bar{y}$ and I given.

81. The maximum shear force in pounds that is sustained by the beam is most nearly

(A) 4000

(B) 9600

(C) 10,400

(D) 12,000

(E) 14,400

82. The maximum moment, expressed in pound-feet, that is sustained by the beam is most nearly

(A) 4800

(B) 23,000

(C) 36,000

(D) 46,000

(E) 58,000

83. The distance in feet from the left-hand support to the point of maximum moment, indicated as x in the diagram, is most nearly at x equal to

(A) 0

(B) 4.8

(C) 5.0

(D) 6.0

(E) 10.0

For problems #84 through #88, assume that this beam is subjected to a bending moment of 30,000 pound-feet and a shearing force of 10,000 pounds.

84. The maximum tensile stress in bending would be most nearly

(A) 625 psi

(B) 920 psi

(C) 1100 psi

(D) 7940 psi

(E) 13,240 psi

85. The maximum compression stress in bending, expressed in pounds/square inch, would be most nearly

(A) 625

(B) 920

(C) 1100

(D) 7940

(E) 13,240

86. The maximum horizontal shear stress, expressed in pounds/square inch, would be most nearly

(A) 0

(B) 625

(C) 880

(D) 920

(E) 1100

87. The flexural stress at the neutral axis, expressed in pounds/square inch, would be most nearly

(A) 0

(B) 625

(C) 880

(D) 920

(E) 1100

88. The average shear stress in this beam, expressed in psi, would be most nearly

(A) 0
(B) 625
(C) 880
(D) 920
(E) 1100

89. The equation of the elastic curve for this beam between $x = 0$ and $x = 10$, where C_1 and C_2 are arbitrary constants, is given by

(A) $1733x^3 - 83.3x^4 + C_1 x + C_2$
(B) $1733x^3 + 83.3x^4 + C_1 x + C_2$
(C) $1600x^3 - 83.3x^4 + C_1$
(D) $1733x^3 + 83.3x^4 + C_1$
(E) $1600x^3 - 83.3x^4 + C_1 x + C_2$

90. The boundary conditions for evaluating the arbitrary constants in problem #89 are

(A) $y(0) = y(10) = 0$
(B) $y(0) = y'(0) = 0$
(C) $y(0) = y(12) = 0$
(D) $y'(0) = y'(10) = 0$
(E) $y(10) = y'(10) = 0$

Thermodynamics/Heat Transfer

The following diagram and description apply to problems #91 through #97, inclusive.

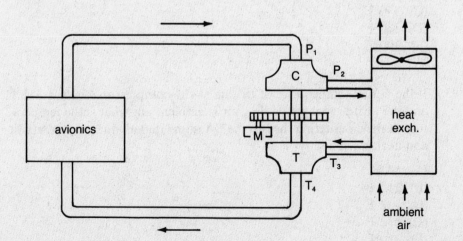

Avionics equipment on board a certain aircraft is cooled by an electric-motor-driven air-cycle machine. The heated air from the avionics equipment is compressed through a pressure ratio of 2.1 : 1 after which it is cooled by a counterflow heat exchanger with an effectiveness of 0.8. The air then expands through a turbine that drives the compressor. Make-up power is supplied to the compressor by an electric motor. During the initial start-up, water is removed after the air leaves the turbine so that the air is completely dry during normal steady-state operation. The cool, dry air is supplied to the avionics equipment. Assume the following operating parameters:

Ambient temperature = 80°F
Ambient pressure = 14.7 psia
The avionics equipment is at ambient pressure
Temperature of air into avionics = 40°F
Avionics heat load = 10 KW (all of which is absorbed by the cooling air)
Compressor efficiency = 0.8
Electric motor efficiency = 0.85
Turbine efficiency = 0.8152
Cooling air flow = 20 lbs/min

91.   The temperature (T_1) of the air leaving the avionics (into the compressor) is approximately

    (A) 70°F
    (B) 88°F
    (C) 103°F
    (D) 120°F
    (E) 158°F

92.   If the actual temperature out of the avionics equipment (into the compressor) is 130°F, the temperature out of the compressor will be most nearly

    (A) 270°F
    (B) 300°F
    (C) 330°F
    (D) 360°F
    (E) 390°F

93.   If the actual temperature of the air at the compressor outlet is 341°F and the heat exchanger cooling air is ambient air, what is the temperature of the air entering the turbine? (Assume that all ducts are adiabatic and neglect friction.)

    (A) 80°F
    (B) 112°F
    (C) 122°F
    (D) 132°F
    (E) 210°F

94. Based on the results of problem #93, what is the temperature of the air coming out of the turbine? (Assume a turbine outlet pressure of 14.7 psia; and that there are no pressure losses in the ducts, in the avionics, or in the heat exchanger.)

    (A) 40°F
    (B) 80°F
    (C) 132°F
    (D) 158°F
    (E) 162°F

95. Assuming that the ducts are sized so that the velocities into and out of the turbine are equal, what is the horsepower delivered from the turbine to the compressor? (Neglect frictional losses.)

    (A) 5.9 HP
    (B) 7.4 HP
    (C) 8.4 HP
    (D) 9.4 HP
    (E) 10.4 HP

96. If the actual temperature of the air out of the compressor is 341°F, and if frictional losses are neglected, the horsepower required for compression will be most nearly

    (A) 15 HP
    (B) 18 HP
    (C) 21 HP
    (D) 23 HP
    (E) 25 HP

97. Referring to the data developed in problems #95 and #96, what is the input power that is required by the electric motor in order to make up the deficit in power between the turbine and compressor?

    (A) 6.4 KW
    (B) 9.0 KW
    (C) 10.3 KW
    (D) 11.6 KW
    (E) 13.0 KW

98. One mole of ethane (C_2H_6) is burned in 100% excess air and complete combustion is assumed. The weight of air in pounds used to burn one pound of ethane is most nearly

    (A) 7.5
    (B) 10.7
    (C) 16.0

(D) 21.4
(E) 32.1

99. For the conditions of problem #98, what is the amount, by weight, of CO_2 in the exhaust when one mole of ethane is burned?

(A) 1.5 lb
(B) 2.9 lb
(C) 44 lb
(D) 88 lb
(E) 132 lb

100. Air exhausted from a building at 80°F and 60% relative humidity (R.H.) is cooled to 40°F. Ninety percent of the liquid water is then removed and the air is reheated to 60°F. Which statement is true of the final condition?

(A) The relative humidity is 55%.
(B) The relative humidity is 80%.
(C) The specific humidity is 0.008 lb H_2O/lb dry air.
(D) The specific humidity is 0.0072 lb H_2O/lb dry air.
(E) The enthalpy is 24.5 Btu/lb.

Answer Key
Practice Examination 1—P.M. Part

Engineering Mechanics

1.	C	6.	A	11.	E
2.	A	7.	C	12.	D
3.	D	8.	E	13.	C
4.	A	9.	D	14.	D
5.	B	10.	B	15.	E

Mathematics

16.	E	21.	B	26.	C
17.	C	22.	C	27.	B
18.	B	23.	A	28.	D
19.	A	24.	B	29.	A
20.	D	25.	E	30.	D

Electrical Circuits

31.	C	35.	B	38.	C
32.	A	36.	D	39.	D
33.	A	37.	C	40.	A
34.	A				

Engineering Economics

41.	E	45.	B	48.	D
42.	D	46.	E	49.	C
43.	C	47.	C	50.	C
44.	A				

Computer Programming

51.	C	55.	B	58.	C
52.	D	56.	E	59.	C
53.	B	57.	D	60.	D
54.	A				

Electronics and Electrical Machinery

61. C	65. D	68. B
62. E	66. C	69. C
63. A	67. C	70. B
64. D		

Fluid Mechanics

71. C	75. B	78. A
72. D	76. C	79. C
73. C	77. E	80. B
74. A		

Mechanics of Materials

81. C	85. E	88. B
82. B	86. D	89. E
83. B	87. A	90. A
84. D		

Thermodynamics/Heat Transfer

91. E	95. E	98. E
92. B	96. C	99. D
93. D	97. B	100. A
94. A		

SOLUTIONS
PRACTICE EXAMINATION 1
P.M. PART

Engineering Mechanics

1. *Answer:* (C)

   Solution: The line of action of the left support is along member AB; its line of action intersects the external 6^K load at $x = 20 + 15 = 35$ and $y = 10 + \frac{1}{2}(15) = 17.5$. The line of action of the other reaction must also pass through this point, the center of concurrence.

2. *Answer:* (A)

   Solution: The sum of the moments about point E equals zero.

   $$50(R_{Ay}) + 10(R_{Ax}) - 15(6) = 0$$

   $$50\left(\frac{R}{\sqrt{5}}\right) + 10\left(\frac{2R}{\sqrt{5}}\right) - 90 = 0$$

   $$R = \frac{90\sqrt{5}}{70} = 2.87^K$$

3. *Answer:* (D)

   Solution: Using the results from solution #2 above,

   a. The sum of the vertical forces is zero,

   $$6 - E_v - \frac{2.87}{\sqrt{5}} = 0$$

   $$E_v = 4.72^K$$

   b. The sum of the horizontal forces is zero,

   $$E_H - \frac{2(2.87)}{\sqrt{5}} = 0$$

   $$E_H = 2.57^K$$

   $$R_E = \sqrt{(E_v)^2 + (E_H)^2} = \sqrt{(4.72)^2 + (2.57)^2} = 5.37^K$$

4. *Answer:* (A)

   Solution: $\sum F_H = 0$

   $$\frac{3}{\sqrt{13}} F_{DE} = 3^K$$

   $$F_{DE} = 3.61^K \text{ compression}$$

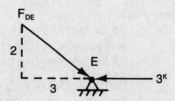

119

5. *Answer:* (B)

   Solution: $\sum F_H = 0$

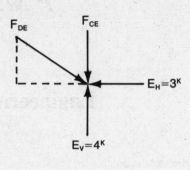

$$\frac{3}{\sqrt{13}} F_{DE} - 3^K = 0$$

$$F_{DE} = \sqrt{13}^K$$

$$\sum F_v = 0$$

$$F_{CE} + \frac{2}{\sqrt{13}}(F_{DE}) - 4 = 0$$

$$F_{CE} + \frac{2\sqrt{13}}{\sqrt{13}} - 4 = 0$$

$$F_{CE} = 2^K$$

6. *Answer:* (A)

   Solution: Since no force is applied at D, bar CD has no force in it.

7. *Answer:* (C)

   Solution: $F_{G_v} = 4 + 2 = 6^K \downarrow$

   $$F_{G_H} = 4 - 3 = 1^K \longrightarrow$$

   $$F_G = \sqrt{6^2 + 1^2} = 6.08^K$$

8. *Answer:* (E)

   Solution: The force on the crate is limited to $(25{,}000\ g)(\mu)$. The impulse on the crate during the short duration is equal to $(25{,}000\ g)(\mu)(\Delta t)$ and is therefore negligible if Δt is very small.

9. *Answer:* (D)

   Solution: Since the crate has no immediate effect on the cars, it may be ignored. From conservation of linear momentum we have

   $$M_{car} V'_{left} + M_{car} V'_{right} = M_{car} V_0 - M_{car} V_0 = 0$$

   $$\therefore V'_{left} = -V'_{right}$$

   From $V'_{left} - V'_{right} = -e(v_0 - (-v_0)) = -2ev_0$

   Hence $V'_{left} = -0.9V_0 = -5.4$ km/hr

   $V'_{right} = 0.9v_0 = 5.4$ km/hr

   $$\Delta E = 2 \times \frac{1}{2}(20{,}000) \times \left[\left(\frac{6000}{3600}\right)^2 - \left(\frac{5400}{3600}\right)^2 \right] = 10{,}555 \text{ joules}$$

   NOTE: Watts is a unit of power, not energy or work.

10. *Answer:* (B)

    Solution: At the instant after impact, the car on the right is moving to the right at 4.8 km/hr, but the crate on this car continues to move to the left at 6.0 km/hr. Applying the conservation of momentum principle:

    $$(20{,}000 + 25{,}000)V_{final} = (20{,}000)(4.8) - (25{,}000)(6)$$

    $$V_{final} = -1.2 \text{ km/hr}$$

11. *Answer:* (E)

   Solution: In solution #10, it is developed that during the instant after impact, the car on the right is moving to the right at 4.8 km/hr, but the crate atop this car is continuing to move to the left at 6.0 km/hr. The final velocity of car and crate is 1.2 km/hr.

   Therefore, the car and crate have a combined kinetic energy immediately after impact which is greater than their final kinetic energy. This loss of energy is equal to the work of the pair of friction forces moving relative to each other a distance of s meters.

$$\text{Initial K.E.} = \frac{1}{2}(20{,}000)\left[\frac{4800}{3600}\right]^2 + \frac{1}{2}(25{,}000)\left[\frac{6000}{3600}\right]^2 = 52{,}500$$

$$\text{Final K.E.} = \frac{1}{2}(20{,}000)\left[\frac{1200}{3600}\right]^2 + \frac{1}{2}(25{,}000)\left[\frac{1200}{3600}\right]^2 = 2500$$

   Loss of energy = $52{,}500 - 2500 = 25{,}000(9.81)(0.5)(s)$

   Distance $s = 0.408$ meters

12. *Answer:* (D)

   Solution: Since $v = 0$ and $a_N = 0$, $N = mg\cos 30° = 100 \times \dfrac{\sqrt{3}}{2} = 86.7$ lbs

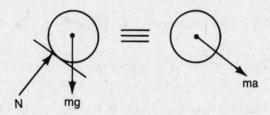

13. *Answer:* (C)

   Solution: From kinematics, $s = r\theta$ where s is the displacement of the center and θ is the angular rotation of the cylinder. Hence $v = rw$, and $a_{\text{tang}} = r\alpha$
   Taking moments about the point of contact

$$r(\sin 30°)mg = I\alpha + mar = (I + mr^2)\alpha = \frac{3}{2}mr^2\alpha$$

$$\text{or}$$

$$mr\alpha = ma = \frac{2}{3}(\sin 30°)mg$$

$$\text{Thus } T = mg(\sin 30°) - ma = \frac{1}{3}mg(\sin 30°)$$

$$N = mg(\cos 30°)$$

$$\mu_{\min} = \frac{T}{N} = \frac{1}{3}(\tan 30°) = 0.192$$

14. *Answer:* (D)

    Solution: The velocity of the center of gravity is given by

$$m\frac{v^2}{2} = mg(5)(1 - \cos 30°).$$

Therefore the normal acceleration of the center of gravity is

$$\frac{v^2}{5} = 2g(1 - \cos 30°).$$

From the equation of motion in the vertical direction

$$R - mg = m\frac{v^2}{5}$$

$$R = mg + 2\,mg(1 - \cos 30°)$$

$$R = 100 + 2(100)(1 - 0.866)$$

$$R = 126.8 \text{ lbs}$$

15. *Answer:* (E)

    Solution: From kinematics, $v_c = r\omega$

From conservation of energy,

$$5(1 - \cos 30°)mg = m\frac{v^2}{2} + \frac{1}{2}I\omega^2$$

$$5(1 - \cos 30°)mg = m\frac{v^2}{2} + \frac{1}{2}\left(\frac{1}{2}\right)mr^2\frac{v^2}{r^2} = \frac{3}{4}mv^2$$

Thus $a_n = \dfrac{v^2}{5} = \dfrac{4}{3}(1 - \cos 30°)g$

From the equation of motion, $R - mg = ma_n = mg\left(\dfrac{4}{3}\right)(1 - \cos 30°)$

$$R = mg\left(1 + \frac{4}{3}(1 - \cos 30°)\right)$$

$$R = 100\left(1 + \frac{4}{3}(1 - \cos 30°)\right) = 117.86 \text{ lbs}$$

Mathematics

16. *Answer:* (E)

    Solution: Using partial fraction expansion,

$$F(s) = \frac{12s + 6}{s(s + 1)(s + 2)} = \frac{A}{s} + \frac{B}{s + 1} + \frac{C}{s + 2}$$

$$\text{where } A = \left.\frac{12s + 6}{(s + 1)(s + 2)}\right|_{s=0} = \frac{6}{(1)(2)} = 3$$

$$B = \left.\frac{12s + 6}{s(s + 2)}\right|_{s=-1} = \frac{-12 + 6}{-1(1)} = 6$$

$$C = \frac{12s + 6}{(s + 1)(s)}\bigg|_{s=-2} = \frac{-24 + 6}{(-1)(-2)} = \frac{-18}{2} = -9$$

$$F(s) = \frac{3}{s} + \frac{6}{s + 1} - \frac{9}{s + 2}$$

$$f(t) = 3 + 6\varepsilon^{-t} - 9\varepsilon^{-2t}$$

17. *Answer:* (C)

Solution: Area $= \displaystyle\int_0^3 \cosh^2\frac{x}{2}dx$

But $\cosh^2\dfrac{x}{2} = 1 + \sinh^2\dfrac{x}{2}$ and $\sinh^2\dfrac{x}{2} = \dfrac{1}{2}[\cosh x - 1]$

$\therefore \cosh^2\dfrac{x}{2} = 1 + \dfrac{1}{2}\cosh x - \dfrac{1}{2} = \dfrac{1}{2}\cosh x + \dfrac{1}{2}$

$$\int_0^3 \cosh^2\frac{x}{2}dx = \int_0^3 \frac{1}{2}\cosh x\, dx + \int_0^3 \frac{1}{2}dx$$

Area $= \dfrac{x}{2}\bigg]_0^3 + \dfrac{1}{2}\sinh x\bigg]_0^3 = \dfrac{3}{2} + \dfrac{1}{2}\sinh 3$

Area $= 1.5 + 0.5[10.01787] = 6.51$

18. *Answer:* (B)

Solution: The real root is 4.93, which may be determined by Horner's method and synthetic division, or by successive trials. The sum of the digits is $4 + 9 + 3 = 16$.

NOTE: The sign of $f(x)$ reverses in going from $f(4)$ to $f(5)$; therefore, the root lies between $x = 4$ and $x = f(5)$.

19. *Answer:* (A)

Solution: Integrating by parts, let $u = x$ and $du = dx$

Let $dv = \varepsilon^{2x}dx$ and $v = \dfrac{1}{2}\varepsilon^{2x}$

$$\int_0^1 x\varepsilon^{2x}dx = uv\bigg]_0^1 - \int_0^1 v\, du$$

$$= x\left(\frac{1}{2}\right)\varepsilon^{2x}\bigg]_0^1 - \int_0^1 \frac{1}{2}\varepsilon^{2x}dx$$

$$= \frac{1}{2}\varepsilon^2 - 0 - \frac{1}{4}\varepsilon^{2x}\bigg]_0^1$$

$$= \frac{1}{2}\varepsilon^2 - \frac{1}{4}\varepsilon^2 + \frac{1}{4}$$

$$= \frac{1}{4}\varepsilon^2 + \frac{1}{4} = 2.10$$

20. *Answer:* (D)

Solution: Using a width W and a length L, the fence perimeter equals $2W + L = 1200$, and the area enclosed is WL.

$$\therefore \text{Area} - W(1200 - 2W) = 1200W - 2W^2$$

For maximum area, $\dfrac{dA}{dW} = 1200 - 4W = 0$

$W = 300$ feet, and $L = 600$ feet.

$\therefore$ Maximum area $= 180,000$ square feet

21. *Answer:* (B)

    Solution: The given expression, $16x^2 - 96x + 25y^2 + 100y - 156 = 0$ can be rearranged as follows:

    $$16[x^2 - 6x + 9] + 25[y^2 + 4y + 4] = 400$$

    $$\frac{(x - 3)^2}{5^2} + \frac{(y + 2)^2}{4^2} = 1$$

    This expression conforms to the classical equation for an ellipse, namely:

    $$\frac{(x - h)^2}{a^2} + \frac{(y - k)^2}{b^2} = 1$$

22. *Answer:* (C)

    Solution: Referring to the solution of problem #21, the center of the ellipse is located at (h, k). Since, in this case, $h = 3$ and $k = -2$, the center is at $(3, -2)$.

23. *Answer:* (A)

    Solution: The equation for this curve conforms to the classical expression $\frac{(x - h)^2}{a^2} + \frac{(y - k)^2}{b^2} = 1$. Since $a > b$, the major axis lies along the x-axis and therefore, is horizontal.

24. *Answer:* (B)

    Solution: $\dfrac{(x - h)^2}{a^2} + \dfrac{(y - k)^2}{b^2} = 1$

    $\dfrac{(x - 3)^2}{5^2} + \dfrac{(y + 2)^2}{4^2} = 1$

    The major axis is defined as 2a which equals $2(5) = 10$.
    The minor axis is defined as 2b which equals $2(4) = 8$.
    The ratio $= 10 : 8 = 1.25$

25. *Answer:* (E)

    Solution: The focus is located a distance c from the center of the ellipse, where

    $c^2 = a^2 - b^2$

    $c^2 = 25 - 16$

    $c = 3$

    Since the major axis is horizontal, the right-hand focus is located 3 units to the right of the center, which is $3 + (3, -2)$ or $(6, -2)$.

26. *Answer:* (C)
    Solution: Transforming the time domain equation into the Laplace equivalent,

$$5\frac{di}{dt} + 200i - 24 = 5[sI(s) - 0.6] + 200I(s) - \frac{24}{s} = 0$$

$$I(s) = \frac{3s + 24}{5s(s + 40)} = \frac{A}{5s} + \frac{B}{s + 40}$$

Using partial fraction expansion,

$$A = \frac{3s + 24}{s + 40}\bigg|_{s=0} = \frac{24}{40} = 0.6$$

$$B = \frac{3s + 24}{5s}\bigg|_{s=-40} = \frac{-120 + 24}{-200} = 0.48$$

$$I(s) = \frac{0.6}{5s} + \frac{0.48}{s + 40}$$

$$i(t) = 0.12 + 0.48\varepsilon^{-40t}$$

At t = 0.05, i = $0.12 + 0.48\varepsilon^{-40(.05)}$

$$i = 0.12 + 0.48(0.1353)$$

$$i = 0.185$$

27. *Answer:* (B)
    Solution: Total area under sine wave $= \int_0^\pi 15\sin x\,dx = -15\cos x\bigg|_0^\pi =$
    $-15[-1 - 1] = 30$

    Area of triangle $= \frac{1}{2}bh = \frac{1}{2}(15\pi) = 7.5\pi$

    Δ Area $= 30 - 7.5\pi = 6.44$ square units

28. *Answer:* (D)
    Solution: $\displaystyle\int_{1.5}^{3.0} \frac{dx}{\sqrt{36 - 4x^2}} = \int_{1.5}^{3.0} \frac{dx}{2\sqrt{9 - x^2}} = \frac{1}{2}\left[\arcsin\frac{x}{3}\right]_{1.5}^{3.0}$

    $$= \frac{1}{2}\left[\arcsin\frac{3}{3} - \arcsin\frac{1.5}{3}\right] = \frac{1}{2}\left[\frac{\pi}{2} - \frac{\pi}{6}\right] = \frac{\pi}{6}$$

29. *Answer:* (A)
    Solution: $\sin x = x - \dfrac{x^3}{3!} + \dfrac{x^5}{5!} - \dfrac{x^7}{7!} + ---$

    $$\cos x = 1 - \frac{x^2}{2!} + \frac{x^4}{4!} - \frac{x^6}{6!} + ------$$

    $$\varepsilon^x = 1 + x + \frac{x^2}{2!} + \frac{x^3}{3!}$$

    $$\therefore (\sin x + \cos x) = 1 + x - \frac{x^2}{2!} - \frac{x^3}{3!} + \frac{x^4}{4!} --------$$

    $$\varepsilon^x(\sin x + \cos x) = 1 + 2x + x^2 + 0 - \frac{5x^4}{24} + -----------$$

30. *Answer:* (D)

 Solution: $m^2 + 9 = 0$

$$m^2 = -9$$

$$m = \pm 3i$$

$$y = C_1 \sin 3x + C_2 \cos 3x$$

Electrical Circuits

31. *Answer:* (C)

 Solution: The solution is developed in the table shown below. The vector summation of the real power in watts and the reactive vars is:

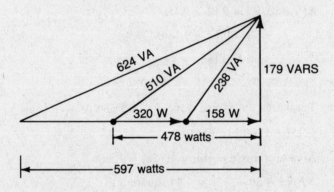

	PRI (80% eff)	PRI (100% eff)	SEC #1	SEC #2
Turns	600	600	400	300
Volts	120v	120v	80v	60v
Amperes	5.196	4.25	4	3.974
R	—	—	20Ω	10Ω
X_L	—	—	0	11.31Ω
Z	23.09	—	20Ω	15.097Ω
P	597.44	477.95	320 watts	157.95 watts
VARS	178.64	178.64	0	178.64
VA	623.57	510.24	320	238.46

32. *Answer:* (A)

 Solution: Referring to the table in solution #31, $Z = \dfrac{V}{I} = \dfrac{V^2}{VA} = \dfrac{(120)^2}{623.6}$

$$Z = 23.09\Omega$$

33. *Answer:* (A)

   Solution: Referring to the table in solution #31, $\theta = \cos^{-1} \dfrac{\text{Power in watts}}{\text{volt-amperes}}$

$$\theta = \cos^{-1} \frac{597.4}{623.6} = 16.6°$$

34. *Answer:* (A)

   Solution: The lagging current in secondary #2 must be exactly offset by the leading current through the capacitor. The current through secondary #2 is

$$i_{sec} = \frac{V}{Z} \left\lfloor -\cos^{-1}\frac{R}{Z} = \frac{60}{15.097} \right\lfloor -\cos^{-1}\frac{10}{15.097} = 3.974 \left\lfloor -48.52° \right.$$

$$\therefore i_c = 3.974 \sin 48.52° = 2.977 \text{ amperes } \lfloor 90°$$

$$x_c = \frac{60v}{2.977} = 20.15 \text{ ohms}$$

$$C = \frac{1}{2\pi fXc} = \frac{1}{2\pi(60)(20.15)} = 132 \text{ microfarads}$$

   Note that it is *incorrect* to set x_c equal to $-X_L$ in this circuit, since the full secondary voltage is applied across X_c while only a partial voltage appears across X_L.

35. *Answer:* (B)

   Solution: The current through the resistor in secondary #2 is 3.974 amperes, notwithstanding the current through the capacitor.

$$P_{SEC-2} = i^2R = (3.974)^2(10) = 157.95 \text{ watts}$$

   Alternatively, $P_{SEC-2} = (60 \text{ volts})(3.974 \cos 48.52°) = 157.95 \text{ watts}$

$$P_{TOT} = 320 + 157.95 = 477.95 \text{ watts}$$

$$P_{IN} = \frac{477.95}{0.80} = 597.44 \text{ watts}$$

$$I_{PRI} = \frac{597.44 \text{ watts}}{120 \text{ volts}} = 4.979 \text{ amperes}$$

36. *Answer:* (D)

   Solution: From solution #31, it was established that the total power drawn by the input equals 597.44 watts. Since $\cos\theta$ equals 0.95, $\tan\theta$ equals 0.3287.

$$\therefore \tan\theta = 0.3287 = \frac{\text{vars}}{\text{watts}} = \frac{\text{vars}}{597.44}$$

   vars = 196.4 (capacitive)

   But existing vars equals 178.64, inductive.

   $\therefore$ vars needed = $196.4 - (-178.64) = 375.0$, capacitive

$$\text{vars} = \frac{V^2 \sec}{X_c}$$

$$X_c = \frac{(60)^2}{375.0} = 9.6 \text{ ohms}$$

$$C = \frac{1}{2\pi f X_c} = \frac{1}{2\pi(60)(9.6)}$$

$$C = 276 \text{ microfarads}$$

37. *Answer:* (C)

    Solution: Volt-amperes drawn by the primary equals $\dfrac{\text{watts}}{\cos\theta}$

    $$VA = \frac{597.44}{0.95} = 628.88$$

    $$\therefore I = \frac{628.88}{120} = 5.24 \text{ amperes}$$

38. *Answer:* (C)

    Solution: Since the reactive "power" drawn by the inductor is 178.64 vars, the capacitor must also draw 178.64 vars.

    $$\therefore \frac{V^2}{X_c} = \frac{(80)^2}{X_c} = 178.64 \text{ vars}$$

    $$X_c = \frac{6400}{178.64} = 35.83 \text{ ohms}$$

    $$\therefore C = \frac{1}{2\pi f X_c} = \frac{1}{2\pi(60)(35.83)} = 74\mu F$$

39. *Answer:* (D)

    Solution: $i_L(0) = -\dfrac{V_1}{30}, \quad i_L(\infty) = \dfrac{V_2}{100}$

    $$i_L = \frac{V_2}{100} - \left[\frac{V_2}{100} - \frac{-V_1}{30} \right] \varepsilon^{-at}$$

    $$\therefore \frac{V_2}{100} = 0.4, \quad V_2 = 40 \text{ volts}$$

    $$\frac{40}{100} - \frac{-V_1}{30} = 2.4, \quad V_1 = 60 \text{ volts}$$

40. *Answer:* (A)

    Solution: The time constant τ appears in the exponent as follows:

    $$\varepsilon^{-\frac{t}{\tau}} = \varepsilon^{-\frac{Rt}{L}} = \varepsilon^{-\frac{t}{L/R}}$$

    $$\therefore \tau = \frac{L}{R} = \frac{2}{100} = 0.02 \text{ seconds}$$

    Note that the branch containing V_1 and the 20-ohm resistor is not in the circuit after time equals zero.

Engineering Economics

41. *Answer:* (E)

    Solution: Converting the cost of construction to an annual basis,

    $$A = (18{,}000 + 30{,}000 + 15{,}000)(A/P, 15\%, 10)$$

    $$A = (49{,}500)(0.1993) = \$9865.35$$

42. *Answer:* (D)

    Solution: Annual depreciation(S.L.) = $1/10(18{,}000 + 30{,}000 + 1500) = \$4950$

    $$\text{Depr}_{(\text{total in first 5 years})} = 5(4950) = \$24{,}750$$

43. *Answer:* (C)

    Solution: Total cost basis = $49,500

End of Year	Depr. Factor	Annual Depr.
1	10/55	9000
2	9/55	8100
3	8/55	7200
4	7/55	6300
5	6/55	5400

    Summation = $36,000

44. *Answer:* (A)

    Solution: S.F. = $(60{,}500 - 0)(A/F, 15\%, 10)$

    $$\text{S.F.} = 60{,}500(0.04925)$$

    $$\text{S.F.} = \$2980$$

45. *Answer:* (B)

    Solution: A valid comparison may be made by reducing all three alternatives to their equivalent annual costs, including both initial expenses and annual operating costs.

    1. Building Option
       a. Equivalent annual worth, from solution #41, is $9685.35.
       b. Annual operating cost = 12,000 + 1000 + 500 = $13,500.
          Total = $9865.35 + $13,500 = $23,365.35
    2. Rental Option
       a. Annual operating cost = $15,000 + 12,000 + 500 = $27,500.
    3. Purchase Option
       a. Equivalent annual worth = $(60{,}000 + 500)(A/P, 15\%, 10)$
          $= (60{,}500)(0.1993) = \$12{,}057.65$
       b. Annual operating cost = $12,000 + 1000 + 500 + $13,400
          Total = $12,057.65 + 13,500 = $25,557.65

46. *Answer:* (E)

    Solution: From the solution to problem #45, the equivalent annual cost of renting is $27,500 and that for building is $23,365.35. The difference is $4,134.65. Converting this annual difference to its present worth or initial cost basis, the excess initial cost would be

    $$\Delta \text{ Initial cost} = \$4134.65(P/A, 15\%, 10)$$

    $$= \$4134.65(5.0188)$$

    $$= \$20,751$$

47. *Answer:* (C)

    Solution: The amount required for building the machine is $49,500. The annual sinking fund amount is therefore $49,500(A/F, 15%, 5).

    $$\text{S.F.} = \$49,500(0.1483) = \$7341$$

48. *Answer:* (D)

    Solution: 1. The present requirement of $49,500 will grow under 5% inflation conditions such that the total amount needed will be

    $$F = \$49,500(F/P, 5\%, 5)$$

    $$F = \$49,500(1.2763) = \$63,177$$

    2. In order to realize $63,177 in cash funds five years hence, the new sinking fund amount will be

    $$\text{S.F.} = \$63,177(0.1483) = \$9369$$

49. *Answer:* (C)

    Solution: The future total of the sinking fund is defined by

    $$F = A\left[\frac{(1+i)^n - 1}{i}\right] \text{ where } i = 15\% \text{ and } A = \$2980, \text{ based on problem}$$

    #44. The future purchase price of the new machine is defined by $F = P(1 + i)^n$, where $P = \$60,500$ and $i = 5\%$ inflation rate. Equating these expressions for F, $60,500(1.05)^n = 2980\left[\frac{(1.15)^n - 1}{0.15}\right]$

    Solving for n, n = 14.
    The sinking fund total for n = 14 is $119,786.
    The inflated purchase cost at n = 14 is $120,704.
    $\therefore$ 14 − 10 = 4 years extra

50. *Answer:* (C)

    Solution: An investment is desirable only if additional increments of capital will result in even greater profits.

Computer Programming

51. *Answer:* (C)

    Solution: The ON ERROR statement in line 10 causes the program to branch to line 170 when an error (such as end-of-file) occurs. The error value for end-of-file (in this system) is 8, and it causes close of files and program termination.

52. *Answer:* (D)
    Solution: Line 50 directs the program to branch to the INPUT LINE statement (line 40) if the line read in (8$) was blank.

53. *Answer:* (B)
    Solution: The INSTR function in line 70 assigns to the variable, X, a value which is one less than the number of the character position (in the string, 8$) at which the first blank space occurs.

54. *Answer:* (A)
    Solution: Line 80 performs the assignment described in answer (A).

55. *Answer:* (B)
    Solution: The lines written out to FILE2 are the variable string, Z$, which, as composed in line 140, consists of the three items described in answer (B).

56. *Answer:* (E)
    Solution: The INSTR function in line 200 looks for a " " (blank space) in the string, B$, starting at the first character position. The value returned by INSTR is equal to the character location of the first blank space, or zero, if no blank is found.

57. *Answer:* (D)
    Solution: The MID$ function, of the form in line 210, returns a value equal to the string of characters in the original string (B$) from the second character position to the right-hand end, inclusive.

58. *Answer:* (C)
    Solution: The STRING$(" ", N) function produces a string containing a number of blank spaces equal in number to the value of N.

59. *Answer:* (C)
    Solution: "X" is equal to the position of the character immediately preceding the first blank space in 8$ (as determined in line 70). "LT" is equal to the length of 8$ (from line 60). The difference, $LT - X$, is therefore equal to the number of characters from the first blank space position to the last character position in the line, inclusive.

60. *Answer:* (D)
    Solution: The hierarchy of operations is:
    1) exponentiation (**)
    2) multiplication and division (*, /)
    3) addition and subtraction (+, −)
    so

    (A) is $A + \dfrac{BD(A - B^{(B-2D)} + C)}{C} = 29$

    (B) is $A + \dfrac{BD}{AC} - B^B - (2D + C) = -1(10)^{10}$ (approx.)

(C) is $\dfrac{(A + B)A}{CD} - B^{(B-2D)} + C = 2.1875$

(D) is $A + \dfrac{ABD}{C} - B^{(B-2D)} + C = 35$

(E) is $A + \dfrac{BD}{(AC - B)^{(B-2D)}} + C = 125.0000065$

Electronics and Electrical Machinery

61. *Answer:* (C)

   Solution: The peak voltage at $V_A = 120(\tfrac{1}{4})\sqrt{2} = 42.4$

$$V_{OMAX} = 42.4 - 0.7 = 41.7 \text{ volts}$$

$$V_{c\,MIN} = 41.7 - 2 = 39.7$$

$$V_c = V_{MAX}\varepsilon^{-t/RC}$$

$$39.7 = 41.7\varepsilon - \dfrac{1/60}{1000C}$$

$$-\dfrac{1}{60,000C} = \ln\left[\dfrac{39.7}{41.7}\right] = -0.04915$$

$$\therefore C = 339\mu F$$

62. *Answer:* (E)

   Solution: Current flows in the secondary only when the diode conducts, which is a very small fraction of the total period. Therefore, the current flow in the transformer secondary consists of a pulse train, one pulse per cycle.

63. *Answer:* (A)

   Solution: The diode conducts only when the voltage at V_A is rising from 39.7 to 41.7 volts.

$$\theta = \cos^{-1}\dfrac{39.7}{41.7} = 17.82°$$

$$\dfrac{\Delta t}{1/60} = \dfrac{17.82}{360}$$

$$\Delta t = 0.825 \text{ milliseconds}$$

64. *Answer:* (D)

   Solution: The average value of the DC output voltage equals

$$V_{OAVG} = \dfrac{41.7 + 39.7}{2} = 40.7 \text{ volts}$$

$$\therefore i_{LOAD\,AVG} = \dfrac{40.7v}{1000\Omega} = 40.7 \text{ milliamperes}$$

$$i_{peak}(\Delta t) = i_{AVG}\left(\frac{1}{60}\right)$$

$$i_{peak} = \frac{0.0407}{60(0.000825)} = 822 \text{ milliamps}$$

65. *Answer:* (D)

Solution: $V_{0ideal} = -12\left[\frac{60K}{80K}\right] + 10\left[\frac{60K}{50K}\right] = -9 + 12 = +3 \text{ volts}$

$$V_{0minimum} = -12\left[\frac{60K(1-0.05)}{80K(1-0.05)}\right] + 10\left[\frac{60K(1-0.05)}{50K(1+0.05)}\right]$$

Note that the minimum output will be achieved if the absolute value of the first term is maximized, and that of the second term is minimized. Note also that the numerator of the first term cannot contain $(1 + 0.05)$ since the feedback resistor can have only one value at any given time.

$$V_{minimum} = -12\left[\frac{3}{4}\right] + 10\left[\frac{57}{52.5}\right] = 1.857 \text{ volts}$$

$$\text{Percentage deviation} = \frac{3 - 1.857}{3} = 0.381 = 38.1\%$$

66. *Answer:* (C)

Solution: $V_{0minimum} = 3 - (0.10)3 = 2.7 \text{ volts}$

Letting $x =$ the tolerance to be specified,

$$2.7 = -12\left[\frac{60K}{80K}\right] + 10\left[\frac{60K}{50K(1+x)}\right]$$

$$2.7 = -9 + \frac{12}{1+x}$$

$$x = 2.56\%$$

67. *Answer:* (C)

Solution: Power losses = 280 watts of core loss + 400 watts of copper loss = 680 watts

$$\text{Efficiency} = \frac{P_{out}}{P_{in}} = \frac{P_{out}}{P_{out} + P_{losses}} = \frac{5000(0.80)}{5000(0.80) + 680} = \frac{4000}{4680}$$

$$\text{Eff} = 85.5\%$$

68. *Answer:* (B)

Solution: At half current, copper loss = $\frac{1}{4}(400) = 100$ watts

At rated voltage, core loss = 280 watts

$\therefore$ Total losses = 380 watts

$$\text{Eff} = \frac{2.5(0.80)}{2.5(0.80) + 380} = \frac{2000}{2380} = 84.0\%$$

69. *Answer:* (C)

Solution: Power $= i_L v_L \sqrt{3} \cos \theta$

$$i_L = \frac{15,000}{208\sqrt{3}(0.8)} = 52.04 \text{ amperes of line current.}$$

$$R = \frac{kL}{A}$$

$$A = \frac{kLi}{Ri} = \frac{10.4(800)(52.04)}{(2/\sqrt{3}) \text{ volts}} = 374,964 \text{ circular mils}$$

70. *Answer:* (B)

 Solution: Using the rated specifications to solve for the reference value of lamp resistance,

$$R_{VR} = \frac{V_R^2}{W_R} = \frac{(120)^2}{500} = 28.8 \text{ ohms}$$

Solving for the rms value of applied voltage,

$$V_{rms} = \frac{320}{2}\left(\frac{1}{\sqrt{2}}\right) = 113.1 \text{ volts}$$

The lamp resistance at this voltage equals

$$R_V = (28.8)\varepsilon^{\frac{1.2(113.1-120)}{120}} = 26.88 \text{ ohms}$$

The power dissipated equals

$$W = \frac{V^2}{R} = \frac{(113.1)^2}{26.88} = 475.9 \text{ watts}$$

Fluid Mechanics

71. *Answer:* (C)

 Solution: The pressure at nozzle A is $25 \text{ psig} - (50')\frac{(62.4)}{144} = 3.3 \text{ psig}$

$$\text{Flow} = VA = A\sqrt{2gh}$$

$$= (0.05)\sqrt{2 \times 32.2\left[\frac{3.3 \times 144}{62.4}\right]} \times 12 \text{ inches/foot}$$

$$= 13.29 \text{ cubic inches per second}$$

$$\text{Flow} = 3.45 \text{ gpm}$$

72. *Answer:* (D)

 Solution: The pressure at nozzle E = $25 \text{ psig} - 10' \times \frac{62.4}{144} = 20.7 \text{ psig}$

$$\text{Flow} = A\sqrt{2gh} = 0.05\sqrt{2(32.2)(20.7)\frac{144}{62.4}} \times 12 \text{ inches/foot}$$

$$\text{Flow} = 8.64 \text{ gpm}$$

73. *Answer:* (C)
    Solution: $\Sigma\text{gpm} = 3 + 5 + 7 + 8 + 9 = 32$

    $$V = \frac{Q}{A} = \left[\frac{32(231)}{0.7854(0.5)^2}\right]\frac{1}{12} \times \frac{1}{60} = 52.3 \text{ fps}$$

    Static pressure $= 25 \text{ psig} - \frac{1}{2}\rho V^2$

    Static pressure $= 25 - \frac{62.4(52.3)^2}{2(32.2)}\left[\frac{1}{144}\right] = 6.60 \text{ psig}$

74. *Answer:* (A)
    Solution: The pressure at E $= 25 \text{ psig} - \Delta P_f - \frac{1}{2}\rho V^2 - \rho h$

    $$\Delta P_f = \frac{fl}{d}\left[\rho\frac{V^2}{2g}\right]$$

    $$V = \frac{32 \text{ gpm} \times 231}{\frac{\pi}{4}(0.75)^2}\left[\frac{1}{12} \times \frac{1}{60}\right] = 23.24 \text{ fps}$$

    $$\frac{1}{2}\rho V^2 = \frac{(62.4)(23.24)^2}{2(32.2)144} = 3.63 \text{ psi}$$

    $$\Delta P_f = \frac{(0.02)(12 \times 12)}{0.75}(3.63) = 13.95 \text{ psi}$$

    $$P_E = 25 - 13.95 - 3.63 - \frac{(62.4)(10')}{144} = 3.1 \text{ psig}$$

75. *Answer:* (B)
    Solution: Hydraulic Radius $R = \dfrac{\text{Flow Area (A)}}{\text{Wetted Perimeter (P)}}$

    $$R = \frac{\frac{5}{6}(\pi r^2) + (0.5)(0.866)}{\frac{5}{6}(2\pi r)} = \frac{3.051 \text{ sq. ft.}}{5.236 \text{ ft.}} = 0.583 \text{ ft.}$$

76. *Answer:* (C)
    Solution: From the Chezy-Manning equation, $Q = \dfrac{1.49}{n}[AR^{2/3}S^{1/2}]$.

    where: Q is flow in cfs
           n is the roughness coefficient $= 0.015$
           A is the flow area $= 3.051$ sq. ft.
           R is the hydraulic radius $= 0.583$ feet
           S is the slope $= 0.0001$ feet/foot

    $Q = 2.115 \text{ cfs}$

77. *Answer:* (E)
    Solution: When flowing full, A $= 3.142$ square feet, and R $= 1$ foot. Using the
    Chezy-Manning equation, $Q = \left(\dfrac{1.49}{0.015}\right)(3.142)(1^{2/3})(0.0001)^{1/2}$
    $Q = 3.121 \text{ cfs.}$

78. *Answer:* (A)

    Solution: $V = \dfrac{Q \text{ cfs}}{A \text{ ft}^2} = \dfrac{(150/60 \text{ gps})(0.1337 \text{ ft}^3/\text{gal})}{\pi \dfrac{(0.5)^2}{4}} = 1.702 \text{ fps}$

    $N_R = \dfrac{\rho V d}{\mu} = \dfrac{(62.4 \text{ lb/ft}^3)(0.8)(1.702 \text{ fps})(0.5 \text{ ft})}{(32.2 \text{ ft/sec}^2)(0.001 \text{ lb/sec/ft})} = 1649$

79. *Answer:* (C)

    Solution: At a Reynolds Number of 1649 the flow is laminar, and $V_c = 2V$.

    $V_c = 2(1.702 \text{ fps}) = 3.40 \text{ fps}$

80. *Answer:* (B)

    Solution: For a one-foot length,

    $\Delta P = \left[\dfrac{0.01(1)}{0.5}\right]\left[\dfrac{(62.4)(0.8)(1.702)^2}{2(32.2)}\right] = 0.0449 \text{ psf}$

    $\text{Shear Stress} = \Delta P \left[\dfrac{\text{cross-sectional area}}{\text{Surface area}}\right]$

    $\tau = 0.0449\left[\dfrac{\pi d^2/4}{\pi d l}\right] = 0.0449\left[\dfrac{0.5}{4(1)}\right] = 0.00561 \text{ psf}$

Mechanics of Materials

81. *Answer:* (C)

    Solution: The right-hand reaction is

    $R_R = \dfrac{2000(12)(6)}{10} = 14{,}400 \text{ pounds}$

    $R_L = 24{,}000 - 14{,}400 = 9600 \text{ pounds}$

    The maximum shear force occurs at the right-hand support, where x equals 10 feet:

    $V_{max} = 9600 - 2000(10) = -10{,}400 \text{ pounds}$

82. *Answer:* (B)

    Solution: The maximum moment equals

    $M_{max} = 9600\dfrac{(9600)}{2000}\left(\dfrac{1}{2}\right) = 23{,}040 \text{ lb-ft}$

    Alternatively,

    $M_{max} = 9600(4.8) - 2000(4.8)(2.4) = 23{,}040 \text{ lb-ft}$

    The maximum moment in the right-hand section is:

    $M_{max} = -2000\dfrac{(2)^2}{2} = -4000 \text{ lb-ft (non-critical value)}$

83. *Answer:* (B)

    Solution: The point of zero shear, and hence maximum moment, occurs at

    $$9600 = 2000x$$

    $$x = 4.8 \text{ feet}$$

84. *Answer:* (D)

    Solution: $\sigma = \dfrac{Mc}{I} = \dfrac{30,000(3)}{136}(12) = 7940 \text{ psi}$

85. *Answer:* (E)

    Solution: $\sigma = \dfrac{Mc}{I} = \dfrac{30,000(5)}{136}(12) = 13,240 \text{ psi}$

86. *Answer:* (D)

    Solution: $\tau = \dfrac{VQ}{It}$ where Q is the moment with respect to the neutral axis, and t is the thickness of the beam.

    $$\tau = \frac{10,000(5)(2)\left(\frac{5}{2}\right)}{136(2)} = 919 \text{ psi}$$

87. *Answer:* (A)

    Solution: $\sigma = \dfrac{My}{I} = \dfrac{30,000(0)}{136} = 0$ where y is the distance measured from the neutral axis.

88. *Answer:* (B)

    Solution: $\tau_{avg} = \dfrac{V}{A} = \dfrac{10,000}{8(2)} = 625 \text{ psi}$

89. *Answer:* (E)

    Solution: $EIy'' = M(x) = 9600x - 2000\dfrac{x^2}{2}$

    $$EIy' = 4800x^2 - \frac{1000}{3}x^3 + C_1$$

    $$EIy = 1600x^3 - \frac{1000}{12}x^4 + C_1x + C_2$$

90. *Answer:* (A)

    Solution: The deflection at the supports is equal to zero; i.e., $y(x = 0)$ equals $y(x = 10)$ equals zero.

Thermodynamics/Heat Transfer

91. *Answer:* (E)

    Solution: The increase in air temperature due to the avionics heat dissipation is:

$$\Delta T = \frac{Q}{wc} = \frac{10 \text{ KW}(56.88)\frac{\text{Btu/min}}{\text{KW}}}{20 \text{ lb/min}(0.24)\text{Btu/lb}^\circ\text{F}}$$

$$\Delta T = 118.5^\circ\text{F}$$

$$T_1 = 40^\circ\text{F} + 118.5 = 158.5^\circ\text{F}$$

92. *Answer:* (B)

    Solution: For the case of isentropic compression:

    $$(T_{out})_{isen} = (130 + 460)(P_2/P_1)^{\frac{\gamma-1}{\gamma}} = 590(2.1)^{0.2857} = 729.3^\circ\text{R}$$

    $$(T_{out})_{isen} = 269.3^\circ\text{F}$$

    For an efficiency of 0.8,

    $$T_{out} = 590 + \frac{T_{isen}}{0.8}$$

    $$= 590 + \frac{139.3}{0.8}$$

    $$= 764.1^\circ\text{R}$$

    $$T_{out} = 304.1^\circ\text{F}$$

93. *Answer:* (D)

    Solution: The heat exchanger effectiveness is 0.8 and is defined as:

    $$E = \frac{T_{HOT} - T_3}{T_{HOT} - T_{COLD}}$$

    $$T_{COLD} = \text{AMBIENT} = 80^\circ\text{F}$$

    $$T_{HOT} = 341^\circ\text{F}$$

    $$T_3 = 341 - 0.8(341 - 80)$$

    $$T_3 = 132.2^\circ\text{F}$$

94. *Answer:* (A)

    Solution: For the case of isentropic expansion:

    $$P_{in} = (2.1)(14.7) = 30.87 \text{ psia}$$

    $$P_{out} = 14.7 \text{ psia}$$

    $$T_{4s} = T_3(P_4/P_3)^{\frac{\gamma-1}{\gamma}} = 592.2\left(\frac{14.7}{30.87}\right)^{0.2857}$$

    $$T_{4s} = 479.1^\circ\text{R}$$

    For an efficiency of 0.8152

    $$\eta = \frac{T_{in} - T_{OUT}}{(T_{in} - T_{out})_{ISENTROPIC}}$$

    $$T_{OUT} = 592.2 - 0.8152(592.2 - 479.1)$$

    $$T_{OUT} = 500^\circ\text{R} = 40^\circ\text{F}$$

95. *Answer:* (E)
    Solution: For the case of no heat losses, work equals the change in enthalpy. Hence,

    $$HP = \dot{w}\,Cp(T_3 - T_4)\left[\frac{0.02357\ HP}{Btu/min}\right]$$

    $$= 20\frac{lb}{min}[0.24\ Btu/lb\text{-}°F](132.2 - 40)°F\left[0.02357\frac{HP}{Btu/min}\right]$$

    $$= 10.43\ HP$$

96. *Answer:* (C)
    Solution: As in problem #95,

    $$HP = \dot{w}\,Cp(T_2 - T_1) = 0.02357$$

    where $T_1 = 158.5°F$ [from problem #91]

    $$HP = (20)(0.24)(341 - 158.5)(0.02357)$$

    $$HP = 20.65$$

97. *Answer:* (B)
    Solution: From problems #95 and #96, the required power is:

    $$HP_{REQD(COMPR)} - HP_{DELIVERED(TURB)} = 20.65 - 10.43 = 10.22$$

    $$\text{Motor Power} = \frac{10.22}{\eta}\left(0.7457\frac{KW}{HP}\right)$$

    $$P_M = \frac{(10.22)(0.7457)}{0.85}$$

    $$P_M = 8.966\ KW$$

98. *Answer:* (E)
    Solution: The chemical reaction equation is:

    $$C_2H_6 + 7O_2 + 7(\tfrac{79}{21})N_2 \Rightarrow 2CO_2 + 3H_2O + 3.5O_2 + 7(\tfrac{79}{21})N_2$$

    The following weights of reactants result from burning one mole of ethane.

    $$30 + 224 + 737.3 \Rightarrow 88 + 54 + 112 + 737.3$$

    The weight of air is $224 + 737.3 = 964.3$ lb

    Ratio $= 964.3/30 = 32.14$ lb of air/lb of ethane

99. *Answer:* (D)
    Solution: From the solution of problem #98, the weight of CO_2 is 88 lbs.

100. *Answer:* (A)

Solution: From the psychrometric charts at the initial condition

$w_s = 0.0132$ lb water/lb dry air

$h = 33.7$ Btu/lb

At 40°F saturated, $w_s = 0.0052$ lb water/lb dry air.
Therefore, 0.0080 lb H_2O/lb air is liquid (0.0132 − 0.0052).
90% of 0.0080 = 0.0072 lb H_2O/lb air removed. This leaves
0.0132 − 0.0072 = 0.0060 lb H_2O/lb air in the final state.
After heating to 60°F, the conditions are:

Specific humidity $(w_s) = 0.0060$ lb water/lb air

Relative humidity (RH) = 55%

Enthalpy (h) = 20.95 Btu/lb

X. SECOND PRACTICE EXAMINATION IN FUNDAMENTALS OF ENGINEERING

This practice examination was developed as a study guide for use by those candidates for the P.E. license who are preparing to take the Fundamentals of Engineering examination given by the National Council of Engineering Examiners. This is a multiple-choice, open-book, open-notes examination in which a battery-operated calculator or a slide rule is permitted.

The following pages present a typical 4-hour Morning Section examination containing 140 questions (all of which must be answered) and a 4-hour Afternoon Section examination containing 100 questions (of which 70 must be answered), together with answers and completely worked out solutions for each problem.

Answer Sheet
Practice Examination 2—A.M. Part

Electrical Circuits

1 Ⓐ Ⓑ Ⓒ Ⓓ Ⓔ   5 Ⓐ Ⓑ Ⓒ Ⓓ Ⓔ   9 Ⓐ Ⓑ Ⓒ Ⓓ Ⓔ   13 Ⓐ Ⓑ Ⓒ Ⓓ Ⓔ   17 Ⓐ Ⓑ Ⓒ Ⓓ Ⓔ

2 Ⓐ Ⓑ Ⓒ Ⓓ Ⓔ   6 Ⓐ Ⓑ Ⓒ Ⓓ Ⓔ   10 Ⓐ Ⓑ Ⓒ Ⓓ Ⓔ   14 Ⓐ Ⓑ Ⓒ Ⓓ Ⓔ   18 Ⓐ Ⓑ Ⓒ Ⓓ Ⓔ

3 Ⓐ Ⓑ Ⓒ Ⓓ Ⓔ   7 Ⓐ Ⓑ Ⓒ Ⓓ Ⓔ   11 Ⓐ Ⓑ Ⓒ Ⓓ Ⓔ   15 Ⓐ Ⓑ Ⓒ Ⓓ Ⓔ

4 Ⓐ Ⓑ Ⓒ Ⓓ Ⓔ   8 Ⓐ Ⓑ Ⓒ Ⓓ Ⓔ   12 Ⓐ Ⓑ Ⓒ Ⓓ Ⓔ   16 Ⓐ Ⓑ Ⓒ Ⓓ Ⓔ

Statics

19 Ⓐ Ⓑ Ⓒ Ⓓ Ⓔ   22 Ⓐ Ⓑ Ⓒ Ⓓ Ⓔ   25 Ⓐ Ⓑ Ⓒ Ⓓ Ⓔ   28 Ⓐ Ⓑ Ⓒ Ⓓ Ⓔ   31 Ⓐ Ⓑ Ⓒ Ⓓ Ⓔ

20 Ⓐ Ⓑ Ⓒ Ⓓ Ⓔ   23 Ⓐ Ⓑ Ⓒ Ⓓ Ⓔ   26 Ⓐ Ⓑ Ⓒ Ⓓ Ⓔ   29 Ⓐ Ⓑ Ⓒ Ⓓ Ⓔ

21 Ⓐ Ⓑ Ⓒ Ⓓ Ⓔ   24 Ⓐ Ⓑ Ⓒ Ⓓ Ⓔ   27 Ⓐ Ⓑ Ⓒ Ⓓ Ⓔ   30 Ⓐ Ⓑ Ⓒ Ⓓ Ⓔ

Dynamics

32 Ⓐ Ⓑ Ⓒ Ⓓ Ⓔ   35 Ⓐ Ⓑ Ⓒ Ⓓ Ⓔ   38 Ⓐ Ⓑ Ⓒ Ⓓ Ⓔ   41 Ⓐ Ⓑ Ⓒ Ⓓ Ⓔ   44 Ⓐ Ⓑ Ⓒ Ⓓ Ⓔ

33 Ⓐ Ⓑ Ⓒ Ⓓ Ⓔ   36 Ⓐ Ⓑ Ⓒ Ⓓ Ⓔ   39 Ⓐ Ⓑ Ⓒ Ⓓ Ⓔ   42 Ⓐ Ⓑ Ⓒ Ⓓ Ⓔ

34 Ⓐ Ⓑ Ⓒ Ⓓ Ⓔ   37 Ⓐ Ⓑ Ⓒ Ⓓ Ⓔ   40 Ⓐ Ⓑ Ⓒ Ⓓ Ⓔ   43 Ⓐ Ⓑ Ⓒ Ⓓ Ⓔ

Mechanics of Materials

45 Ⓐ Ⓑ Ⓒ Ⓓ Ⓔ   48 Ⓐ Ⓑ Ⓒ Ⓓ Ⓔ   51 Ⓐ Ⓑ Ⓒ Ⓓ Ⓔ   54 Ⓐ Ⓑ Ⓒ Ⓓ Ⓔ   57 Ⓐ Ⓑ Ⓒ Ⓓ Ⓔ

46 Ⓐ Ⓑ Ⓒ Ⓓ Ⓔ   49 Ⓐ Ⓑ Ⓒ Ⓓ Ⓔ   52 Ⓐ Ⓑ Ⓒ Ⓓ Ⓔ   55 Ⓐ Ⓑ Ⓒ Ⓓ Ⓔ

47 Ⓐ Ⓑ Ⓒ Ⓓ Ⓔ   50 Ⓐ Ⓑ Ⓒ Ⓓ Ⓔ   53 Ⓐ Ⓑ Ⓒ Ⓓ Ⓔ   56 Ⓐ Ⓑ Ⓒ Ⓓ Ⓔ

Fluid Mechanics

58 Ⓐ Ⓑ Ⓒ Ⓓ Ⓔ   61 Ⓐ Ⓑ Ⓒ Ⓓ Ⓔ   64 Ⓐ Ⓑ Ⓒ Ⓓ Ⓔ   67 Ⓐ Ⓑ Ⓒ Ⓓ Ⓔ   70 Ⓐ Ⓑ Ⓒ Ⓓ Ⓔ

59 Ⓐ Ⓑ Ⓒ Ⓓ Ⓔ   62 Ⓐ Ⓑ Ⓒ Ⓓ Ⓔ   65 Ⓐ Ⓑ Ⓒ Ⓓ Ⓔ   68 Ⓐ Ⓑ Ⓒ Ⓓ Ⓔ   71 Ⓐ Ⓑ Ⓒ Ⓓ Ⓔ

60 Ⓐ Ⓑ Ⓒ Ⓓ Ⓔ   63 Ⓐ Ⓑ Ⓒ Ⓓ Ⓔ   66 Ⓐ Ⓑ Ⓒ Ⓓ Ⓔ   69 Ⓐ Ⓑ Ⓒ Ⓓ Ⓔ

Thermodynamics/Heat Transfer

72 Ⓐ Ⓑ Ⓒ Ⓓ Ⓔ   75 Ⓐ Ⓑ Ⓒ Ⓓ Ⓔ   78 Ⓐ Ⓑ Ⓒ Ⓓ Ⓔ   81 Ⓐ Ⓑ Ⓒ Ⓓ Ⓔ   84 Ⓐ Ⓑ Ⓒ Ⓓ Ⓔ

73 Ⓐ Ⓑ Ⓒ Ⓓ Ⓔ   76 Ⓐ Ⓑ Ⓒ Ⓓ Ⓔ   79 Ⓐ Ⓑ Ⓒ Ⓓ Ⓔ   82 Ⓐ Ⓑ Ⓒ Ⓓ Ⓔ   85 Ⓐ Ⓑ Ⓒ Ⓓ Ⓔ

74 Ⓐ Ⓑ Ⓒ Ⓓ Ⓔ   77 Ⓐ Ⓑ Ⓒ Ⓓ Ⓔ   80 Ⓐ Ⓑ Ⓒ Ⓓ Ⓔ   83 Ⓐ Ⓑ Ⓒ Ⓓ Ⓔ

Mathematics

86 Ⓐ Ⓑ Ⓒ Ⓓ Ⓔ   89 Ⓐ Ⓑ Ⓒ Ⓓ Ⓔ   92 Ⓐ Ⓑ Ⓒ Ⓓ Ⓔ   95 Ⓐ Ⓑ Ⓒ Ⓓ Ⓔ

87 Ⓐ Ⓑ Ⓒ Ⓓ Ⓔ   90 Ⓐ Ⓑ Ⓒ Ⓓ Ⓔ   93 Ⓐ Ⓑ Ⓒ Ⓓ Ⓔ   96 Ⓐ Ⓑ Ⓒ Ⓓ Ⓔ

88 Ⓐ Ⓑ Ⓒ Ⓓ Ⓔ   91 Ⓐ Ⓑ Ⓒ Ⓓ Ⓔ   94 Ⓐ Ⓑ Ⓒ Ⓓ Ⓔ   97 Ⓐ Ⓑ Ⓒ Ⓓ Ⓔ

Chemistry

98 Ⓐ Ⓑ Ⓒ Ⓓ Ⓔ   100 Ⓐ Ⓑ Ⓒ Ⓓ Ⓔ   102 Ⓐ Ⓑ Ⓒ Ⓓ Ⓔ   104 Ⓐ Ⓑ Ⓒ Ⓓ Ⓔ   106 Ⓐ Ⓑ Ⓒ Ⓓ Ⓔ

99 Ⓐ Ⓑ Ⓒ Ⓓ Ⓔ   101 Ⓐ Ⓑ Ⓒ Ⓓ Ⓔ   103 Ⓐ Ⓑ Ⓒ Ⓓ Ⓔ   105 Ⓐ Ⓑ Ⓒ Ⓓ Ⓔ   107 Ⓐ Ⓑ Ⓒ Ⓓ Ⓔ

Computer Programming

108 Ⓐ Ⓑ Ⓒ Ⓓ Ⓔ   110 Ⓐ Ⓑ Ⓒ Ⓓ Ⓔ   112 Ⓐ Ⓑ Ⓒ Ⓓ Ⓔ   114 Ⓐ Ⓑ Ⓒ Ⓓ Ⓔ

109 Ⓐ Ⓑ Ⓒ Ⓓ Ⓔ   111 Ⓐ Ⓑ Ⓒ Ⓓ Ⓔ   113 Ⓐ Ⓑ Ⓒ Ⓓ Ⓔ   115 Ⓐ Ⓑ Ⓒ Ⓓ Ⓔ

Mathematical Modeling of Engineering Systems

116 Ⓐ Ⓑ Ⓒ Ⓓ Ⓔ   118 Ⓐ Ⓑ Ⓒ Ⓓ Ⓔ   120 Ⓐ Ⓑ Ⓒ Ⓓ Ⓔ   122 Ⓐ Ⓑ Ⓒ Ⓓ Ⓔ

117 Ⓐ Ⓑ Ⓒ Ⓓ Ⓔ   119 Ⓐ Ⓑ Ⓒ Ⓓ Ⓔ   121 Ⓐ Ⓑ Ⓒ Ⓓ Ⓔ   123 Ⓐ Ⓑ Ⓒ Ⓓ Ⓔ

Engineering Economics

124 Ⓐ Ⓑ Ⓒ Ⓓ Ⓔ   126 Ⓐ Ⓑ Ⓒ Ⓓ Ⓔ   128 Ⓐ Ⓑ Ⓒ Ⓓ Ⓔ

125 Ⓐ Ⓑ Ⓒ Ⓓ Ⓔ   127 Ⓐ Ⓑ Ⓒ Ⓓ Ⓔ   129 Ⓐ Ⓑ Ⓒ Ⓓ Ⓔ

Materials Science

130 Ⓐ Ⓑ Ⓒ Ⓓ Ⓔ   132 Ⓐ Ⓑ Ⓒ Ⓓ Ⓔ   134 Ⓐ Ⓑ Ⓒ Ⓓ Ⓔ

131 Ⓐ Ⓑ Ⓒ Ⓓ Ⓔ   133 Ⓐ Ⓑ Ⓒ Ⓓ Ⓔ   135 Ⓐ Ⓑ Ⓒ Ⓓ Ⓔ

The Structure of Matter

136 Ⓐ Ⓑ Ⓒ Ⓓ Ⓔ   137 Ⓐ Ⓑ Ⓒ Ⓓ Ⓔ   138 Ⓐ Ⓑ Ⓒ Ⓓ Ⓔ   139 Ⓐ Ⓑ Ⓒ Ⓓ Ⓔ   140 Ⓐ Ⓑ Ⓒ Ⓓ Ⓔ

PRACTICE EXAMINATION 2
A.M. PART

Electrical Circuits

1. Two separately excited 240-volt DC shunt generators are to be connected in parallel to share a 600-ampere load. The first generator has a no-load terminal voltage of 255 volts and a total armature resistance of 0.08 ohms. The second generator has a no-load terminal voltage of 248 volts and an armature resistance of 0.12 ohms. Neglecting contact resistances and brush drops, the first generator will have an armature current in amperes that is most nearly

   (A) 105
   (B) 240
   (C) 300
   (D) 360
   (E) 395

2. The rms level of the voltage wave shape as shown is most nearly

   (A) 2.3
   (B) 5.1
   (C) 6.1
   (D) 6.3
   (E) 7.1

   volts

   10

   5

   0   0   5   7   10   15   time in
                                      seconds

   −6   −6

3. In the circuit shown, the output voltage V_0 is most nearly equal to

   (A) 70
   (B) 80
   (C) 90
   (D) 100
   (E) 110

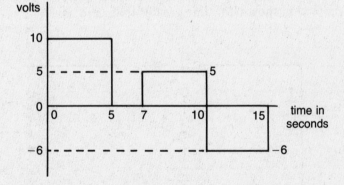

   120 volts
   60 Hz   100 Ω   0.1 h V_0

   200 Ω

   0.5 h

4. The frequency in Hertz of the AC voltage produced by a 440-volt 3-phase 24-pole alternator rotating at 600 rpm is most nearly

   (A) 30
   (B) 60
   (C) 120
   (D) 240
   (E) 1000

5. A 120-volt battery is connected across a 400-ohm resistor, a 10-milli-henry inductor, and 3 capacitors, all of which are in series. The capacitors are $10\mu F$, $20\mu F$, and $50\mu F$, respectively. After a very long time, the DC voltage across the $50\mu F$ capacitor will be most nearly

   (A) 0
   (B) 14
   (C) 15
   (D) 75
   (E) 106

6. In the circuit shown, the switch is thrown to the DOWN position at time equals zero. It had previously been UP for a very long time. The mathematical expression for the current through the inductor, in the direction shown, for time greater than zero, is:

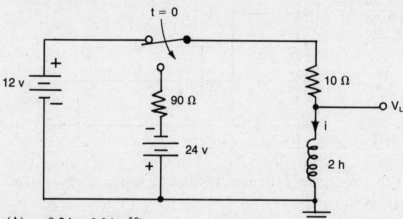

   (A) $-0.24 - 0.24\varepsilon^{-50t}$
   (B) $-0.24 + 0.24\varepsilon^{-50t}$
   (C) $-0.24 + 0.96\varepsilon^{-50t}$
   (D) $-0.24 - 1.44\varepsilon^{-50t}$
   (E) $-0.24 + 1.44\varepsilon^{-50t}$

7. In the preceding problem, starting from time equals zero, the time in milliseconds that will be required for the current through the inductor to reach zero amperes is most nearly

   (A) 36

(B) 60
(C) 100
(D) 120
(E) 140

8. In the circuit shown for the preceding two problems, the maximum voltage that is developed across the inductor is most nearly

(A) 24
(B) 36
(C) 96
(D) 120
(E) 144

9. A 120-volt 60-Hertz source is connected to the primary winding of a transformer that has two independent secondary windings, one supplying 90 volts and the other 60 volts. Each secondary is connected to a separate 10-ohm resistive load. If the overall efficiency of the transformer is 75 percent, the current in amperes drawn by the primary will be most nearly

(A) 6
(B) 8
(C) 13
(D) 15
(E) 20

10. The Zener diode voltage regulator circuit shown in the diagram has an input voltage which varies between 30 volts and 40 volts DC, and a variable load resistor which can vary between 500 ohms and infinity ohms. The maximum instantaneous power in watts dissipated in the Zener diode is most nearly

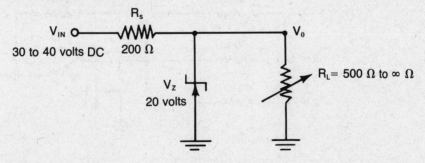

(A) 0.2
(B) 1.0
(C) 1.2
(D) 1.6
(E) 2.0

11. In the Zener diode voltage regulator circuit shown in problem #10, the variable load resistor is removed and is now replaced by a fixed load resistor of 200 ohms. The new output voltage

    (A) is constant at 15 volts
    (B) is constant at 18 volts
    (C) is constant at 20 volts
    (D) varies between 15 and 20 volts
    (E) varies between 18 and 20 volts

12. For the operational amplifier circuit shown, the output voltage V_0 is most nearly at

    (A) +4 volts
    (B) −4 volts
    (C) 0 volts
    (D) positive saturation
    (E) negative saturation

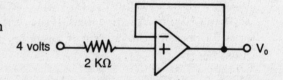

13. In the operational amplifier shown, all of the resistors have a tolerance of plus or minus 5%. Under these conditions, the maximum voltage that can be expected at the output under normal operating conditions is most nearly

    (A) 4.0
    (B) 4.4
    (C) 4.8
    (D) 5.1
    (E) 5.4

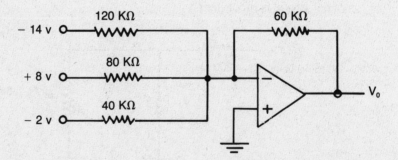

14. At time equals zero, the voltage waveshape shown above is applied to the input of the operational amplifier circuit as indicated. The feedback capacitor is initially uncharged. At the end of exactly 12 seconds the output voltage V_0 will be most nearly

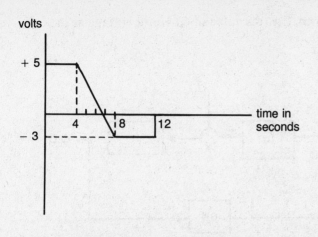

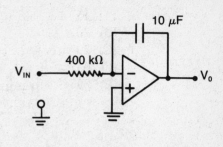

(A) −3
(B) +3
(C) −12
(D) +12
(E) 0

15. An industrial plant has a 3-phase 440-volt 60-Hertz supply. One portion of this plant draws 120 kilowatts at a power factor of 0.8 lagging. The other portion draws 50 kilowatts at unity power factor. The overall line current in amperes drawn by this plant is most nearly

(A) 220
(B) 250
(C) 280
(D) 440
(E) 480

16. A factory building draws an average current of 360 amperes daily from a single-phase 120-volt 60-Hertz line, at a power factor of 0.80 lagging. If this power factor were to be corrected to unity by connecting a bank of ideal capacitors directly across the line, the total value of capacitance in microfarads that would be required is most nearly

(A) 4420
(B) 4780
(C) 5210
(D) 6370
(E) 7950

17. In the feedback circuit shown, the rms value of 60-Hertz voltage at the output C is most nearly

   (A) 15
   (B) 20
   (C) 29
   (D) 63
   (E) 89

$R = 20 + 10 \sin 377t$

$U_1 = 40 + 30 \sin 377t$

18. A 60-volt battery source is applied as an input to a negative feedback system whose forward gain G equals $\dfrac{30}{4s + 5}$ in Laplace notation, and whose feedback element H equals unity. In this system, the final (or steady-state) value of error voltage is most nearly

   (A) 6
   (B) 7
   (C) 9
   (D) 30
   (E) 60

Statics

19. A ladder of length L leans against a frictionless wall and rests on a floor with a friction coefficient of 0.25. The most shallow angle of repose α that is possible for equilibrium is most nearly

   (A) 27°
   (B) 34°
   (C) 45°
   (D) 56°
   (E) 63°

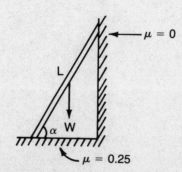

20. Three force vectors are given by

$$\vec{F}_1 = 10\vec{i} - 10\vec{k}$$
$$\vec{F}_2 = 20\vec{i} + 10\vec{j} + 10\vec{k}$$
$$\vec{F}_3 = -10\vec{i} + 10\vec{j} - 20\vec{k}$$

The magnitude of the resultant force is most nearly

(A) 20
(B) 28
(C) 35
(D) 40
(E) 60

21. For the system shown, the coefficient of rolling friction is 0.1 and that of sliding friction is 0.2. What is the maximum angle of inclination α for which the system will not move?

(A) 0°
(B) 5.7°
(C) 10°
(D) 11.3°
(E) 30°

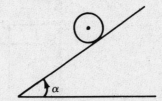

22. Determine the x-coordinate in inches of the centroid of the cross-section shown.

(A) 1.0
(B) 1.5
(C) 1.8
(D) 2.0
(E) 2.5

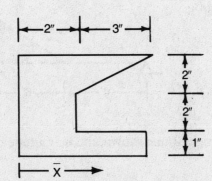

23. Which of the following principles or methods is not one pertaining to statics?

(A) Method of Joints
(B) Method of Sections
(C) Newton's First Law
(D) Maxwell's Polygon
(E) d'Alembert's Principle

24. Determine the minimum coefficient of friction, μ, required to hold the 20-pound block in equilibrium on the inclined surface. (Friction factor is assumed equal on all surfaces.)

   (A) 0.0
   (B) 0.1
   (C) 0.2
   (D) 0.25
   (E) 0.29

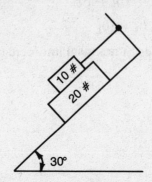

25. Determine the moment of inertia for the cross-section shown about the axis x — x through the centroid.

   (A) 40 in⁴
   (B) 96 in⁴
   (C) 136 in⁴
   (D) 184 in⁴
   (E) 736 in⁴

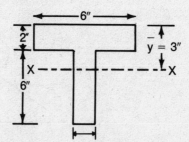

26. The left-hand reaction of the beam shown, expressed in pounds, is most nearly

   (A) −180
   (B) 0
   (C) 60
   (D) 180
   (E) 720

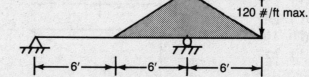

27. For the rigid frame shown, the magnitude of the reaction at A is most nearly

   (A) 0
   (B) 7.5ᴷ
   (C) 10ᴷ
   (D) 12.5ᴷ
   (E) 25ᴷ

28. Which of the following statements about suspended cables is false?

    (A) A cable loaded by a uniformly distributed load on a horizontal projection will hang in the shape of a parabola.
    (B) A cable loaded by its own weight will hang in the shape of a catenary.
    (C) A cable will be incapable of sustaining moment and will adjust its shape to accommodate lateral loads.
    (D) A cable will adjust its height to account for thermal deformations.
    (E) A cable loaded by a series of concentrated loads will hang in the shape of a circular arc.

29. In the rigid system shown, the magnitude of the reaction at B is most nearly

    (A) 0
    (B) 10^K
    (C) 15^K
    (D) 20^K
    (E) 25^K

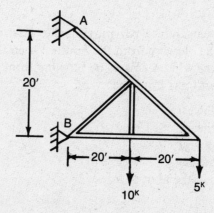

30. A force vector $\vec{F} = 10\vec{i} + 5\vec{j} + 10\vec{k}$ acts in a plane, the normal to which is given by $\vec{n} = \vec{i} + c\vec{k}$. The coefficient c is equal to

    (A) -1
    (B) $-1/2$
    (C) 0
    (D) $1/2$
    (E) 1

31. The moment, expressed in pound-feet, at the left support of the hinged beam which is uniformly loaded at 1000 pounds/foot, is most nearly

    (A) 30,000
    (B) 48,000
    (C) 50,000
    (D) 80,000
    (E) 128,000

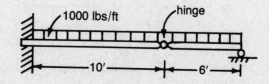

Dynamics

32. A weight of 50 lbs is hanging from a cable connected by a frictionless pulley to a spring of $k = 50$ lb/ft. The work required to lift the weight 0.5 feet above its equilibrium position is most nearly

    (A) 6.3 ft-lb
    (B) 12.5 ft-lb
    (C) 18.8 ft-lb
    (D) 25 ft-lb
    (E) cannot be determined without knowing the undeformed length of the spring

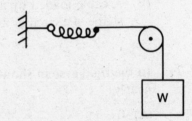

33. To a passenger in a car moving due East at 30 mph, a steady wind seems to be blowing from the South. When the car moves due North at 60 mph, the wind seems to be blowing from the Northwest. The actual wind direction is from the

    (A) Northwest
    (B) Northeast
    (C) Southwest
    (D) Southeast
    (E) none of the above

34. A small object moves along a horizontal circle inside a smooth frictionless paraboloid of revolution. If the speed needed to move in a plane $z = H$ is equal to v, the speed needed to move in a plane $z = 2H$ is most nearly

    (A) $\dfrac{v}{\sqrt{2}}$
    (B) v
    (C) $2\sqrt{2}\,v$
    (D) $2v$
    (E) $2\sqrt{2}\,v$

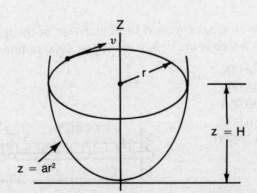

35. Knowing that the radius of the earth is approximately 6370 kilometers, the escape velocity, i.e., the smallest initial velocity in meters per second which a projectile needs to escape the gravitational pull of the earth (ignoring air resistance), is most nearly

    (A) 11,179
    (B) 11,679
    (C) 12,179
    (D) 13,179
    (E) 24,358

36. A 3-foot long homogeneous bar has its ends constrained to move in a vertical plane without friction around the inner surface of a hollow cylinder having a 3-foot radius. The bar is released from rest in a vertical position, and is allowed to fall freely. When it reaches a horizontal position, the velocity of its midpoint in feet per second is most nearly

    (A) 8.8
    (B) 9.3
    (C) 11.0
    (D) 12.3
    (E) cannot be determined without knowing the weight of the bar

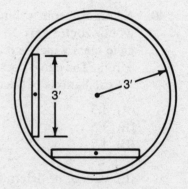

37. A small object slides down a frictionless chute consisting of a 90° circular arc of radius R. It is released from rest at point A ($\theta = 90°$) and emerges horizontally from the chute at point B ($\theta = 0°$), a distance h above the ground. Measuring from point B, the horizontal distance L traveled before the object strikes the ground is

    (A) $\dfrac{\sqrt{Rh}}{2}$

    (B) $\sqrt{\dfrac{Rh}{2}}$

    (C) $\sqrt{Rh}$

    (D) $\sqrt{2Rh}$

    (E) $2\sqrt{Rh}$

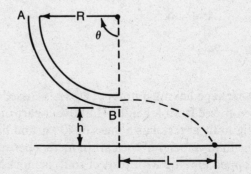

38. Three subway cars each weighing 50 kips have a rolling friction of 5 kips each. If the front car exerts a traction equal to 21 kips, the force in the coupling between the first and the second car is most nearly

    (A) 12^k
    (B) 13^k
    (C) 14^k
    (D) 15^k
    (E) 16^k

39. A ball bounces on a floor. If the coefficient of restitution is e, the ratio of the successive heights to which the ball rises is

    (A) $\sqrt{e}$
    (B) e
    (C) $e^{3/2}$
    (D) e^2
    (E) $1 - e^2$

40. A homogeneous cylinder weighing 200 pounds can rotate freely about its horizontal axis. It has wrapped around it a flexible cable of negligible mass which is connected at its two ends with springs whose k = 3 lb/in. The cable does not slip with respect to the drum. The period of the oscillations of the drum in seconds is most nearly

    (A) 1.3
    (B) 1.5
    (C) 1.7
    (D) 1.9
    (E) cannot be determined without knowing the radius R

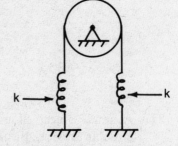

41. A small body with coordinates $(2, 0, 0)$ has a mass of 3 kg and a velocity in m/sec of $\vec{v} = 4\hat{i} + 4\hat{k}$. Its angular momentum about the origin in consistent units is

    (A) $-24\hat{i}$
    (B) $24\hat{k}$
    (C) $-24\hat{i} + 24\hat{k}$
    (D) $-24\hat{j}$
    (E) $-24\hat{k}$

42. A package having a mass of 20 kg is tossed with horizontal velocity v_0 = 6 m/sec from a height H above a cart on which it lands. The cart is originally at rest, has a mass of 40 kg, and has negligible rolling friction. The final velocity of the cart in meters per second (after the package has stopped moving with respect to it) is most nearly

(A) 1
(B) 2
(C) 3
(D) 4
(E) cannot be determined
without knowing H

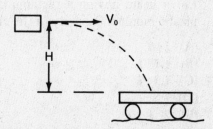

43. A homogeneous disc 18 inches in diameter weighing 80 pounds rotates about its axis at an angular speed of 400 rpm. The normal force P, in pounds, which must be exerted through a brake shoe having a coefficient of friction $\mu = 0.50$ in order to bring the disc to rest in 2 seconds is most nearly

(A) 39
(B) 41
(C) 43
(D) 45
(E) 52

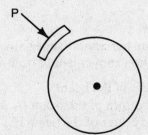

44. A wheel having a radius of 2 feet can rotate freely about its fixed horizontal axis and is initially at rest. It is struck tangentially by a 1/4 ounce bullet having a velocity of 3000 ft/sec. The bullet becomes lodged in the wheel which acquires an angular velocity of 0.03 ft/sec. The moment of inertia of the wheel, expressed in lb-ft-sec^2, is most nearly

(A) 85
(B) 97
(C) 107
(D) 117
(E) 130

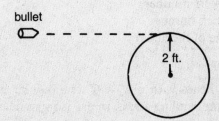

Mechanics of Materials

45. For a beam having a rectangular cross-section, the ratio of the fully plastic moment capacity to the elastic moment capacity is

   (A) 1 : 1
   (B) 1.1 : 1
   (C) 1.3 : 1
   (D) 1.5 : 1
   (E) 2 : 1

46. The total axial elongation in inches that will be noted at the bottom end of an oil well drill due to its own weight, if the drill is six inches in diameter and 2000 feet long, with a density γ of 0.282 pounds per cubic inch and a modulus of elasticity E of $30(10)^6$ psi, is most nearly

   (A) 2.7
   (B) 5.4
   (C) 6.0
   (D) 10
   (E) 30

47. The maximum horizontal shear stress due to a vertical load on the cruciform section shown would occur at the

   (A) neutral axis of the beam
   (B) top and bottom of the beam (A & E)
   (C) geometric center of the beam (C)
   (D) vertical edges of the beam (H & G)
   (E) junction of the beam (B & D)

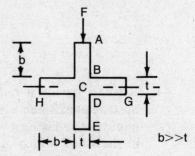

48. Rockwell hardness testers usually measure hardness by means of

   (A) B and C scales
   (B) A and D scales
   (C) Vickers number
   (D) Brinell number
   (E) none of the above

49. For the beam with a 2″ × 6″ rectangular cross-section as shown, the maximum bending stress, in psi, is most nearly

(A) 125
(B) 250
(C) 1500
(D) 3000
(E) 6000

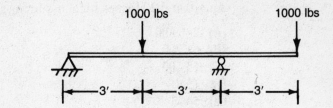

50. For the beam in problem #49, the maximum shear stress, in psi, is most nearly

(A) 83
(B) 125
(C) 250
(D) 1500
(E) 3000

51. A concentrated load P is applied to a rigid slab which is supported by three identical wires of equal length, as shown. The actual weight of the slab may be neglected compared to the load P. Determine the distance x in terms of the dimension "a" such that the left-hand wire will just be slack under the action of the concentrated load.

(A) $\dfrac{a}{2}$

(B) a

(C) $\dfrac{4a}{3}$

(D) $\dfrac{5a}{3}$

(E) 2a

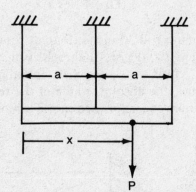

52. A material has the following properties: Tensile ultimate strength = 250 psi; shear ultimate strength = 500 psi; compressive ultimate strength = 2000 psi. If a cylindrical shaft made of this material is loaded in torsion it will fail

(A) along a shear plane perpendicular to the longitudinal axis
(B) along a plane inclined at 45° to the longitudinal axis
(C) along a helix inclined at 45° to the longitudinal axis
(D) by splitting along a longitudinal axial plane
(E) none of the above

53. The elastic buckling load in pounds of a pin-ended steel column 1 inch square and 20 inches high, assuming $E = 30 \times 10^6$ psi, is most nearly

    (A) 246,800
    (B) 61,700
    (C) 15,400
    (D) 1540
    (E) 5400

54. Which of the sketches shown below most nearly portrays the idealized stress-strain curve of an elastic perfectly plastic material? (The symbol + denotes the failure point.)

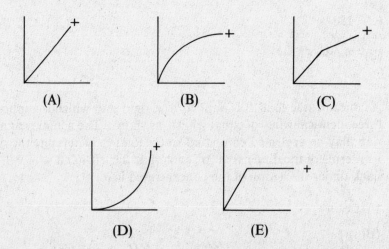

55. An aluminum rod 30 inches long at room temperature is heated to a temperature 100 degrees Fahrenheit higher. If $E = 10(10)^6$ psi and $\alpha = 12(10)^{-6}$ in/in $-$ °F, and if the initial gap between rigid supports is 0.006 inches, the absolute value of the resulting compressive stress in the aluminum rod, expressed in psi, is most nearly

    (A) 0
    (B) 6000
    (C) 10,000
    (D) 12,000
    (E) 15,000

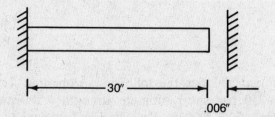

56. Stress concentrations occur at

    (A) holes in plates
    (B) places where cross-sectional size changes
    (C) points of application of concentrated loads

(D) some of the above

(E) all of the above

57. A steel reinforced square concrete column measuring a total of 10 inches on each side is reinforced by 4 bars each having a cross-sectional area of 1 square inch. If the ratio of the modulus of elasticity of steel to that of concrete is 10 to 1, what percentage of an axial load applied to the column is carried by the steel?

(A) 4%

(B) 9%

(C) 29%

(D) 91%

(E) 100%

Fluid Mechanics

58. The absolute viscosity of a fluid

(A) equals its kinematic viscosity times the gravitational constant g_0

(B) equals its kinematic viscosity divided by density

(C) causes a shear stress on the upper surface of a wing in flight

(D) always decreases with increasing temperature

(E) usually increases with increasing pressure

59. An open-topped rectangular tank that is three feet high, two feet wide, and ten feet long contains a 10-inch depth of water. This tank is then accelerated horizontally along its longitudinal axis at a constant rate of 7 feet/sec/sec. At steady-state conditions, the height of water at the rear end of the tank, expressed in inches, will be most nearly

(A) 16.1

(B) 22.8

(C) 23.1

(D) 23.4

(E) 26.1

60. Calculate the pressure gauge reading in psia assuming sea level conditions:

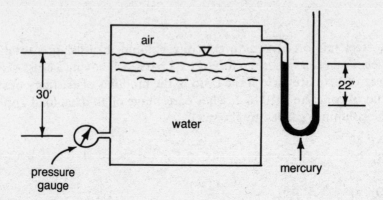

(A) 13
(B) 16.9
(C) 23.7
(D) 28.5
(E) 38.5

61. A scale model of a 20-foot actual prototype aircraft wing is to be constructed and then tested at its operating temperature in a sea-level wind tunnel. The aircraft is designed to fly at an altitude corresponding to a pressure of 3.5 psi and at a speed of 700 feet/second. The available airspeed in the tunnel is 250 mph, what length of the model aircraft wing in feet will be required in order to achieve dynamic similarity?

(A) 1.3
(B) 4.8
(C) 5.3
(D) 9.1
(E) 10.5

62. The pressure drop due to a square-edged entrance (K = 0.5) of a 6-inch diameter pipe with a flow rate of 5 cfs of water is most nearly

(A) 0.5 psi
(B) 2.2 psi
(C) 4.3 psi
(D) 12.3 psf
(E) 24.6 psf

63. A high-pressure low-velocity water distribution system has two nearly identical branches emanating from a common source. The only difference is that one branch has a smooth convergent-divergent venturi with a throat of 1/2 diameter. The ratio of the total flow through the branch without the venturi to the flow through the branch with the venturi will be approximately

   (A) 1 : 1
   (B) 2 : 1
   (C) 4 : 1
   (D) 8 : 1
   (E) 16 : 1

64. The electric power in kilowatts necessary to pump 4 cfs of water to a height of 20 feet above the pump, using an electric motor with an efficiency of 85% to drive a pump whose efficiency is 70%, is most nearly

   (A) 5.5
   (B) 7.1
   (C) 7.9
   (D) 10.2
   (E) 11.4

65. The stagnation temperature in degrees Fahrenheit of a plane flying at Mach 1.7 at an ambient temperature of $-60°F$ is most nearly

   (A) 76
   (B) 148
   (C) 171
   (D) 235
   (E) 247

66. The water that flows in the large circular 6-inch diameter duct, as shown in the diagram, has a velocity, expressed in feet per second, of most nearly

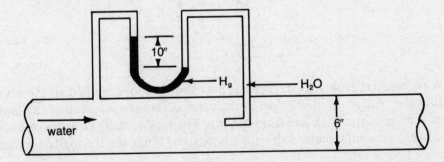

   (A) 25
   (B) 26
   (C) 27
   (D) 28
   (E) 29

67. Which of the following statements is true for internal duct flow?

    (A) The friction factor is $32/N_R$ for laminar flow.
    (B) Transition usually occurs at a Reynolds Number based on diameters of $1.5(10)^6$ to $3.0(10)^6$.
    (C) In turbulent flow, head loss due to friction varies directly with velocity.
    (D) In laminar flow, head loss due to friction varies directly with the square of the velocity.
    (E) In laminar flow, head loss due to friction varies directly with velocity.

68. The velocity in feet per second of the water flowing through the 2-inch diameter port is most nearly

    (A) 24
    (B) 30
    (C) 36
    (D) 43
    (E) 52

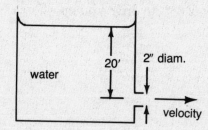

Problems #69 through #71 inclusive, are based on the following:

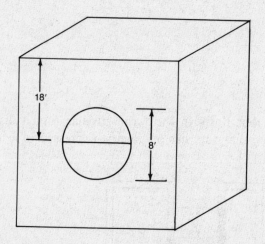

A rectangular tank with an open top as shown above is filled to the brim with water. A circular disc 8 feet in diameter is set into one side of the tank such that its center is 18 feet from the top. The disc actually consists of a top and a bottom semi-circular half with a horizontal hinge pin through its center.

69. The distance in feet from the center of the circular disc to the centroid of the lower semi-circular half is most nearly

    (A) 0

(B) 1.3
(C) 1.5
(D) 1.7
(E) 2.0

70. The force in tons on the lower semi-circular half of the disc is most nearly

A) 12.5
(B) 12.8
(C) 14.1
(D) 15.4
(E) 15.7

71. If the circular disc were free to rotate about its horizontal axis, the torque in pound-feet required to keep it in place would be most nearly

(A) 0
(B) 5400
(C) 9100
(D) 10,000
(E) 12,800

Thermodynamics/Heat Transfer

72. What is the thermal conductivity of a plastic sheet 1/8″ thick that transfers 20,000 Btu/hr-ft^2 with a 100°F temperature difference between the upper and lower surfaces?

(A) 2 Btu/hr-ft-°F
(B) 16 Btu/hr-ft-°F
(C) 25 Btu/hr-ft-°F
(D) 2 Btu-in/hr-ft^2-°F
(E) 16 Btu-in/hr-ft^2-°F

73. A perfect gas at 70°F and 1000 psia has a volume of 1 cubic foot. If the pressure changes to 800 psia in a frictionless, constant-volume process, the resulting temperature will be most nearly

(A) 70°F
(B) 37°F
(C) 32°F
(D) 0°F
(E) −36°F

74. Air at 70°F is compressed during a polytropic process (n = 1.2) from a pressure of 14.7 psia to 100 psia. If the process is adiabatic, the resulting temperature will be most nearly

   (A) 70°F
   (B) 170°F
   (C) 270°F
   (D) 370°F
   (E) 457°F

75. A three-inch diameter piston moves through a stroke of 2 inches due to a pressure that decreases linearly from 100 psig to 40 psig. The work done on the piston in foot-pounds is most nearly

   (A) 0
   (B) 43
   (C) 47
   (D) 82
   (E) 118

76. The four-stroke cycle of an internal combustion engine (automobile engine using a spark plug) is best simulated by the

   (A) Carnot cycle
   (B) Ericsson cycle
   (C) Otto cycle
   (D) Brayton cycle
   (E) Rankine cycle

77. Water at 70°F flows through a 6-inch diameter pipe with a velocity of 20 fps. In a 100-foot length of this pipe, the pressure drop is 1 psig. If the pipe is perfectly insulated the change in the internal energy of the water, expressed in Btu/lb, is most nearly

   (A) 0
   (B) 0.003
   (C) 0.03
   (D) 0.30
   (E) 0.50

78. The maximum coefficient of performance (COP) for any refrigeration unit operating between temperatures of 800°R and 1000°R is

   (A) 0.2
   (B) 0.25
   (C) 0.8
   (D) 4
   (E) 5

79. The humidity ratio is best expressed

    (A) as a ratio of two percentages
    (B) in terms of pounds of water per unit volume of dry air
    (C) in terms of pounds of water per unit weight of dry air
    (D) in terms of unit volume of water per unit volume of dry air
    (E) in terms of unit volume of water per unit weight of dry air

80. Which of the following statements about thermodynamic cycles is true?

    (A) The Diesel cycle is similar to the Otto cycle except that heat is added at constant pressure.
    (B) A Diesel cycle cannot be idealized because combustion occurs during parts of the compression and expansion processes.
    (C) The Brayton cycle is similar to the Otto cycle except that heat is added at constant pressure.
    (D) The Brayton and Rankine cycles are identical.
    (E) Theoretically the Rankine cycle can develop the same efficiency as a Carnot cycle operating between the same temperatures.

81. If the quality of steam in a certain process is 0.95, which of the following statements is true?

    (A) The entrained liquid droplets are uniformly dispersed throughout the liquid/vapor mixture.
    (B) The entrained liquid droplets are of uniform size in which one standard deviation of diameter is ± 0.05.
    (C) The steam contains 5% of its water in the vapor phase.
    (D) The steam contains 5% of its water in the liquid phase.
    (E) 95% of the enthalpy of the mixture is due to the liquid water.

82. Air passing through a turbine that drives an electrical generator will

    (A) condense moisture
    (B) be heated
    (C) always be isothermal
    (D) be cooled
    (E) be isothermal if the process is also adiabatic

83. Which of the following is not true for humid air with a relative humidity of 90%?

    (A) wet bulb temperature < dry bulb temperature
    (B) wet bulb temperature = dew point temperature
    (C) humidity ratio ≠ relative humidity
    (D) enthalpy at the wet bulb temperature ≠ enthalpy of saturated water vapor at the same temperature
    (E) dry bulb temperature > dew point temperature

84. A pan of water at 35°F is on a roof exposed to a clear sky with an effective temperature of $-50°F$. The rate of heat transfer from the water (assuming emissivity of water to be 0.95) in Btu/hr-ft^2 is most nearly

(A) 0
(B) 10
(C) 40
(D) 48
(E) 52

85. If ice and water are assumed to have infinite conductivity, how many pounds of water will freeze if the pan in problem #84 has an area of one square foot, a depth of 6 inches, and stands for 8 hours at the conditions described? (Assume a constant heat transfer rate of 48 Btu/hr-ft^2.)

(A) 0
(B) 1
(C) 2
(D) 3
(E) 4

Mathematics

86. Given a family of exponential curves described by $y = K - K\varepsilon^{-ax}$. The numerical value of "a" that will cause all of these curves to reach exactly 50% of their final amplitude when x equals 2.5 is most nearly

(A) 0.28
(B) 0.37
(C) 0.50
(D) 0.63
(E) 0.69

87. The equation that best describes the set of all points in a plane that are equidistant from a given line and a given point not on that line is

(A) $y^2 + x^2 = 3$
(B) $y^2 + 8x = 2$
(C) $4y^2 + 2x^2 = 5$
(D) $3y^2 - 2x^2 = 7$
(E) $4y - 3x = 9$

88. If a line segment is drawn between points $(-6, 1)$ and $(-1, 8)$, the equation of a line which is perpendicular to this line segment, and which passes through the origin, is

    (A) $7y = 5x + 1$
    (B) $5y = 7x$
    (C) $5y = -7x$
    (D) $7y = -5x$
    (E) $7y = 5x$

89. The derivative, with respect to t, of the function $w = K(\varepsilon)^{x^2}(\varepsilon)^{y^2}$ (where $x = \sin t$ and $y = \cos t$) is

    (A) 0
    (B) 1
    (C) ε
    (D) $\varepsilon \sin t$
    (E) $\varepsilon \cos t$

90. Given the equation $x^2 + 4x + y^2 + 6y + 16 = 0$. The graph of this equation

    (A) is a circle
    (B) is an ellipse
    (C) is a parabola
    (D) is a hyperbola
    (E) does not exist

91. In a normal Gaussian distribution, the variance is defined as

    (A) one standard deviation
    (B) two standard deviations
    (C) three standard deviations
    (D) the square of the rms deviation
    (E) the square root of the rms deviation

92. Which of the following determinants is equivalent to the determinant $\begin{vmatrix} a_{11} & a_{12} \\ a_{21} & a_{22} \end{vmatrix}$?

    (A) $\begin{vmatrix} a_{11} & a_{12} & 0 \\ a_{21} & a_{22} & 1 \\ 0 & 0 & 0 \end{vmatrix}$

    (B) $\begin{vmatrix} a_{11} & a_{12} & 1 \\ a_{21} & a_{22} & 0 \\ 1 & 0 & 1 \end{vmatrix}$

(C) $\begin{vmatrix} a_{11} & a_{12} & 1 \\ a_{21} & a_{22} & 0 \\ 1 & 0 & 0 \end{vmatrix}$

(D) $\begin{vmatrix} a_{11} & a_{12} & 0 \\ a_{21} & a_{22} & 0 \\ 0 & 0 & 1 \end{vmatrix}$

(E) $\begin{vmatrix} a_{11} & a_{12} & 1 \\ a_{21} & a_{22} & 1 \\ 1 & 1 & 0 \end{vmatrix}$

93. The definite integral $\int_0^1 \varepsilon^{-2x}\, dx$ is equal to

(A) ε^2
(B) $\frac{1}{2}\varepsilon^{-2}$
(C) $\frac{1}{2} - \frac{1}{2}\varepsilon^{-2}$
(D) $\frac{1}{2}\varepsilon^{-2} - \frac{1}{2}$
(E) $1 - \varepsilon^{-2}$

94. The sum of the following geometric series, $\frac{4}{10}, \frac{1}{10}, \frac{1}{40}, \frac{1}{160}, \ldots$ is exactly equal to a rational fraction whose numerator, when the fraction is reduced to its simplest form, is

(A) 5
(B) 8
(C) 10
(D) 12
(E) 15

95. The trigonometric expression $\cos 3x\,[\cos^3 x]^{-1}$ is equal to

(A) $1 - 3\tan^2 x$
(B) $1 - 2\sin^3 x$
(C) $\cos 2x - 1$
(D) $1 - 3\sin^2 x$
(E) $1 - 3\sec^2 x$

96. The nappe of a right circular cone is

(A) the portion nearest the vertex
(B) the angle between the axis and the slant height
(C) the area enclosed within a given conic section
(D) the volume of the cone bounded by the vertex and a given conic section
(E) the part of the cone on one side of the vertex

97. The average value of an exponential growth function and a related exponential decay function may be expressed as a

(A) hyperbolic sine
(B) hyperbolic cosine
(C) hyperbolic tangent
(D) hyperbolic secant
(E) hyperbolic cosecant

Chemistry

98. The category known as the alkaline earth metals includes which one of the following elements?

(A) Na
(B) Cl
(C) Li
(D) Al
(E) Mg

99. C_4H_{10} is the symbol for

(A) butane
(B) ethane
(C) propane
(D) carbohydrate
(E) quartane

100. When the equation below

$$KMnO_4 + H_2SO_4 + FeSO_4 \rightarrow K_2SO_4 + MnSO_4 + Fe_2(SO_4)_3 + H_2O$$

is correctly balanced, the sum of all the coefficients is equal to

(A) 9
(B) 18
(C) 27
(D) 36
(E) 48

101. The symbol H_3C CH_3 represents

(A) orthoxylene
(B) metaxylene

(C) orthobenzene

(D) metabenzene

(E) paraxylene

102. The hydroxyl ion concentration of a given solution is 17×10^{-11} gm/cc. What is the pH?

(A) -10

(B) -6

(C) 6

(D) 10

(E) 12

103. The symbol CH_3—O—CH_3 is the formula for

(A) acetone

(B) acetylene

(C) methanol

(D) formaldehyde

(E) methyl ether

104. The solubility product for silver chromate is 9.0×10^{-12}. Its solubility in mols/liter, assuming complete ionization in water, is most nearly

(A) 0.65×10^{-4}

(B) 1.3×10^{-4}

(C) 3.0×10^{-4}

(D) 3.0×10^{-6}

(E) 4.5×10^{-6}

105. The lowest pH for the precipitation of Fe(II) hydroxide is most nearly

(A) 3

(B) 4

(C) 5

(D) 6

(E) 7

106. Approximately how many pounds of lime (as CaO) are required to neutralize 1000 gallons of 10% (by weight) waste sulfuric acid?

(A) 320

(B) 450

(C) 500

(D) 550

(E) 700

107. If it takes one square foot of filter area to filter 10 pounds/hour of precipitated calcium sulfate, the filter area in square feet that would be required to clarify 1000 gallons/hour of spent acid after the neutralization of problem #106 is most nearly

    (A) 120
    (B) 240
    (C) 300
    (D) 450
    (E) 520

Computer Programming

108. In a BASIC program containing the following IF statement, what action does the program take in the event the condition referred to by the IF is false (i.e., if X is not equal to 0)?

    50 IF X = 0 THEN LET X = X + 1

    (A) The program terminates.
    (B) An action opposite to the prescribed one (LET X = X − 1, instead of LET X = X + 1) takes place.
    (C) The program "falls through" to the next statement.
    (D) The computer "hangs up," unable to handle this condition.
    (E) None of the above.

109. Which of the following is the decimal equivalent of binary 10011110?

    (A) 158
    (B) 130
    (C) 176
    (D) 151
    (E) 212

110. Which of the following is the same as decimal 47?

    (A) hex 31
    (B) 55 base eight
    (C) binary 111001
    (D) octal 57
    (E) 100111 base two

111. What is the decimal equivalent of the 7 bit 1's complement binary number, 1001011?

    (A) −75
    (B) −52
    (C) −53
    (D) 75
    (E) −11

112. Which of the following is a valid FORTRAN logical expression?

    (A) ((A.LT.B).AND.(C.GE.A)
    (B) (A < B) & (C > A)
    (C) (A.LT.B) AND (C.GT.A)
    (D) (A.LT.B.AND.C.GT.A)
    (E) (A < B) AND (C > A)

113. The following two statements are in BASIC:

    10 LET X = 33
    20 PRINT CHR$(X)

    The resulting display will be

    (A) a row of thirty-three X's
    (B) the single character having an ASCII value of 33 in decimal
    (C) the single character having an ASCII value of 33 in hexadecimal
    (D) the two digits "33"
    (E) the hexadecimal value of the decimal number "33"

114. What is the sum of $(A53)_{16} + (7BE)_{16}$ expressed in hexadecimal?

    (A) 4625
    (B) 1412
    (C) 1211
    (D) 231A
    (E) 1121

115. Which of the following is not a legal FORTRAN operator?

    (A) .NOT.
    (B) ↑
    (C) *
    (D) /
    (E) +

Mathematical Modeling of Engineering Systems

116. The block of concrete shown in the diagram is suspended by a spring and connected to a dash pot so that it is free to vibrate vertically. The spring constant K_s is 4 pounds per half-inch, and the dash pot coefficient K_D is 20 pounds per foot/second. An externally applied force F_A of 10 pounds is exerted upward, and the resulting displacement is y.

   If the concrete block has a natural undamped frequency of vibration equal to 3.0 radians per second, the weight of this block in pounds is most nearly

   (A) 10
   (B) 32
   (C) 100
   (D) 340
   (E) 1030

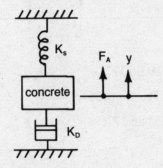

117. In problem #116, the system response is

   (A) appreciably underdamped
   (B) slightly underdamped
   (C) critically damped
   (D) slightly overdamped
   (E) appreciably overdamped

118. Given an analog temperature transducer that develops an electrical output of 0.1 volts per degree Fahrenheit as shown above. The operational amplifier stages as connected constitute a special-purpose analog computer that will convert this output to a voltage proportional to degrees Centigrade. The resulting number of volts per degree Centigrade will be most nearly

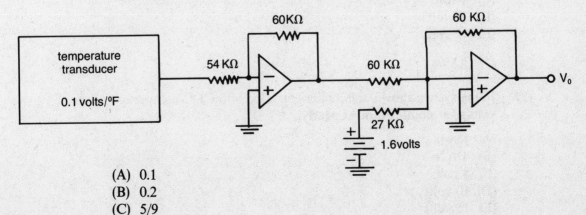

   (A) 0.1
   (B) 0.2
   (C) 5/9
   (D) 10/9
   (E) 2.2

The system shown in the block diagram below applies to problems #119 through #121, inclusive.

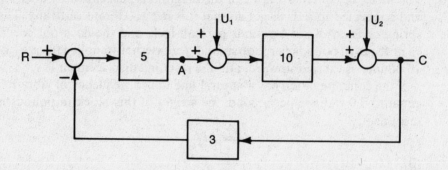

$$R = 100 + 10 \sin 377t$$

$$U_1 = 3 \sin 377t + 6 \sin 754t$$

$$U_2 = 20 + 120 \sin 377t$$

119. In the system shown, the *rms* value of the 60-Hertz component of the voltage at point A is most nearly

(A) 3 volts
(B) 4 volts
(C) 10 volts
(D) 15 volts
(E) 20 volts

120. In the system shown, the *rms* value of the 120-Hertz component of the voltage at point A is most nearly

(A) 4 volts
(B) 6 volts
(C) 8 volts
(D) 10 volts
(E) 12 volts

121. In the system shown, the numerical value of the DC component of the voltage at point A is most nearly

(A) 1 volt
(B) 4 volts
(C) 8 volts
(D) 10 volts
(E) 15 volts

122. The mathematical equation that is modeled or simulated by the operational amplifier circuit shown is

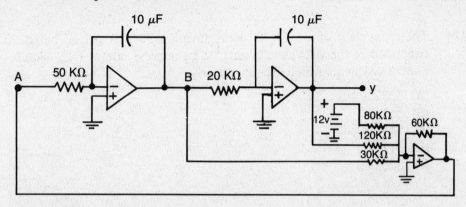

(A) $\dfrac{d^2y}{dt^2} - 2\dfrac{dy}{dt} + \dfrac{y}{2} + 9 = 0$

(B) $\dfrac{d^2y}{dt^2} + 2\dfrac{dy}{dt} - \dfrac{y}{2} - 9 = 0$

(C) $\dfrac{d^2y}{dt^2} + \dfrac{dy}{dt} + \dfrac{y}{20} - \dfrac{9}{10} = 0$

(D) $\dfrac{d^2y}{dt^2} + 4\dfrac{dy}{dt} - 5y - 90 = 0$

(E) $\dfrac{d^2y}{dt^2} - 4\dfrac{dy}{dt} + 5y + 90 = 0$

123. In order for the operational amplifier circuit shown below at the left to correctly model or simulate the block diagram shown at the right, the resistance R_x in ohms must be most nearly

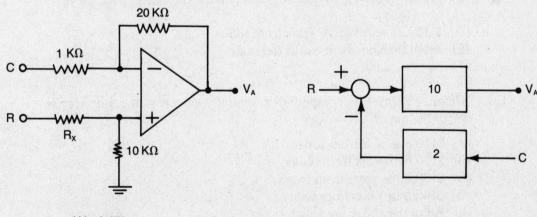

(A) 0.5K
(B) 1K
(C) 5K
(D) 10K
(E) 11K

Engineering Economics

124. The repayment of a $100,000 loan during a 30-year period based on equal end-of-the-year installments, at an interest rate of 15%, requires annual payments which are most nearly

    (A) $3333
    (B) $13,833
    (C) $15,230
    (D) $17,500
    (E) $20,080

125. If $2800 was borrowed exactly 5 years ago, the lump sum amount which must now be paid back, based on a 12% interest rate compounded monthly, is most nearly

    (A) $2943
    (B) $3920
    (C) $4934
    (D) $5087
    (E) $5200

126. If money earns 10% compounded annually, which of the following is worth the most?

    (A) $614.46 received today.
    (B) $100.00 received each year for 10 years, starting one year from today.
    (C) $506.44 received 5 years from today plus $778.12 received 10 years from today.
    (D) $1593.75 received 10 years from today.
    (E) All of the above are worth the same.

127. If money earns 10% compounded annually, which of the following is worth the most?

    (A) $110 one year from today.
    (B) $120 two years from today.
    (C) $130 three years from today.
    (D) $140 four years from today.
    (E) All of the above are worth the same.

128. If the interest rate is 12% compounded monthly, the effective rate per annum is most nearly

    (A) 12.0%

(B) 12.12%
(C) 12.34%
(D) 12.68%
(E) 12.96%

129. Three banks offer the same savings interest rate of 5%. Bank #1 compounds the interest continuously, bank #2 compounds daily, and bank #3 compounds quarterly. Into which bank or banks should you deposit your savings in order to earn the most interest?

(A) Bank 1
(B) Bank 2
(C) Bank 3
(D) Equally in Banks 1 and 2
(E) Equally in Banks 1, 2, and 3

Materials Science

130. The Curie temperature for a given material is the point at which

(A) its electromagnetic radiation activity increases sharply
(B) its net electron spin reaches a maximum
(C) an alloy just reaches the 100% liquid state
(D) a ferromagnetic material loses its magnetic properties
(E) the total area enclosed within the hysteresis loop reaches a maximum

131. In the heat treatment of steel, quenching in oil rather than water

(A) provides maximum hardness for a given carbon content
(B) provides superior surface hardness properties
(C) is preferable for small-size pieces
(D) is preferable for low carbon steel
(E) is preferable for high carbon steel

132. In a crystalline material which is exposed to a constant stress at high temperature, the creep process, once started, usually

(A) progresses toward failure at a relatively constant rate
(B) progresses toward failure at a roughly linearly increasing rate of acceleration
(C) is the greatest in the initial and final stages only
(D) is initially negligible, but builds up exponentially to an eventual maximum
(E) is too erratic to permit a generalized conclusion

133. The purity of distilled water used in the laboratory can be most easily determined by

    (A) measuring the absorption spectra
    (B) measuring the boiling point
    (C) measuring the electrical conductivity
    (D) measuring the thermal conductivity
    (E) performing a chemical analysis for impurities

134. The freezing point depression caused by the introduction of a solute can be used to calculate the

    (A) equilibrium constant
    (B) molecular weight of the solute
    (C) molecular weight of the solvent
    (D) solubility of the solute in the solvent
    (E) solubility product

135. A solution containing one mol of magnesium chloride and one mol of sodium sulfate is compared with a second solution containing one mol of magnesium sulfate and one mol of sodium chloride. These solutions

    (A) differ in sulfate content
    (B) differ in chloride content
    (C) differ in sodium content
    (D) differ in magnesium content
    (E) are identical

The Structure of Matter

136. The shape of the BF_3 molecule is

    (A) planar
    (B) linear
    (C) pyramidal
    (D) tetrahedral
    (E) octahedral

137. If the half-life of a certain radioactive isotope is 8.6 days, approximately how long will it take to decay to 1.0 percent of the original amount?

    (A) 29 days
    (B) 57 days
    (C) 66 days
    (D) 86 days
    (E) 860 days

138. In the ammonium ion, the hydrogen and nitrogen atoms are held together by

    (A) covalent bonds
    (B) electrovalent bonds
    (C) covalent and coordinate bonds
    (D) electrostatic bonds
    (E) Van der Waal's attraction

139. If a radioactive nucleus decays emitting alpha radiation, its

    (A) atomic weight decreases, but its atomic number remains the same
    (B) atomic number decreases, but its atomic weight remains about the same
    (C) atomic weight and atomic number remain the same
    (D) atomic weight and atomic number both decrease
    (E) atomic weight remains about the same, but its atomic number increases

140. The highest bond energy in kilo-calories/mole is found in which of the following crystalline or molecular structures?

    (A) Se_6 : Se-Se bond
    (B) S_8 : S-S bond
    (C) Ge : Ge-Ge bond
    (D) P_4 : P-P bond
    (E) Sn : Sn-Sn bond

Answer Key
Practice Examination 2—A.M. Part

Electrical Circuits

1.	E	7.	A	13.	D
2.	E	8.	E	14.	A
3.	C	9.	C	15.	B
4.	C	10.	E	16.	B
5.	B	11.	D	17.	B
6.	E	12.	A	18.	C

Statics

19.	E	24.	E	28.	E
20.	C	25.	C	29.	D
21.	B	26.	B	30.	A
22.	C	27.	D	31.	D
23.	E				

Dynamics

32.	B	37.	E	41.	D
33.	C	38.	C	42.	B
34.	B	39.	D	43.	A
35.	A	40.	A	44.	B
36.	D				

Mechanics of Materials

45.	D	50.	B	54.	E
46.	A	51.	D	55.	C
47.	E	52.	C	56.	E
48.	A	53.	B	57.	C
49.	D				

Fluid Mechanics

58.	C	63.	A	68.	C
59.	B	64.	E	69.	D
60.	B	65.	C	70.	D
61.	D	66.	B	71.	C
62.	B	67.	E		

Thermodynamics/Heat Transfer

72.	A	77.	B	82.	D
73.	E	78.	D	83.	B
74.	C	79.	C	84.	E
75.	D	80.	A	85.	C
76.	C	81.	D		

Mathematics

86.	A	90.	E	94.	B
87.	B	91.	D	95.	A
88.	D	92.	D	96.	E
89.	A	93.	C	97.	B

Chemistry

98.	E	102.	C	105.	D
99.	A	103.	E	106.	C
100.	D	104.	B	107.	A
101.	B				

Computer Programming

108.	C	111.	B	114.	C
109.	A	112.	D	115.	B
110.	D	113.	B		

Mathematical Modeling of Engineering Systems

116.	D	119.	C	122.	E
117.	A	120.	A	123.	E
118.	B	121.	A		

Engineering Economics

124.	C	126.	E	128.	D
125.	D	127.	A	129.	A

Materials Science

130.	D	132.	C	134.	B
131.	E	133.	C	135.	E

The Structure of Matter

136.　A	138.　C	140.　B
137.　B	139.　D	

SOLUTIONS
PRACTICE EXAMINATION 2
A.M. PART

Electrical Circuits

1. *Answer:* (E)
   Solution: Under load-sharing conditions, the terminal voltages of both generators must be equal. Therefore,

   $$V_1 - i_1 R_1 = V_2 - i_2 R_2$$

   But $i_2 = 600 - i_1$

   $$\therefore 255 - 0.08 i_1 = 248 - 0.12(600 - i_1)$$

   $$i_1 = 395 \text{ amperes}$$

2. *Answer:* (E)
   Solution: $\text{rms} = \sqrt{\dfrac{1}{t} \Sigma v^2 \, dt}$

   $$\text{rms} = \sqrt{\frac{1}{15}[10^2(5) + 0^2(2) + 5^2(3) + 6^2(5)]}$$

   $$\text{rms} = \sqrt{\frac{1}{15}[500 + 0 + 75 + 180]}$$

   $$\text{rms} = 7.09 \text{ volts}$$

3. *Answer:* (C)
   Solution: The total impedance $Z_{TOT} = 100 + 200 + j(2\pi)(60)[0.1 + 0.5]$

   $$Z_{TOT} = 300 + j226.2$$

   $$Z_{TOT} = \sqrt{(300)^2 + (226.2)^2} = 375.7\Omega$$

   $$\therefore i = \frac{120}{375.7} = 0.3194 \text{ amperes}$$

   $$V_0 = i[200 + j(2\pi)(60)(0.5)]$$

   $$V_0 = 0.3194\sqrt{(200)^2 + (188.5)^2}$$

   $$V_0 = 0.3194(274.8)$$

   $$V_0 = 87.8 \text{ volts}$$

4. *Answer:* (C)
   Solution: If the speed were 60 rpm (1 rps), and if the alternator had 2 poles, the frequency would be 1 Hz.

For speed at 600 rpm, and if 2 poles, frequency would be 10 Hz.
For speed at 600 rpm, and for 24 poles, frequency equals 120 Hz.

NOTE: $f = \dfrac{(rpm)(pole\ pairs)}{60}$

$$f = \frac{(600)(12)}{60}$$

$$f = 120Hz$$

5. *Answer:* (B)

   Solution: After a very long time, there will be no DC voltage across the inductor, and none across the resistor. The voltage across each capacitor is $v_c = \dfrac{1}{c}\displaystyle\int i\,dt$, or inversely proportional to the value of capacitance. The integral of the current is the same constant for each capacitor.

   $$v_{10\mu F} + v_{20\mu F} + v_{50\mu F} = 120$$

   $$\frac{K}{10} + \frac{K}{20} + \frac{K}{50} = 120$$

   $$K = \frac{12,000}{17}$$

   $$v_{50\mu F} = \frac{K}{50} = \frac{12,000}{17(50)} = 14.1 \text{ volts}$$

6. *Answer:* (E)

   Solution: The initial value of current is $+1.2$ amperes and the final value is -0.24 amperes. The overall amplitude of the exponential is $1.2 - (-0.24) = 1.44$ amperes. The equation that satisfies these conditions for time $= 0$ and time $= \infty$ is:

   $$i = -0.24 + 1.44\varepsilon^{-50t}$$

   NOTE: Time Constant $= \dfrac{L}{R_1 + R_2} = \dfrac{2}{10 + 90} = \dfrac{1}{50}$ seconds

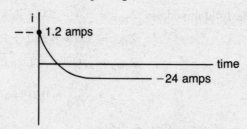

7. *Answer:* (A)

   Solution: $i = -0.24 + 1.44\varepsilon^{-50t}$

   $$0 = -0.24 + 1.44\varepsilon^{-50t}$$

   $$\varepsilon^{-50t} = \frac{0.24}{1.44} = 0.1667$$

   $$-50t = \ln 0.1667 = -1.792$$

   $$t = 35.8 \text{ milliseconds}$$

8. *Answer:* (E)

   Solution: Using Kirchoff's voltage law around the circuit at time equals zero plus,

   $$-24 - (90 + 10)(1.2) = v_L$$

   $$v_L = -24 - 120$$

   $$v_L = -144 \text{ volts}$$

   Alternatively $v_L = L\dfrac{di}{dt} = 2(1.44\varepsilon^{-50t})(-50)\Big|_{t=0} = -144$ volts

9. *Answer:* (C)

   Solution: The total power dissipated in the secondary loads equals 810 watts plus 360 watts, which is 1170 watts. Since the efficiency is 75 percent, the power required by the input is 1560 watts.

   $$i_{pri} = \frac{P}{V} = \frac{1560}{120} = 13 \text{ amperes}$$

10. *Answer:* (E)

    Solution: Under no-load conditions, the load resistor is at infinity ohms, and the load current equals zero. Therefore, the Zener diode branch absorbs the total current flow.

    $$i_{ZMAX} = i_{sMAX} = \frac{40 - 20}{200} = 100 \text{ ma}$$

    $$P_{ZMAX} = 20 \text{ volts} \times 100 \text{ ma} = 2.0 \text{ watts}$$

11. *Answer:* (D)

    Solution: The series resistor and the load resistor form a voltage divider network whose output voltage never succeeds the Zener voltage. Therefore no current will flow through the Zener diode. The resistance ratio of 1 : 1 will result in an output voltage that halves the input voltage and thus varies between 15 and 20 volts.

12. *Answer:* (A)

    Solution: Since the applied voltage is connected to the non-inverting input, and since the feedback is connected to the inverting input, the circuit becomes a voltage follower, and the output is maintained at +4 volts, independent of the resistance values.

13. *Answer:* (D)

    Solution: $V_{0_{MAX}} = +14\left[\dfrac{60K(1.05)}{120K(0.95)}\right] - 8\left[\dfrac{60K(1.05)}{80K(1.05)}\right] + 2\left[\dfrac{60K(1.05)}{40K(0.95)}\right]$

    $$V_{0_{MAX}} = +14[0.5526] - 8[0.75] + 2[1.658]$$

    $$V_{0_{MAX}} = 5.05 \text{ volts}$$

14. *Answer:* (A)

    Solution: The output of the op amp integrator is $V_0 = -\dfrac{1}{RC}\displaystyle\int_0^t V_{IN}\,dt$

    The total output, based on the 3 separate segments of the input voltage, is

$$V_0 = -\frac{1}{4}\int_0^4 5\,dt - \frac{1}{4}\int_4^8 (13 - 2t)\,dt - \frac{1}{4}\int_8^{12} -3\,dt$$

$$V_0 = -\frac{5}{4}\Big[t\Big]_0^4 - \frac{1}{4}\Big[13t - \frac{2t^2}{2}\Big]_4^8 + \frac{3}{4}\Big[t\Big]_8^{12}$$

$$V_0 = -\frac{5}{4}(4) - \frac{1}{4}[13(8 - 4) - (64 - 16)] + \frac{3}{4}(12 - 8)$$

$$V_0 = -5 - \frac{1}{4}[52 - 48] + \frac{3}{4}(4)$$

$$V_0 = -5 - 1 + 3$$

$$V_0 = -3 \text{ volts}$$

15. *Answer:* (B)

   Solution: $KVA_{TOT} = \sqrt{170^2 + 90^2} = 192.4 \text{ KVA}$

$$I_{TOT} = \frac{1000(KVA)}{V\sqrt{3}} = \frac{192,400}{440\sqrt{3}} = 252 \text{ amps}$$

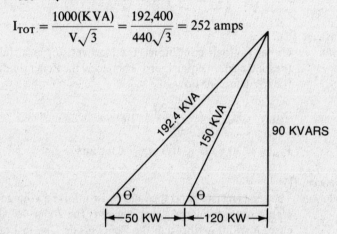

16. *Answer:* (B)

   Solution: The reactive current i_c that must be drawn by the capacitor is
   $i_c = 360\sin(\cos^{-1} 0.8) = 360(0.6) = 216 \text{ amperes}$

   Therefore $X_c = \dfrac{120 \text{ volts}}{216 \text{ amps}} = 0.5556 \text{ ohms}$

$$C = \frac{1}{2\pi f X_c} = \frac{1}{2\pi(60)(0.5556)} = 4775 \text{ microfarads}$$

17. *Answer:* (B)

   Solution: $C = \left[\dfrac{G_1 G_2}{1 + G_1 G_2 H}\right]\left[R + \dfrac{U_1}{G_1}\right]$

   Based on superposition, using only the peak amplitudes of the 60-Hertz inputs,

$$C = \frac{10(2)}{1 + 10(2)(0.4)}\left[10 + \frac{30}{10}\right]$$

$$C = \frac{20}{9}[13] = 28.89 \text{ peak value}$$

$$C_{rms} = 28.89(.7071) = 20.4 \text{ volts}$$

18. *Answer:* (C)

Solution: Error voltage $e = \dfrac{R}{1 + GH}$; $E(s) = \dfrac{R(s)}{1 + GH(s)}$

$$e_{ss} = sE(s)|_{s=0} = \left.\dfrac{s\left(\dfrac{60}{s}\right)}{1 + \dfrac{30}{4s + 5}}\right|_{s=0} = \dfrac{60}{1 + \dfrac{30}{5}} = 8.57 \text{ volts}$$

Statics

19. *Answer:* (E)

Solution: Since $\Sigma F_H = 0$, $F_H = 0.25W$. Taking moments about point 0, $WL \cos \alpha$
$- W\dfrac{L}{2}\cos \alpha - 0.25\,WL \sin \alpha = 0$. Solving, $\tan \alpha = 2$. $\alpha = 63.4°$

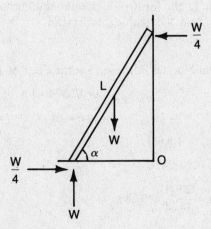

20. *Answer:* (C)

Solution: Addition of the $\vec{i}, \vec{j}$, and $\vec{k}$ components of all 3 forces yields

$$\vec{R} = 20\vec{i} + 20\vec{j} - 20\vec{k}$$

$$|\vec{R}| = \sqrt{20^2 + 20^2 + 20^2} = 34.6$$

21. *Answer:* (B)

Solution: $W \sin \alpha = \mu W \cos \alpha$. Thus, $\tan \alpha = \mu = 0.1$. $\alpha = \tan^{-1} 0.1 = 5.7°$

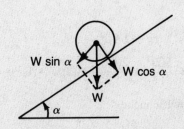

22. *Answer:* (C)

   Solution: $\bar{x} = \dfrac{\Sigma Ax}{\Sigma A} = \dfrac{2(5)(\frac{2}{2}) + 3(\frac{2}{2})(2 + \frac{3}{3}) + 3(1)(2 + \frac{3}{2})}{10 + 3 + 3}$

   $\bar{x} = 1.84$ inches

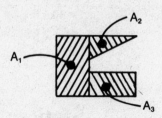

   NOTE: In the above solution the cross-section is analyzed as the composite summation of two rectangles and one triangle.

23. *Answer:* (E)

   Solution: The d'Alembert's Principle is a method of writing Newton's Second Law in the form of a pseudo-equilibrium equation, and hence is a principle of dynamics, not statics.

24. *Answer:* (E)

   Solution: Total Normal Force = {1 surface at 8.66 lbs} + {1 surface at 8.66 lbs

   $+ 17.32$ lbs}

   $= 34.64$ lbs

   $N_{TOT} = 4(8.66)$

   $\mu N = 20 \sin 30°$

   $\mu = \dfrac{20(\frac{1}{2})}{34.64} = 0.289$

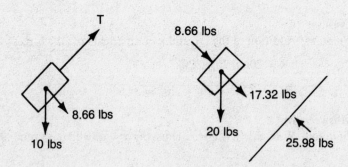

25. *Answer:* (C)

   Solution: $I_{x-x} = \Sigma Icg + \Sigma Ad^2$

   $I_{x-x} = \dfrac{6(2)^3}{12} + \dfrac{2(6)^3}{12} + 6(2)(1 + 1)^2 + 6(2)(3 - 1)^2$

   $I_{x-x} = 136$ inches^4

26. *Answer:* (B)

    Solution: The resultant of the distributed load passes through the right-hand reaction. Hence the left-hand reaction obtained by taking moments about the right-hand support is zero.

27. *Answer:* (D)

    Solution: Based on horizontal equilibrium, $H_A = 10^K \rightarrow$

    Since the summation of the moments taken about point B equals zero,

    $$V_A(8) - 10(6) = 0$$

    $$V_A = 7.5^K \uparrow$$

    Resultant magnitude $= \sqrt{(7.5)^2 + (10)^2} = 12.5^K$

28. *Answer:* (E)

    Solution: Concentrated loads will cause discontinuities in the slope of a hanging cable, hence a circular arc shape is impossible.

29. *Answer:* (D)

    Solution: The sum of the moments taken about point A equals zero.

    $$\Sigma M_A = H_B(20) - 10(20) - 5(40) = 0$$

    $$H_B = 20^K \rightarrow$$

30. *Answer:* (A)

    Solution: Since $\vec{F}$ and $\vec{n}$ are perpendicular, the dot product $\vec{n} \cdot \vec{F}$ must equal zero.

    $$\vec{n} \cdot \vec{F} = (\vec{i} + c\vec{k}) \cdot (10\vec{i} + 5\vec{j} + 10\vec{k}) = 0$$

    $$\vec{n} \cdot \vec{F} = 10 + 10c = 0$$

    $$c = -1$$

31. *Answer:* (D)

    Solution: For the section to the right of the hinge, taking moments about the right support,

    $$R(6) - 1000(6)(3) = 0$$

    $$R = 3000 \text{ pounds}$$

    For the section to the left of the hinge, taking moments about the left support,

    $$M = 1000(10)(\tfrac{10}{2}) + 3000(10)$$

    $$M = 80,000 \text{ lb/ft}$$

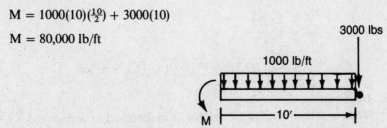

Dynamics

32. *Answer:* (B)

    Solution: The original extension of the spring is $\frac{50}{50}$ = one foot. The final extension is $1 - 0.5 = 0.5$ ft. The change in total potential energy of the system is $\frac{50}{2}(0.5)^2 - \frac{50}{2}(1)^2 + 50(0.5) = 12.5$ ft/lb.

33. *Answer:* (C)

    Solution: Since $\vec{v}_w = \vec{v}_{car} + \vec{v}_{w/car}$ the diagram shows that $\vec{v}_w$ is from the Southwest.

    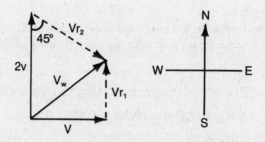

34. *Answer:* (B)

    Solution: From the equation of motion $\frac{mg}{mv^2/r} = \tan\theta = \frac{dz}{dr} = 2ar$

    Therefore $v^2 = \frac{g}{2a}$ (independent of H)

    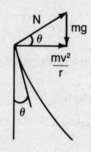

35. *Answer:* (A)

    Solution: $\frac{1}{2}mv^2 = \int_R^\infty -\frac{GmM}{r^2}dr = \frac{GmM}{R}$

    or $v^2 = \frac{2GM}{R}$

    but $g = \frac{GM}{r^2}$ $\therefore v^2 = 2gR$

    or $v = \sqrt{2(9.81)(6,370,000)} = 11,179$ m/sec

36. *Answer:* (D)

    Solution: The midpoint of the bar is maintained at a distance $\frac{R\sqrt{3}}{2}$ from the center of the cylinder.

The velocity $V_G = r\omega = \left(R\dfrac{\sqrt{3}}{2}\right)(\omega)$.

From the principle of conservation of energy $\dfrac{1}{2}m(V_G)^2 + \dfrac{1}{2}I\omega^2 = hW$

or $\dfrac{1}{2}mV_G^2 + \dfrac{1}{2}\left(m\dfrac{L^2}{12}\right)\left(\dfrac{V_G^2}{R^2}\right)\left(\dfrac{4}{3}\right) = 3\left(\dfrac{\sqrt{3}}{2}\right)W$.

With $L = R$ and $W = mg$ we have

$\dfrac{1}{2}V_G^2\left(1 + \dfrac{1}{9}\right) = 2.598g$

$V_G = 12.3$ ft/sec.

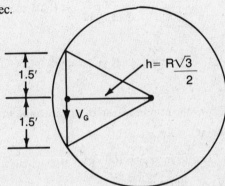

37. *Answer:* (E)

    Solution: The velocity of the object as it emerges from the chute is $V = \sqrt{2gR}$. The time needed to strike the ground is found from $\frac{1}{2}gt^2 = h$ or

    $t = \sqrt{\dfrac{2h}{g}}$. Since the horizontal component of the velocity is constant

    and equal to $\sqrt{2gR}$, $L = V_x t = \sqrt{2gR}\sqrt{\dfrac{2h}{g}} = 2\sqrt{Rh}$.

38. *Answer:* (C)

    Solution: The net force = (mass)(acceleration).

    $$21^K - 3(5^K) = \left(\dfrac{150}{g}\right)a$$

    The acceleration of the cars is $\dfrac{21 - 3(5)}{150/g} = \dfrac{g}{25}$

    The coupling force equals the total load which the last 2 cars impose on the first car. It consists of the rolling friction plus the force required to produce their acceleration.

    $\therefore F_c = 2(5) + Ma = 10 + \left(\dfrac{100}{g}\right)\left(\dfrac{g}{25}\right)$

    $F_c = 14$ kips

39. *Answer:* (D)

    Solution: The ratio of the velocities before and after a bounce is e. The height to

    which the ball rises is $\dfrac{v^2}{2g}$. Thus the ratio of heights is e^2.

40. *Answer:* (A)

    Solution: If θ is the angle of rotation of the drum, the equation of motion is

    $$\frac{MR^2}{2}\frac{d^2\theta}{dt^2} + (2kR\theta)R = 0$$

    $$\text{or } \frac{d^2\theta}{dt^2} + \frac{4k\theta}{M} = 0$$

    $$\omega = \sqrt{\frac{4k}{M}} \quad T = \frac{2\pi}{\omega} = 2\pi\sqrt{\frac{M}{4k}}$$

    $$T = \pi\sqrt{\frac{M}{k}} = \pi\sqrt{\frac{200/32.2}{3 \times 12}} = 1.305 \text{ sec}$$

    KRθ KRθ

41. *Answer:* (D)

    Solution: $H_0 = 2\hat{i} \times (4\hat{i} + 4\hat{k})3 = -24\hat{j}$

42. *Answer:* (B)

    Solution: From the conservation of linear momentum in the direction of v_0

    $$M_1V_1 = M_2V_2$$

    $$(20 \text{ kg})(6 \text{ m/sec}) = (60 \text{ kg})(V_2)$$

    $$V_2 = 2 \text{ m/sec}$$

43. *Answer:* (A)

    Solution: From the principle of angular impulse and momentum

    $$M(\Delta t) = I\omega \quad P\mu R(\Delta t) = \tfrac{1}{2}MR^2\omega$$

    $$\text{or } P = \frac{1}{2\mu}\frac{MR\omega}{\Delta t} = \frac{1}{2 \times 0.5} \times \frac{80}{32.2} \times 0.75 \times \frac{400 \times 2\pi}{60} \times \frac{1}{2}$$

    $$P = 39.03 \text{ lb}$$

44. *Answer:* (B)

    Solution: From conservation of angular momentum,

    $$mrv = [mr^2 + I]w, \text{ where } m = \frac{W}{g}$$

    $$\frac{1}{4}\left[\frac{1}{16}\right]\left[\frac{1}{32.2}\right][3000][2] = \left[\frac{1}{4}\left(\frac{1}{16}\right)\left(\frac{1}{32.2}\right)(2^2) + I\right](0.03)$$

    Solving, $I = 97.05$ lb-ft-sec^2

Mechanics of Materials

45. *Answer:* (D)

    Solution: $M_{\text{plastic}} = \sigma \times bh/2 \times 2h/4$

    $M_{\text{elastic}} = \sigma \times bh^2/6$

    $$\text{Ratio} = \frac{2bh^2/8}{bh^2/6} = \frac{1/4}{1/6} = \frac{6}{4} = \frac{1.5}{1}$$

46. *Answer:* (A)

    Solution: $\delta = \int_0^L \dfrac{\gamma A x \, dx}{AE} = \dfrac{1}{2} \dfrac{\gamma L^2}{E} = \dfrac{0.282}{2} \left[\dfrac{(2 \times 10^3)^2}{30 \times 10^6} \right] 144$

    $\delta = 0.141 \dfrac{(4)(144)}{30} = 2.71$ inches

47. *Answer:* (E)

    Solution: Normally, maximum shear stress occurs at the neutral axis, provided that the minimum thickness also occurs at that point. Since $\tau = \dfrac{VQ}{It}$, when b ≫ t, the maximum shear stress will occur at the point closest to the neutral axis where minimum thickness occurs, namely B and D.

48. *Answer:* (A)

    Solution: Rockwell hardness testers have two scales, different because of varying weights of the penetrator. The scales are usually labeled B and C.

49. *Answer:* (D)

    Solution: $\sigma = \dfrac{Mc}{I}$ $M_{max} = 1000 \times 3$, since R at left equals 0.

    $\sigma = \dfrac{3000 \times 12 \times 3}{\dfrac{(2)(6)^3}{12}} = 3000$ psi

50. *Answer:* (B)

    Solution: τ max for rectangular section $= \dfrac{3}{2} \dfrac{V}{A} = \dfrac{3}{2} \times \dfrac{1000}{2 \times 6} = 125$ psi

    (Maximum shear force equals either of the loads)

51. *Answer:* (D)

    Solution: The deflected position of the slab shows zero elongation of the left wire, δ in the middle wire, and 2δ in the right wire, due to the rigidity of the slab. As a result, note that

    $P_1 = 0$

    $P_3 = 2P_2$

    $P_1 + P_2 + P_3 = P$

    $\therefore P_2 = \dfrac{P}{3}$ and $P_3 = \dfrac{2P}{3}$

    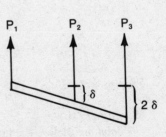

    Taking moments about the left end,

    $2a\left(\dfrac{2P}{3}\right) + a\left(\dfrac{P}{3}\right) = P(x)$

    $\therefore x = \dfrac{4}{3}a + \dfrac{1}{3}a = \dfrac{5}{3}a$

52. *Answer:* (C)

    Solution: Since the material is weakest in tension, a pure shear loading will generate tension stresses along directions inclined at 45° to the longitudinal axis. Stresses will decrease with depth, hence generating a failure along a helical surface (not a plane) inclined at 45° to the longitudinal axis.

53. *Answer:* (B)

Solution: $P_{cr} = \dfrac{EI\pi^2}{L^2} = \dfrac{30 \times 10^6 \times \pi^2}{12(20)^2} = 61,700$ lbs

54. *Answer:* (E)

Solution: Elastic perfectly plastic materials remain linearly elastic up to the yield point and at yield they experience indefinite strain without increase in stress until failure.

55. *Answer:* (C)

Solution: $\dfrac{\sigma L}{E} = \alpha L(\Delta T) - 0.006$

$\therefore \sigma = [12(10)^{-6}(30)(100) - 0.006]\left[\dfrac{10(10)^6}{30}\right] = 10,000$ psi

56. *Answer:* (E)

Solution: Holes, cross-sectional changes, and concentrated loads all cause stress concentrations.

57. *Answer:* (C)

Solution: $\delta_{steel} = \delta_{concrete}$ $P_{steel} + P_{concrete} = P_{total}$

$\dfrac{P_s L_s}{A_s E_s} = \dfrac{P_c L_c}{A_c E_c}$

$\dfrac{P_s}{P_c} = \dfrac{A_s E_s}{A_c E_c} = \dfrac{4}{96}\left(\dfrac{10}{1}\right) = \dfrac{40}{96}$

% carried by steel $= \dfrac{40}{136}(100) = 29.3\%$

Fluid Mechanics

58. *Answer:* (C)

59. *Answer:* (B)

Solution: Before the tank undergoes its acceleration, the area of a vertical cross-section of water, taken through the longitudinal axis, is the product of the height of water and the length of the tank. It is rectangular in shape. A = (10 inches)(10 feet)(12) = 1200 square inches. Under constant acceleration, this cross-sectional area will remain constant, but will assume a triangular shape having a slope of 7/32.2, as shown in the diagram.

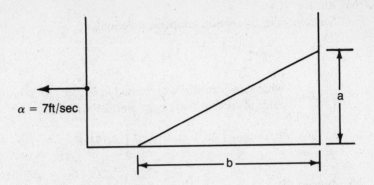

$$\frac{1}{2}ab = 1200 \text{ square inches}$$

$$\frac{a}{b} = \frac{7}{32.2}$$

$$\therefore a = 22.8 \text{ inches}$$

60. *Answer:* (B)

   Solution: $P = \gamma h_{\text{water}} - \gamma h_{\text{mercury}} + P_{\text{ambient}}$

   $$P = \frac{62.4(30)}{144} - \frac{(13.55)(62.4)(22)}{144(12)} + 14.7$$

   $$P = 13 - 10.76 + 14.7 = 16.94 \text{ psia}$$

61. *Answer:* (D)

   Solution: The Reynolds Number ($PV\ell/\mu$) of the model and that of the actual prototype must be equal. Since the temperature of the test is the same as the operational temperature, this equality reduces to:

   $$\ell_m V_m P_m = \ell_P V_P P_P$$

   $$\ell_m = \frac{20(700)(3.5)}{(367)(14.7)} = 9.08 \text{ feet}$$

62. *Answer:* (B)

   Solution: $\Delta P = K\left(\frac{1}{2}\right)\rho V^2 = 0.5\left(\frac{1}{2}\right)\left(\frac{62.4}{32.2}\right)\left(\frac{5}{0.196}\right)^2\left(\frac{1}{144}\right)$

   $$\Delta P = 2.18 \text{ psi}$$

63. *Answer:* (A)

   Solution: A smooth venturi in a low-velocity system will have very little effect on overall flow.

64. *Answer:* (E)

   Solution: $HP = \frac{Q\Delta P}{n(550)}, \quad KW = 0.746 \text{ HP}$

   $$\therefore KW = \frac{0.746(4 \text{ cfs})(62.4 \text{ lb/ft}^3)(20 \text{ ft})}{(0.7)(0.85)(550)} = 11.4 \text{ KW}$$

65. *Answer:* (C)

 Solution: The stagnation temperature equals

$$T_s = T_\infty \left(1 + \frac{k-1}{2} M^2 \right)$$

where temperature is expressed in degrees Rankine, and where k is the ratio of specific heats c_P/c_v and equals 1.4 for air.

$$T_s = 400 \left[1 + \frac{1.4-1}{2}(1.7)^2 \right] = 171°F$$

66. *Answer:* (B)

 Solution: Ten inches of mercury minus ten inches of water equals

$$\Delta P = (13.55 - 1.0)(62.4)\left(\frac{10}{12}\right) = 652.6 \text{ psf}$$

$$V = \sqrt{\frac{2\Delta P}{\rho}} = \sqrt{\frac{2 \times 32.2 \times 652.6}{62.4}} = 25.95 \text{ fps}$$

67. *Answer:* (E)

 Solution: In laminar flow, the friction factor is $64/N_R$, and the head loss due to friction is directly proportional to velocity. The transition usually occurs at a Reynolds Number of approximately 2100. In turbulent flow, the head loss due to friction is directly proportional to the square of the velocity.

68. *Answer:* (C)

 Solution: $V = \sqrt{2gh} = \sqrt{2(32.2)(20)} = 35.9 \text{ fps}$

69. *Answer:* (D)

 Solution: $y_c = \frac{4r}{3\pi} = \frac{4(4)}{3\pi} = 1.7 \text{ feet}$

70. *Answer:* (D)

 Solution: $F = h\rho A$

where h is the vertical depth of the centroid below the surface of the water.

$$F = (18 + 1.7)(62.4)(\pi)\left(\frac{4^2}{2}\right)\left(\frac{1}{2000}\right) \text{ tons}$$

$$F = 15.4 \text{ tons}$$

71. *Answer:* (C)

 Solution: The force on the bottom semi-circular half is 15.45 tons; the force on the top half is 12.78 tons. Therefore, the net torque is

$$T = F_B y_C - F_T y_C = 15.45(2000)(1.7) - 12.78(2000)(1.7)$$

$$T = 9080 \text{ lb-ft}$$

Thermodynamics/Heat Transfer

72. *Answer:* (A)
    Solution: This is a problem in one-dimensional heat conduction.

$$Q = \frac{k}{x}(A\Delta T)$$

$$k = \frac{(20,000)(1/8'')}{100°F}$$

$$k = 25 \text{ Btu-in/hr-ft}^2\text{-°F}$$

$$k = 2.08 \text{ Btu/hr-ft-°F}$$

73. *Answer:* (E)
    Solution: $\dfrac{P_1}{P_2} = \dfrac{T_1}{T_2}$

$$T_2 = T_1\left(\frac{P_2}{P_1}\right) = 530\left(\frac{800}{1000}\right)$$

$$T_2 = 424°R = -36°F$$

74. *Answer:* (C)
    Solution: $TP^{\frac{1-n}{n}} = \text{constant}$

$$\frac{T_2}{T_1} = \left(\frac{P_2}{P_1}\right)^{\frac{n-1}{n}}$$

$$T_2 = 530\left(\frac{100}{14.7}\right)^{0.167}$$

$$T_2 = 729.6°R = 269.6°F$$

75. *Answer:* (D)
    Solution: $\text{Work} = \displaystyle\int_{x=0}^{x=L} pA\,dx$

$$\text{where } p = 100 - \left(\frac{60}{L}\right)x$$

$$\text{Work} = (70 \text{ psig})(\pi)\left(\frac{3^2}{4}\right)\left(\frac{2}{12}\right)$$

$$\text{Work} = 82.466 \text{ ft-lb}$$

76. *Answer:* (C)
    Solution: The Otto cycle.

77. *Answer:* (B)
    Solution: The steady flow energy equation is:

$$\frac{V_1^2}{2g_0} + Z_1 + U_1 + \frac{p_1}{\rho_1} + Q = \frac{V_2^2}{2g_0} + Z_2 + U_2 + \frac{p_2}{\rho_2} + W_x$$

which reduces to:

$$\Delta U = \frac{\Delta p}{\rho} = \frac{144 \text{ psf}}{62.4 \text{ lb/ft}^3}$$

$$\Delta U = 2.308 \text{ ft-lb/lb}$$

$$U = 0.002966 \text{ Btu/lb}$$

78. *Answer:* (D)

   Solution: $(COP)_{max} = \dfrac{T_2}{T_1 - T_2} = \dfrac{800}{1000 - 800} = 4$

79. *Answer:* (C)

   Solution: Specific humidity (or humidity ratio) is expressed in terms of pounds of water (or grains of water) per pound of dry air.

80. *Answer:* (A)

81. *Answer:* (D)

82. *Answer:* (D)

83. *Answer:* (B)

   Solution: At 70°F dry bulb and 90% relative humidity, the wet bulb is 68°F and the dew point is less than 67°F.

84. *Answer:* (E)

   Solution: $q/A = 0.173 \times 10^{-8} \varepsilon (T_1^4 - T_2^4)$ Btu/hr-ft^2

   $$q/A = 0.173 \times 0.95 \left[\left(\frac{495}{100}\right)^4 - \left(\frac{410}{100}\right)^4 \right]$$

   $$q/A = 52.23 \text{ Btu/hr-ft}^2$$

85. *Answer:* (C)

   Solution: Heat transferred = 48 Btu/hr-ft^2 × 1 ft^2 × 8 hours = 384 Btu
   1/2 cu ft of water weighs 31.2 lb. C = 1 Btu/lb°F
   To cool the water from 35°F to 32°F

   $$Q = (31.2 \text{ lb})(1 \text{ Btu/lb-°F})(35 - 32) = 93.6 \text{ Btu}$$

   The latent heat of fusion of water is 143 Btu/lb

   $$Q = 384 - 93.6 = W \times 143$$

   $$W = 2.03 \text{ lb}$$

Mathematics

86. *Answer:* (A)

   Solution: The final amplitude in each case equals K. For 50% of the final amplitude,

$$y = 0.50K = K - K\varepsilon^{-a(2.5)}$$

$$0.50 = \varepsilon^{-2.5a}$$

$$-2.5a = \ln 0.5 = -0.693$$

$$a = 0.277$$

87. *Answer:* (B)

 Solution: The problem statement defines a parabola, which is represented by $y^2 + 8x = 2$. The other choices represent a circle, ellipse, hyperbola, and straight line, respectively, none of which are valid for the given description.

88. *Answer:* (D)

 Solution: The slope of the given line segment is

$$m = \frac{y_2 - y_1}{x_2 - x_1} = \frac{8 - 1}{-1 - (-6)} = \frac{7}{5}$$

Therefore, since the slope of the desired equation must be the negative reciprocal of m, the slope will be $-\frac{5}{7}$; and since the y-intercept is zero,

$$y = -\frac{5}{7}x + 0$$

$$7y = -5x$$

89. *Answer:* (A)

 Solution: Since $\sin^2 t + \cos^2 t = 1$,

$$w = K\varepsilon^{(\sin^2 t + \cos^2 t)} = K\varepsilon$$

$$\frac{dw}{dt} = 0$$

90. *Answer:* (E)

 Solution: Factoring the equation, it becomes $(x + 2)^2 + (y + 3)^2 = -3$. This equation describes a circle with its center at $(-2, -3)$, but with a radius of $\sqrt{-3}$, which of course does not exist.

91. *Answer:* (D)

92. *Answer:* (D)

 Solution: $\begin{vmatrix} a_{11} & a_{12} \\ a_{21} & a_{22} \end{vmatrix} = a_{11}a_{22} - a_{12}a_{21}$

$$\begin{vmatrix} a_{11} & a_{12} & 0 \\ a_{21} & a_{22} & 0 \\ 0 & 0 & 1 \end{vmatrix} = a_{11}a_{22} + 0 + 0 - a_{12}a_{21} - 0 - 0$$

93. *Answer:* (C)

 Solution: $\int_0^1 \varepsilon^{-2x}\,dx = -\frac{1}{2}\varepsilon^{-2x}\Big|_0^1 = -\frac{1}{2}[\varepsilon^{-2} - 1] = \frac{1}{2} - \frac{1}{2}\varepsilon^{-2}$

94. *Answer:* (B)

    Solution: The sum of a converging geometric series is given by

    $$\Sigma = \frac{a}{1 - r},$$ where a is the first term and r is the geometric ratio.

    $$\Sigma = \frac{0.4}{1 - 0.25} = \frac{0.40}{0.75} = \frac{8}{15}$$

95. *Answer:* (A)

    Solution: $\cos 3x [\cos^3 x]^{-1} = \dfrac{\cos 3x}{\cos^3 x} = \dfrac{\cos 2x \cos x - \sin 2x \sin x}{\cos^3 x}$

    $$= \frac{(\cos^2 x - \sin^2 x)\cos x - 2\sin^2 x \cos x}{\cos^3 x} = \frac{\cos^2 x - 3\sin^2 x}{\cos^2 x}$$

    $$= 1 - 3\tan^2 x$$

96. *Answer:* (E)

97. *Answer:* (B)

    Solution: A hyperbolic cosine is defined as $\cosh u = \frac{1}{2}[\varepsilon^u + \varepsilon^{-u}]$, which is the average value of an exponential growth function and a related exponential decay function.

Chemistry

98. *Answer:* (E)

99. *Answer:* (A)

100. *Answer:* (D)

    Solution: The balanced equation is

    $$2KMnO_4 + 8H_2SO_4 + 10FeSO_4 \longrightarrow K_2SO_4 + 2MnSO_4$$
    $$+ 5Fe_2(SO_4)_3 + 8H_2O$$

    The sum of the coefficients $= 2 + 8 + 10 + 1 + 2 + 5 + 8 = 36$

101. *Answer:* (B)

102. *Answer:* (C)

    Solution: 17×10^{-11} gm/cc $= 1 \times 10^{-11}$ mols/cc $= 1 \times 10^{-8}$ mols/1

    $$[H^+] \times [OH^-] = 10^{-14}$$

    $$[H^+] = 10^{-14} \times 10^8 = 10^{-6}$$

    $$pH = \log \frac{1}{[H^+]} = \log \frac{1}{10^{-6}} = 6$$

103. *Answer:* (E)

104. *Answer:* (B)
    Solution: $2Ag^+ + (Cr_2O_7)^= \rightleftharpoons Ag_2Cr_2O_7$

    $$[Ag^+]^2 \times [Cr_2O_7^=] = 9(10)^{-12}$$

    Let $[Cr_2O_7^=] = x$, and $[Ag] = 2x$

    $$(2x)^2(x) = 9(10)^{-12}$$

    $$4x^3 = 9(10)^{-12}$$

    $$x = 1.3(10)^{-4}$$

105. *Answer:* (D)

106. *Answer:* (C)
    Solution: The specific gravity of 10% sulfuric acid is 1.06. Its weight is

    $$(8.33 \text{ lb/gal})(1.06)(1000)(0.1) = 883 \text{ lbs of } H_2SO_4$$

    $$\begin{matrix} & 883 & & & \\ H_2SO_4 & + & CaO & \longrightarrow & CaSO_4\downarrow + H_2O \\ 98 & & 56 & & 136 \end{matrix}$$

    Weight of $CaO = \dfrac{56}{98}(883) = 505$ pounds/1000 gallons acid

107. *Answer:* (A)
    Solution: Since the calcium sulfate has a molecular weight of 136, and the sulfuric acid has a weight of 98, the rate of flow of the calcium sulfate is

    $$\frac{136}{98}(883) = 1225 \text{ lbs/hour}$$

    The filter area $= 1225 \div 10 = 122 \text{ ft}^2$

Computer Programming

108. *Answer:* (C)

109. *Answer:* (A)
    Solution: $(10011110)_2 = (1 \times 2^7 + 0 \times 2^6 + 0 \times 2^5 + 1 \times 2^4 + 1 \times 2^3 + 1 \times 2^2 + 1 \times 2^1 + 0 \times 2^0)_{10} = 158_{10}$

110. *Answer:* (D)
    Solution: (A) $3 * 16 + 1 = 49$
    (B) $5 * 8 + 5 = 45$
    (C) $32 + 16 + 8 + 1 = 57$
    (D) $5 * 8 + 7 = 47$
    (E) $32 + 4 + 2 + 1 = 39$

111. *Answer:* (B)

    Solution: The leftmost bit is a 1 so the number is negative. To get the magnitude of a 1's complement number which is negative, one complements the number and finds the equivalent of the result.

    The complement of $(1001011)_2$ is $(0110100)_2$

$$(0110100)_2 = (0*64 + 1*32 + 1*16 + 0*8 + 1*4 + 0*2 + 0*1)_{10}$$
$$= (52)_{10}$$

    So $(1001011)_{1's} = (-52)_{10}$

112. *Answer:* (D)

    Solution: (A) missing a right parenthesis.

              (B) $<, >$ are not logical operators; & is not AND.

              (C) AND operator is .AND.

              (D) This is correct.

              (E) This is not FORTRAN due to improper relational operators $<$, $>$, and improper "AND".

113. *Answer:* (B)

114. *Answer:* (C)

    Solution:

$$
\begin{array}{ccc}
1 & 1 & \\
A & 5 & 3 \\
+\,7 & B & E \\
\hline
(12)_{16} & (11)_{16} & (11)_{16}
\end{array}
$$

    so the answer is $(1211)_{16}$

115. *Answer:* (B)

    Solution: The legal FORTRAN operators are:

           **   exponentiation

           *   multiplication

           /   division

           +   addition

           −   subtraction

           .AND.   logical and

           .OR.   logical or

           .NOT.   logical not

Mathematical Modeling of Engineering Systems

116. *Answer:* (D)

    Solution: The net summation of the forces equals mass times acceleration.

$$F_A - F_s - F_D = Ma$$

    Letting y equal the vertical displacement, $F_A = M\dfrac{d^2y}{dt^2} + K_D\dfrac{dy}{dt} + K_s y$

    But K_D equals 20 pounds per foot/second and Ks equals $\dfrac{4(12)}{0.5}$ or 96 pounds/foot.

The characteristic equation is, in Laplace notation:

$$Ms^2 + 20s + 96 = 0$$

$$s^2 + \frac{20s}{M} + \frac{96}{M} = 0$$

Therefore $W_n^2 = \frac{96}{M} = \frac{96}{W/g}$

$$\omega = \frac{96(32.2)}{(3)^2} = 343 \text{ pounds}$$

117. *Answer:* (A)

   Solution: $2\zeta\omega_n = \frac{20}{M}$

$$\zeta = \frac{20}{2\omega_n M} = \frac{20(32.2)}{2(3)(343)} = 0.313$$

   $\therefore$ System is appreciably underdamped

118. *Answer:* (B)

   Solution: From the op amp stages,

$$V_0 = {}^\circ F(0.1)\left(-\frac{60K}{54K}\right)\left(-\frac{60K}{60K}\right) - \frac{60K}{27K}(1.6)$$

$$V_0 = (0.1)^\circ F\left(\frac{10}{9}\right) - \frac{32}{9}$$

$$V_0 = \frac{1}{9}[{}^\circ F - 32]$$

   but $^\circ C = 5/9(^\circ F - 32)$

   $\therefore V_0 = \frac{1}{5}(^\circ C) = 0.2(^\circ C)$

119. *Answer:* (C)

   Solution: Superposition permits the consideration of only the 60-Hertz components of the applied signals, while excluding the DC components. The system output may be expressed as:

$$C = (\text{Transfer Function})\left[R + \frac{U_1}{G_1} + \frac{U_2}{G_1 G_2}\right]$$

   which verifies the concept that each input is reduced by a factor equal to the forward gain that precedes this input. Using peak values of the 60-Hertz inputs,

$$C = \frac{5(10)}{1 + 5(10)(3)}\left[10 + \frac{3}{5} + \frac{120}{50}\right] = \left[\frac{50}{151}\right][13]$$

$$= 4.305 \text{ volts peak}$$

$$V_A = (4.305 - 120)\left(\frac{1}{10}\right) - 3 = -14.57 \text{ volts peak}$$

$$V_{A_{RMS}} = 14.57(0.7071) = 10.3 \text{ volts}$$

120. *Answer:* (A)

   Solution: Using the approach outlined in problem #119,

$$V_c = \frac{5(10)}{1 + 5(10)(3)}\left[0 + \frac{6}{5} + 0\right] = \frac{50}{151}\left[\frac{6}{5}\right] = 0.3974 \text{ volts peak}$$

$$V_A = (0.3974)\left[\frac{1}{10}\right] - 6 = -5.96 \text{ volts peak}$$

$$V_{A_{RMS}} = 5.96(0.7071) = 4.21 \text{ volts rms}$$

121. *Answer:* (A)

   Solution: $V_{C_{DC}} = \dfrac{5(10)}{1 + 5(10)(3)}\left[100 + 0 + \dfrac{20}{50}\right] = \dfrac{50}{151}[100.4] = 33.25 \text{ volts}$

$$V_{A_{DC}} = [33.25 - 20]\left[\frac{1}{10}\right] = 1.325 \text{ volts}$$

122. *Answer:* (E)

   Solution: For the voltage at point B, $y = -\dfrac{1}{RC}\displaystyle\int V_B \, dt$

$$\therefore \frac{dy}{dt} = -\frac{V_B}{RC}, \quad V_B = -RC\frac{dy}{dt} = -0.2\frac{dy}{dt}$$

   Similarly, $V_A = -R'C'\dfrac{d}{dt}(V_B) = -0.5(-0.2)\dfrac{d^2y}{dt^2} = 0.1\dfrac{d^2y}{dt^2}$

$$V_A = 0.1\frac{d^2y}{dt^2} = -V_B\left[\frac{60K}{30K}\right] - y\left[\frac{60K}{120K}\right] - 12\left[\frac{60K}{80K}\right]$$

$$0.1\frac{d^2y}{dt^2} = +0.2\frac{dy}{dt}[2] - y\left[\frac{1}{2}\right] - 12\left[\frac{3}{4}\right]$$

$$\frac{d^2y}{dt^2} - 4\frac{dy}{dt} + 5y + 90 = 0$$

123. *Answer:* (E)

   Solution: From the block diagram, $V_A = 10[R - 2C] = 10R - 20C$. In the operational amplifier circuit, using superposition, the output V_A is the summation of the output component due to C alone plus that due to R alone.

$$V_A = -C\left[\frac{20K}{1K}\right] + R\left[\frac{10K}{10K + R_x}\right]\left[\frac{20K + 1K}{1K}\right]$$

$$V_A = \left[\frac{10K(21)}{10K + R_x}\right]R - 20C = 10R - 20C$$

$$\left[\frac{10K(21)}{10K + R_x}\right]R = 10R$$

$$10(10K + R_x) = 21(10K)$$

$$R_x = 11K \text{ ohms}$$

Engineering Economics

124. *Answer:* (C)

    Solution: $A = P(A/P, 15\%, 30)$

$$A = 100,000(0.1523)$$

$$A = \$15,230$$

125. *Answer:* (D)

    Solution: $F = P\left(F/P, \dfrac{12\%}{12}, 5 \times 12\right)$

$$F = \$2800(F/P, 1\%, 60)$$

$$F = \$2800(1.8167)$$

$$F = \$5087$$

126. *Answer:* (E)

    Solution: The present worth of each choice is \$614.46, as follows:

        (B) $\$100(P/A, 10\%, 10) = \$614.46$

        (C) $\left.\begin{cases} \$506.44(P/F, 10\%, 5) = \$314.46 \\ \$778.12(P/F, 10\%, 10) = \$300.00 \end{cases}\right\}$ Total $= \$614.46$

        (D) $\$1593.75(P/F, 10\%, 10) = \$614.46$

127. *Answer:* (A)

    Solution: All of the indicated amounts are the same for 10% simple interest. However, when considering compound interest, present worth becomes \$100 now for (A), and ever smaller amounts for (B), (C), and (D). The calculations show:

        (A) $\$110 \times (PW_1\ 0.9091) = \$100.00$

        (B) $\$120 \times (PW_2\ 0.8264) = \$99.17$

        (C) $\$130 \times (PW_3\ 0.7513) = \$97.67$

        (D) $\$140 \times (PW_4\ 0.6830) = \$95.62$

128. *Answer:* (D)

    Solution: $F = 1\left(F/P, \dfrac{12\%}{12}, 12\right)$

$$F = 1.1268$$

$$\therefore i_{eff} = 1.1268 - 1 = 0.1268 = 12.68\%$$

129. *Answer:* (A)

    Solution: Calculation is actually unnecessary because in principle the more often the interest rate is compounded, the more money you earn. For reference, however:

        (A) $e^{0.05} = 1.0512711$

        (B) $\left(1 + \dfrac{0.05}{365}\right)^{365} = 1.0512675$

        (C) $\left(1 + \dfrac{0.05}{4}\right)^{4} = 1.0509453$

Materials Science

130. *Answer:* (D)

131. *Answer:* (E)

132. *Answer:* (C)

133. *Answer:* (C)

134. *Answer:* (B)

135. *Answer:* (E)

The Structure of Matter

136. *Answer:* (A)

137. *Answer:* (B)

   Solution: $\left(\dfrac{1}{2}\right)^x = 0.01$

   $x(\log 0.5) = \log 0.01$

   $x = \dfrac{-2}{-0.30103} = 6.644$

   Since each unit of x represents 8.6 days, t = 6.644(8.6) = 57.1 days

138. *Answer:* (C)

139. *Answer:* (D)

140. *Answer:* (B)
   Solution: Se-Se bond = 41 kilo-calories/mole
                 S-S bond = 54 kilo-calories/mole
                 Ge-Ge bond = 45 kilo-calories/mole
                 P-P bond = 48 kilo-calories/mole
                 Sn-Sn bond = 36 kilo-calories/mole

Answer Sheet
Practice Examination 2—P.M. Part

Engineering Mechanics

1 Ⓐ Ⓑ Ⓒ Ⓓ Ⓔ   4 Ⓐ Ⓑ Ⓒ Ⓓ Ⓔ   7 Ⓐ Ⓑ Ⓒ Ⓓ Ⓔ   10 Ⓐ Ⓑ Ⓒ Ⓓ Ⓔ   13 Ⓐ Ⓑ Ⓒ Ⓓ Ⓔ

2 Ⓐ Ⓑ Ⓒ Ⓓ Ⓔ   5 Ⓐ Ⓑ Ⓒ Ⓓ Ⓔ   8 Ⓐ Ⓑ Ⓒ Ⓓ Ⓔ   11 Ⓐ Ⓑ Ⓒ Ⓓ Ⓔ   14 Ⓐ Ⓑ Ⓒ Ⓓ Ⓔ

3 Ⓐ Ⓑ Ⓒ Ⓓ Ⓔ   6 Ⓐ Ⓑ Ⓒ Ⓓ Ⓔ   9 Ⓐ Ⓑ Ⓒ Ⓓ Ⓔ   12 Ⓐ Ⓑ Ⓒ Ⓓ Ⓔ   15 Ⓐ Ⓑ Ⓒ Ⓓ Ⓔ

Mathematics

16 Ⓐ Ⓑ Ⓒ Ⓓ Ⓔ   19 Ⓐ Ⓑ Ⓒ Ⓓ Ⓔ   22 Ⓐ Ⓑ Ⓒ Ⓓ Ⓔ   25 Ⓐ Ⓑ Ⓒ Ⓓ Ⓔ   28 Ⓐ Ⓑ Ⓒ Ⓓ Ⓔ

17 Ⓐ Ⓑ Ⓒ Ⓓ Ⓔ   20 Ⓐ Ⓑ Ⓒ Ⓓ Ⓔ   23 Ⓐ Ⓑ Ⓒ Ⓓ Ⓔ   26 Ⓐ Ⓑ Ⓒ Ⓓ Ⓔ   29 Ⓐ Ⓑ Ⓒ Ⓓ Ⓔ

18 Ⓐ Ⓑ Ⓒ Ⓓ Ⓔ   21 Ⓐ Ⓑ Ⓒ Ⓓ Ⓔ   24 Ⓐ Ⓑ Ⓒ Ⓓ Ⓔ   27 Ⓐ Ⓑ Ⓒ Ⓓ Ⓔ   30 Ⓐ Ⓑ Ⓒ Ⓓ Ⓔ

Electrical Circuits

31 Ⓐ Ⓑ Ⓒ Ⓓ Ⓔ   33 Ⓐ Ⓑ Ⓒ Ⓓ Ⓔ   35 Ⓐ Ⓑ Ⓒ Ⓓ Ⓔ   37 Ⓐ Ⓑ Ⓒ Ⓓ Ⓔ   39 Ⓐ Ⓑ Ⓒ Ⓓ Ⓔ

32 Ⓐ Ⓑ Ⓒ Ⓓ Ⓔ   34 Ⓐ Ⓑ Ⓒ Ⓓ Ⓔ   36 Ⓐ Ⓑ Ⓒ Ⓓ Ⓔ   38 Ⓐ Ⓑ Ⓒ Ⓓ Ⓔ   40 Ⓐ Ⓑ Ⓒ Ⓓ Ⓔ

Engineering Economics

41 Ⓐ Ⓑ Ⓒ Ⓓ Ⓔ   43 Ⓐ Ⓑ Ⓒ Ⓓ Ⓔ   45 Ⓐ Ⓑ Ⓒ Ⓓ Ⓔ   47 Ⓐ Ⓑ Ⓒ Ⓓ Ⓔ   49 Ⓐ Ⓑ Ⓒ Ⓓ Ⓔ

42 Ⓐ Ⓑ Ⓒ Ⓓ Ⓔ   44 Ⓐ Ⓑ Ⓒ Ⓓ Ⓔ   46 Ⓐ Ⓑ Ⓒ Ⓓ Ⓔ   48 Ⓐ Ⓑ Ⓒ Ⓓ Ⓔ   50 Ⓐ Ⓑ Ⓒ Ⓓ Ⓔ

Computer Programming

51 Ⓐ Ⓑ Ⓒ Ⓓ Ⓔ   53 Ⓐ Ⓑ Ⓒ Ⓓ Ⓔ   55 Ⓐ Ⓑ Ⓒ Ⓓ Ⓔ   57 Ⓐ Ⓑ Ⓒ Ⓓ Ⓔ   59 Ⓐ Ⓑ Ⓒ Ⓓ Ⓔ

52 Ⓐ Ⓑ Ⓒ Ⓓ Ⓔ   54 Ⓐ Ⓑ Ⓒ Ⓓ Ⓔ   56 Ⓐ Ⓑ Ⓒ Ⓓ Ⓔ   58 Ⓐ Ⓑ Ⓒ Ⓓ Ⓔ   60 Ⓐ Ⓑ Ⓒ Ⓓ Ⓔ

Electronics and Electrical Machinery

61 Ⓐ Ⓑ Ⓒ Ⓓ Ⓔ   63 Ⓐ Ⓑ Ⓒ Ⓓ Ⓔ   65 Ⓐ Ⓑ Ⓒ Ⓓ Ⓔ   67 Ⓐ Ⓑ Ⓒ Ⓓ Ⓔ   69 Ⓐ Ⓑ Ⓒ Ⓓ Ⓔ

62 Ⓐ Ⓑ Ⓒ Ⓓ Ⓔ   64 Ⓐ Ⓑ Ⓒ Ⓓ Ⓔ   66 Ⓐ Ⓑ Ⓒ Ⓓ Ⓔ   68 Ⓐ Ⓑ Ⓒ Ⓓ Ⓔ   70 Ⓐ Ⓑ Ⓒ Ⓓ Ⓔ

Fluid Mechanics

71 (A) (B) (C) (D) (E) 73 (A) (B) (C) (D) (E) 75 (A) (B) (C) (D) (E) 77 (A) (B) (C) (D) (E) 79 (A) (B) (C) (D) (E)

72 (A) (B) (C) (D) (E) 74 (A) (B) (C) (D) (E) 76 (A) (B) (C) (D) (E) 78 (A) (B) (C) (D) (E) 80 (A) (B) (C) (D) (E)

Mechanics of Materials

81 (A) (B) (C) (D) (E) 83 (A) (B) (C) (D) (E) 85 (A) (B) (C) (D) (E) 87 (A) (B) (C) (D) (E) 89 (A) (B) (C) (D) (E)

82 (A) (B) (C) (D) (E) 84 (A) (B) (C) (D) (E) 86 (A) (B) (C) (D) (E) 88 (A) (B) (C) (D) (E) 90 (A) (B) (C) (D) (E)

Thermodynamics/Heat Transfer

91 (A) (B) (C) (D) (E) 93 (A) (B) (C) (D) (E) 95 (A) (B) (C) (D) (E) 97 (A) (B) (C) (D) (E) 99 (A) (B) (C) (D) (E)

92 (A) (B) (C) (D) (E) 94 (A) (B) (C) (D) (E) 96 (A) (B) (C) (D) (E) 98 (A) (B) (C) (D) (E) 100 (A) (B) (C) (D) (E)

PRACTICE EXAMINATION 2
P.M. PART

Engineering Mechanics

The accompanying diagram applies to problems #1 through #7, inclusive.

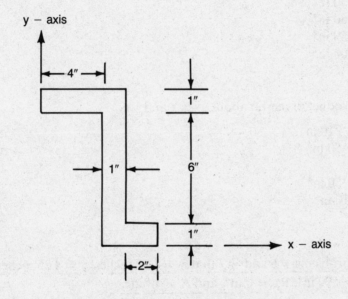

The section shown is referenced with respect to x and y axes.

1. The x location of the centroid, expressed in inches, is most nearly

   (A) 3.0
   (B) 4.0
   (C) 4.5
   (D) 4.6
   (E) 5.0

2. The y location of the centroid, expressed in inches, is most nearly

   (A) 3.0
   (B) 4.0
   (C) 4.5
   (D) 4.6
   (E) 5.0

3. The moment of inertia of the cross-section about the x-axis is most nearly

   (A) 50 in^4
   (B) 250 in^4
   (C) 260 in^4
   (D) 350 in^4
   (E) 400 in^4

4. The moment of inertia of the cross-section about the y-axis is

   (A) 50 in^4
   (B) 250 in^4
   (C) 260 in^4
   (D) 350 in^4
   (E) 400 in^4

5. The product of inertia about axes x and y is

   (A) -210 in^4
   (B) -50 in^4
   (C) 0
   (D) $+50$ in^4
   (E) 210 in^4

Assume for problems #6 and #7 that $\bar{x} = 4.25$ inches, $\bar{y} = 4.25$ inches, $I_{xx} = 500$ in^4, $I_{yy} = 500$ in^4, $P_{xy} = 0$ in^4, and $A = 14$ in^2.

6. Under these assumptions, the moment of inertia about the centroid is most nearly

   (A) 0
   (B) 125 in^4
   (C) 247 in^4
   (D) 253 in^4
   (E) 443 in^4

7. Under the same assumptions, the product of inertia about the centroid is

   (A) -250 in^4
   (B) -125 in^4
   (C) 0
   (D) $+125$ in^4
   (E) $+250$ in^4

The diagram and description below apply to problems #8 through #11, inclusive.

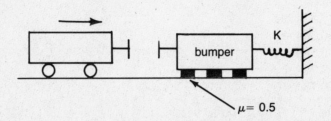

A 2000-pound track vehicle is to be stopped by a 10,000-pound bumper which is mounted on brake shoes having a coefficient of friction $\mu = 0.5$, and a spring which can exert either tension or compression. The vehicle and the bumper become linked upon impact. Their common velocity immediately after impact is 50 ft/sec. The rolling friction of the vehicle may be neglected. The spring constant is $K = 100,000$ lb/ft.

8. If the impact lasts 0.2 sec, the average force, in pounds, exerted between vehicle and bumper during this time is most nearly

    (A) 31,580
    (B) 32,385
    (C) 51,580
    (D) 53,385
    (E) 77,640

9. The maximum compression of the spring, expressed in feet, will be most nearly

    (A) 2.5
    (B) 3.0
    (C) 3.5
    (D) 4.0
    (E) 4.5

10. After the maximum compression, the spring will rebound. The bumper-cart assembly will then reach a maximum velocity when the spring compression, measured in feet, is most nearly

    (A) 0.05
    (B) 0.15
    (C) 0.20
    (D) 0.26
    (E) 0.35

11. It can be shown that the presence of the frictional force will not affect the period of vibrations following the impact. This period is most nearly

(A) 0.324 sec
(B) 0.384 sec
(C) 0.684 sec
(D) 0.724 sec
(E) 0.784 sec

The following diagram and description apply to problems #12 through #15, inclusive.

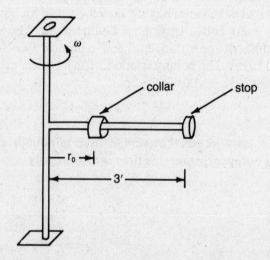

A vertical bar with a rigidly connected horizontal arm having a stop at its end can rotate freely about its axis as shown. The moment of inertia of the two bars and the stop about the axis of the vertical bar is 0.50 ft-lb/sec². A small cylindrical collar weighing 5 lb can slide without friction along the horizontal bar.

12. The collar is restrained by a string at a distance $r_0 = 1$ ft from the vertical axis. The entire assembly rotates with an angular velocity of 150 rpm. The power needed to bring the system from rest to this motion in 5 seconds is most nearly

(A) 0.029 HP
(B) 0.032 HP
(C) 0.29 HP
(D) 0.32 HP
(E) 2.90 HP

13. With the entire assembly rotating as specified in problem #12, and with no external forces exerted, the restraining string breaks. The radial velocity of the collar as it reaches the stop is most nearly

(A) 11 ft/sec

(B) 16 ft/sec
(C) 21 ft/sec
(D) 26 ft/sec
(E) 31 ft/sec

14. If a constant-speed motor is used to maintain the angular velocity of the assembly at 150 rpm, and if the string which keeps the collar at a distance r_0 should break, the law of variation of r with t will be

(A) linear
(B) quadratic
(C) sinusoidal
(D) exponential
(E) none of the above

15. Suppose a constant-speed motor maintains the assembly at an angular velocity of 300 rpm. The collar is restrained by a spring attached to the axis and having a spring constant $k = 60$ lb/ft and an undeformed length of $r_0 = 1$ ft. The resultant stretching of the spring will be most nearly

(A) 0.77 ft
(B) 1.27 ft
(C) 1.77 ft
(D) 2.00 ft
(E) 2.50 ft

Mathematics

16. A cable which is suspended between two support towers of equal height and spaced 200 feet apart hangs in the form of a catenary defined by $y = a \cosh(x/a)$, where x is measured in feet from the center of the span, y is the height in feet above a proper reference level, and a is equal to 250. No point along the cable may be less than 120 feet above the ground. The minimum height in feet required for the support towers, therefore, is most nearly

(A) 140
(B) 200
(C) 250
(D) 270
(E) 330

17. The indefinite integral $\int \left(\dfrac{x^2}{1 + x^2} \right) dx$ is equal to

   (A) $\ln(1 + x^2) + c$
   (B) $x - \tan^{-1} x + c$
   (C) $\dfrac{x^3}{3} \ln(1 + x^2) + c$
   (D) $\left[\dfrac{1 + x^2}{2} \right] \tan^{-1} x$
   (E) $\ln \left[\dfrac{x^2}{1 + x^2} \right] + c$

18. Given the differential equation $0.5 \dfrac{dy}{dx} + 30y = 60$, with the initial conditions that y equals 1.2 at x equal to zero. The solution of this equation when x is equal to 0.015 is most nearly

   (A) 0.8
   (B) 1.0
   (C) 1.2
   (D) 1.7
   (E) 2.0

19. The volume in the first (positive) octave only under the solid surface described by $z = 4 - 4x^2 - y^2$ is

   (A) 1/3
   (B) 2/3
   (C) 1
   (D) 2
   (E) 4

The following mathematical expression applies to problems #20 through #23, inclusive.

$$4x^2 + 32x - 9y^2 + 36y - 8 = 0$$

20. The graph of this mathematical expression on Cartesian coordinates is

   (A) a circle only
   (B) an ellipse only
   (C) a parabola only
   (D) a hyperbola only
   (E) none of the above

21. The Cartesian coordinates of the center of the curve defined in problem #20 (as well as the center of its transverse axis) are

    (A) $(0,0)$
    (B) $(4,-2)$
    (C) $(-4,2)$
    (D) $(3,2)$
    (E) $(9,4)$

22. Referring to the curve established in problem #20, the mathematical equation defining the transverse axis, which goes through both foci, is

    (A) $y = 0$
    (B) $y = 2$
    (C) $y = \dfrac{2x}{3} + \dfrac{14}{3}$
    (D) $xy = 1$
    (E) $y = \dfrac{4x}{9} + \dfrac{14}{3}$

23. The equation that describes one of the asymptotes to the curve defined in problem #20 is

    (A) $y = \frac{2}{3}x + \frac{14}{3}$
    (B) $y = \frac{4}{9}x + \frac{14}{3}$
    (C) $xy = 1$
    (D) $y = \frac{2}{3}x + \frac{8}{3}$
    (E) $y = \frac{4}{9}x + \frac{8}{3}$

24. The ratio of the average amplitude of the sine wave shown in the diagram to the average amplitude of the triangular wave is most nearly

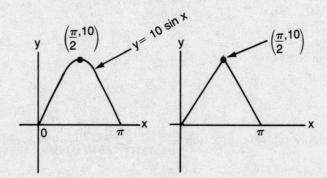

    (A) 1.1
    (B) 1.2
    (C) 1.3
    (D) 1.4
    (E) 1.5

25. Given is the Laplace expression $V(s) = \dfrac{5000(s + 1)}{s(s + 51)}$. In the time domain, the ratio of the initial value to the final value is

   (A) 1:5
   (B) 5:1
   (C) 5
   (D) 5000 : 51
   (E) 5000 : 98

26. The evaluation of the integral $\displaystyle\int_0^1 \dfrac{\log(2x + 1)}{2x + 1}\, dx$ is equal to

   (A) 1
   (B) $\log 3$
   (C) $0.25(\log 3)^2$
   (D) $0.50(\log 3)^2$
   (E) $2(\log 3)^2$

27. The repeating decimal 0.273273273... is exactly equal to a rational fraction which, when expressed in simplest form, has a numerator and denominator whose sum equals

   (A) 424
   (B) 591
   (C) 643
   (D) 717
   (E) 751

28. A solid cube measuring 5 feet along each edge just fits snugly inside a hollow sphere. The volume in cubic feet within this sphere that is not occupied by the cube is most nearly

   (A) 190
   (B) 320
   (C) 400
   (D) 520
   (E) 1440

29. The trigonometric expression $\dfrac{1 + \cos x}{\sin x} + \dfrac{\sin x}{1 + \cos x}$ is equal to

   (A) $2 \sin x$
   (B) $2 \cos x$
   (C) $2 \tan x$
   (D) $2 \sec x$
   (E) $2 \csc x$

30. Using only the first 2 terms of the appropriate Maclaurin series, the best accuracy can be realized for the computation of

    (A) $\sin 45°$
    (B) $\cos 45°$
    (C) $\varepsilon^{0.5}$
    (D) $\ln 1.1$
    (E) $\sinh 1.5$

Electrical Circuits

The following diagram applies to problems #31 through #37, inclusive.

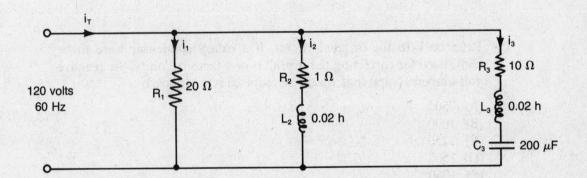

31. The total rms current i_T in amperes that is drawn by this circuit is most nearly

    (A) 10
    (B) 12
    (C) 15
    (D) 17
    (E) 20

32. The phase angle of the total current drawn by this circuit, considering the applied voltage to be a reference source whose phase angle is zero degrees, is most nearly

    (A) $-31°$
    (B) $-20°$
    (C) $0°$
    (D) $+20°$
    (E) $+31°$

33. Under steady-state conditions, the rms voltage across the capacitor C_3 is most nearly

    (A) 44
    (B) 52
    (C) 68
    (D) 120
    (E) 138

34. A bank of shunt capacitors is to be used to change the overall power factor from its present value to 0.95 lagging. The total value of capacitance in microfarads that must be connected directly across the voltage source to accomplish this is most nearly

    (A) 85
    (B) 107
    (C) 168
    (D) 231
    (E) 253

35. Refer back to the original circuit. If a rotary condenser were to be considered for correcting the overall power factor to unity, the reactive volt-amperes (vars) that would be required is most nearly

    (A) 750
    (B) 1000
    (C) 1250
    (D) 1500
    (E) 1750

36. Refer back to the original circuit. If a bank of ideal capacitors were connected directly across the voltage source such that the overall power factor were corrected to unity, the total rms current in amperes that would be drawn from the voltage source would be most nearly

    (A) 17
    (B) 20
    (C) 22
    (D) 25
    (E) 28

37. Refer back to the original circuit. How many light bulbs rated at 120 volts, 120 watts, and unity power factor must be connected across the voltage source in order for the overall power factor to be improved to approximately 0.91 lagging?

    (A) 4

(B) 6
(C) 10
(D) 15
(E) 23

38. A transformer whose overall efficiency is 75% consists of a primary winding having 200 turns and two independent secondary windings. Secondary #1 has 400 turns and is connected to a resistive load. Secondary #2 has 300 turns and is connected to a resistive load having half the resistance of that used in secondary #1. The value of load resistance in ohms that must be used for secondary #2, in order that the primary winding may draw exactly 20.0 amperes from a single-phase 120-volt 60-Hertz source, is most nearly

(A) 4 ohms
(B) 10 ohms
(C) 17 ohms
(D) 34 ohms
(E) 68 ohms

39. In the circuit shown, the switch is thrown to the DOWN position at time equals zero, after having been in the UP position for a very long time. Assume instantaneous switching. Also, assume an ideal diode with no voltage drop in the forward direction and infinite resistance in the reverse direction. When time equals 0.5 seconds, the value of resistance R in ohms that will cause the current in the inductor to subside to 2.0 amperes, is most nearly

(A) 5
(B) 9
(C) 12
(D) 15
(E) 25

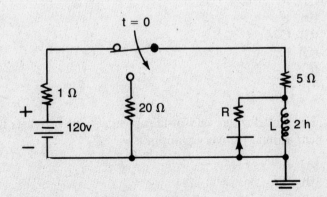

40. Referring to problem #39, the numerical value for the time constant τ in seconds for this circuit, starting with time equals zero, is most nearly

   (A) 0.04
   (B) 0.2
   (C) 3
   (D) 7
   (E) 13

Engineering Economics

The following paragraph applies to problems #41 through #50, inclusive.

Several possible models of new automation equipment have been proposed to reduce the production costs of an automotive parts manufacturer. The pertinent data on 5 different equipment models are presented in the table below. Each model produces identical units. Assume that the prevailing interest rate is 10% compounded annually.

	INITIAL COST	ESTIMATED LIFE	SALVAGE VALUE AT END OF LIFE	PRODUCTION RATE UNITS/YEAR	ANNUAL MAINTENANCE
Model A	$30,000	10 years	$2000	10,200	$1400
Model B	32,000	12 years	3000	10,400	1300
Model C	35,000	14 years	4000	10,600	1200
Model D	38,000	16 years	5000	10,800	1100
Model E	40,000	18 years	6000	11,000	1000

41. Neglecting salvage recovery values, the model exhibiting the lowest equivalent annual cost is

   (A) A
   (B) B
   (C) C
   (D) D
   (E) E

42. The model whose end-of-life salvage value provides the highest equivalent annual recovery amount is

   (A) A
   (B) B
   (C) C

(D) D
(E) E

43. The model with the lowest equivalent annual cost, taking salvage recovery into account, is

(A) A
(B) B
(C) C
(D) D
(E) E

44. Neglecting the costs of labor, maintenance, and materials, the model capable of manufacturing units having the lowest cost for a full year's production is

(A) A
(B) B
(C) C
(D) D
(E) E

45. If the additional costs of operation are $4000 annually per machine for labor, $0.30 per unit for material, and 80% of direct labor for overhead, the lowest break-even cost per unit that can be obtained is most nearly

(A) $1.48
(B) $1.51
(C) $1.53
(D) $1.56
(E) $1.61

46. The automation equipment model that provides the lowest manufacturing cost per unit is

(A) A
(B) B
(C) C
(D) D
(E) E

47. If model E were to be selected, the total depreciation at the end of 5 full years, using the sum-of-the-digits method, would be most nearly

(A) $13,500

(B) $14,500
(C) $15,100
(D) $15,900
(E) $16,900

48. If model B were to be selected, the book value at the end of the third year, using straight-line depreciation, would be most nearly

(A) $22,500
(B) $24,250
(C) $24,750
(D) $25,250
(E) $27,500

49. If Model D were to be selected, the annual sinking fund amount would be most nearly

(A) $920
(B) $980
(C) $1020
(D) $1150
(E) $1250

50. If the applicable interest rate should be changed from 10% compounded annually to 10% compounded continuously, the percentage decrease in the annual sinking fund amount calculated in problem #49 would be most nearly

(A) 3.2%
(B) 3.6%
(C) 4.0%
(D) 4.4%
(E) 5.0%

Computer Programming

The following BASIC program is used to reformat a listing, and applies to problems #51 through #59, inclusive.

```
10 INPUT "INPUT FILENAME:", FI$
20 OPEN OLD FI$ AS 1
30 OPEN NEW "TEMP" AS 2
40 INPUT "MESSAGE 1", EL
```

```
 50 INPUT "MESSAGE 2", L
 60 INPUT "MESSAGE 3", SP
 70 DIM E$(EL, L)
 80 ON ERROR GOTO 350
 90 FOR X = 1 TO EL
100 FOR Y = 1 TO L
110 INPUT LINE #1, I$
120 IF LEN(I$) > CM THEN CM = LEN(I$)
130 E$(X, Y) = I$
140 NEXT Y
150 NEXT X
160 T$ = ".TA"
170 FOR I = 1 TO EL
180 T$ = T$ + STR$((CM + SP) * I)
190 NEXT I
200 PRINT LINE #2, ".PL 0"
210 PRINT LINE #2, ".TC &"
220 PRINT LINE #2, T$
230 PRINT LINE #2, ".NF"
240 FOR Y = 1 TO L
250 L$ = ""
260 FOR X = 1 TO EL
270 IF X = 1 GOTO 290
280 L$ = L$ + "&"
290 L$ = L$ + E$(X, Y)
300 NEXT X
310 PRINT LINE #2, L$
320 NEXT Y
330 CLOSE 1, 2
340 EXIT
350 IF ERR < > 8 THEN ON ERROR GOTO 0
360 RESUME 160
```

51. How is the end-of-file condition handled?

    (A) The program terminates automatically when no more data are available.
    (B) The program branches to line 330 upon reaching the end-of-file.
    (C) An end-of-file condition causes an error code of "8", which causes the program to continue at line 160.
    (D) The program terminates automatically after reading 80 lines.
    (E) The program restores the input file to its starting position and begins reading it again.

52. Which line in the program determines the length of the longest line read from the input file?

    (A) 70

(B) 120
(C) 130
(D) 180
(E) 290

53. Array subscripts for the system on which this program runs start at the value "1". How many elements are in the array "E\$"?

(A) 10
(B) 20
(C) EL + L
(D) EL * L
(E) 2

54. If the input file does not run out of data, how many times will the INPUT LINE statement of line 110 be executed during this program?

(A) L
(B) EL
(C) L + EL
(D) L * EL
(E) 80

55. What action ensues if the line read in from the input file is blank?

(A) A blank line is immediately written to the output file.
(B) A null value is assigned to the appropriate element in array E\$.
(C) The program writes out the preceding line once again.
(D) A string of 40 blank spaces is written to the output file.
(E) None of the above.

56. What function do the three lines 170 through 190 perform?

(A) To assign the character whose ASCII value is CM + SP to the variable T\$.
(B) To assign to the variable T\$ a string that looks like: "T\$ + T\$ + T\$ + ···"
(C) To assign a string to T\$ which looks like: ".TA 1 5 7 8 ..."
(D) To assign a string to T\$ which looks like: ".TA 7 14 21 28 ..."
(E) To assign a string to T\$ which looks like: ".TA A B C D ..."

57. What function is performed by lines 240 through 320, inclusive?

(A) Creates strings (L\$) consisting of elements of array E\$, with the character "&" separating them, for output.

(B) Creates strings (L$) consisting of lines read from the input file and assigns them to elements of array E$.

(C) Creates strings (L$) composed of the characters "L" and "&" followed by a line read from the input file.

(D) Creates strings (L$) consisting of the character "L" followed by an element of the array E$.

(E) None of the above.

58. When, during the execution of the program, are lines 200 through 230, inclusive, executed?

(A) Every time a line is read from the input file.
(B) Once, before anything else is printed out.
(C) Once, after everything else is printed out.
(D) Every time "L" elements of array E$ have been assigned.
(E) None of the above.

59. What happens if the input file contains more data than the program expects to receive?

(A) The program terminates with an error before producing output.
(B) Output is produced which is "all garbled."
(C) The program "hangs."
(D) The program runs perfectly and handles all the data available.
(E) The program produces proper results, but only for the amount of input data expected.

60. Which of the following BASIC programs will set the fifty variables of an array "AA" to the sequential values 1 through 50, respectively? (Assume the first element of an array is identified by the subscript "1".)

```
(A) 10 N = 1
    20 LET AA(N) = N
    30 LET N = N + 1
    40 IF N > 50 THEN END
    50 GOTO 20
(B) 10 DIM AA(50)
    20 LET AA(X) = X
    30 LET AA(X + 1) = X + 1
    40 IF X > 50 THEN END
    50 GOTO 30
(C) 10 DIM AA(50)
    20 FOR Q = 1 TO 50
    30 LET AA(Q) = Q + 1
    40 NEXT Q
    50 END
```

```
(D) 10 DIM AA(50)
    20 FOR Z = 1 TO 50
    30 LET AA(Z + 1) = AA(Z)
    40 NEXT Z
    50 END
(E) 10 DIM AA(50)
    20 FOR X = 1 TO 50
    30 LET AA(X) = X
    40 NEXT X
    50 END
```

Electronics and Electrical Machinery

61. In the circuit shown, the step-down transformer has a 2 : 1 turns ratio. Under no load or very light load conditions, the DC voltage level at V_B is most nearly

    (A) 40 volts
    (B) 60 volts
    (C) 85 volts
    (D) 120 volts
    (E) 170 volts

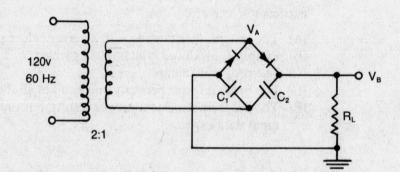

62. Refer to the circuit in problem #61. If R_L equals 1000 ohms and if C_1 equals C_2 equals 100 microfarads, the time constant of this circuit, expressed in seconds, is most nearly

    (A) 0.05
    (B) 0.1
    (C) 0.2
    (D) 0.3
    (E) 0.5

63. In the circuit described in problems #61 and #62, the peak-to-peak ripple voltage that will appear across each capacitor is most nearly

    (A) 1.5 volts
    (B) 3 volts
    (C) 6 volts
    (D) 12 volts
    (E) 24 volts

64. The 3-terminal integrated-circuit voltage-regulator unit by itself normally provides a DC output of 20 volts. Its quiescent current i_q is nominally 10 milliamperes. The resistors R_1 and R_2 are designed to increase this DC output to $+24$ volts. If the value of quiescent current should then change by 20%, the percentage error introduced in the 24-volt output voltage level will be most nearly

(A) 0.7%
(B) 1.5%
(C) 3%
(D) 6%
(E) 20%

65. The operational amplifier circuit shown in the diagram uses an integrated circuit "chip" having an extremely high input impedance. Its forward gain decreases, however, as the frequency of the input voltage increases. Assume that both resistors are ideally accurate. At a forward gain of 100, the percentage by which the output voltage level falls below its nominally ideal value is most nearly

(A) 0.1%
(B) 1%
(C) 1.5%
(D) 3%
(E) 5%

66. The integrated circuit "chip" used in the operational amplifier circuit shown in the diagram has a mid-band forward gain of 10,000 up to a frequency of 10 kilo-Hertz, and falls off at higher frequencies. Assume an infinitely high input impedance, and also assume that both resistors are ideally accurate. The decibel drop in forward gain that would cause the output voltage to drop to 11.0 volts is most nearly

(A) 25 dB
(B) 30 dB
(C) 35 dB
(D) 40 dB
(E) 45 dB

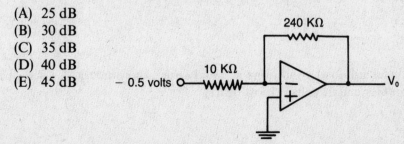

67. Three identical 10 KVA transformers, connected delta-to-delta, supply 440 volts to a three-phase balanced load. One of these transformers is removed, and the other two remain connected to the load, in an open delta configuration. The maximum KVA that can be thus supplied, without overloading either transformer, is most nearly

    (A) 14.1
    (B) 15.7
    (C) 17.3
    (D) 18.6
    (E) 20

The following statement applies to problems #68 through #70, inclusive.

A 220-volt 5-HP direct current compound motor, connected long shunt, operates at full-load with 85% efficiency. The shunt field resistance is 100 ohms, the series field resistance is 0.35 ohms, and the armature resistance is 0.64 ohms. A 3-point starting box is used so that this motor may be safely started under full-load conditions. System specifications require that the armature current shall not exceed 175% of its full-load value.

68. The total external resistance in ohms that will be required for this starter is most nearly

    (A) 4
    (B) 5
    (C) 6
    (D) 7
    (E) 8

69. The calculation of the individual resistance steps required in the starting box is formulated on the condition that while starting under full-load conditions, the armature current shall never exceed 175%, and shall never drop below 100%, of its full-load rating. As such, the minimum number of discrete resistance steps that will be required in the starting box in order for this motor to start safely and correctly will be

    (A) 1
    (B) 2
    (C) 3
    (D) 4
    (E) 5

70. Under full-load conditions at rated speed, the numerical value of the counter emf in volts is most nearly

    (A) 0

(B) 94
(C) 112
(D) 202
(E) 220

Fluid Mechanics

The diagram shown below applies to problems #71 through #75, inclusive.

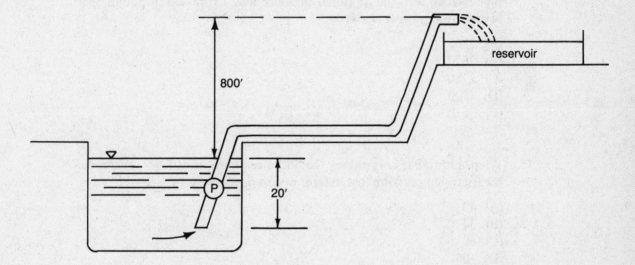

71. Determine the power required to pump 10 cfs of fresh water (62.4 lb/ft³) through a six-inch I.D. pipe to a reservoir 800 feet above the level of the lake. (Neglect friction.)

(A) 850 HP
(B) 890 HP
(C) 910 HP
(D) 950 HP
(E) 975 HP

72. If the pump is 10 feet below the level of the lake, what is the static pressure in psig at the upstream side of the pump? (Neglect frictional losses.)

(A) 4.3
(B) 0
(C) −4.3
(D) −8.6
(E) −13.1

73. If a 12-inch diameter pipe were to be selected for the application in problems #71 and #72, and if it were an uncoated cast iron (e = 0.01 inch) type, what would the Darcy friction factor be, assuming a water temperature of 60°F?

    (A) 0.015
    (B) 0.017
    (C) 0.019
    (D) 0.021
    (E) 0.023

74. If the 12-inch pipe of problem #73 is used, and if the total length of pipe is 1000 feet, the frictional pressure loss, expressed in pounds per square foot, is most nearly

    (A) 2360
    (B) 2670
    (C) 2980
    (D) 3300
    (E) 3610

75. What additional horsepower would be required in order to overcome the frictional pressure loss determined in problem #74?

    (A) 43
    (B) 54
    (C) 60
    (D) 108
    (E) 131

This paragraph and the diagram shown below apply to problems #76 through #80, inclusive.

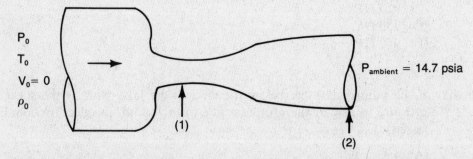

Air flows from left to right through a converging-diverging nozzle, from a source with stagnation conditions of $P_0 = 50$ psia and $T_0 = 530°R$. The throat (1) is 1 inch in diameter and the exit (2) is 2 inches in diameter. The air discharges to the atmosphere which is at an ambient pressure of 14.7 psia.

76. The velocity of the air at the throat V_1, in feet per second, is most nearly

    (A) 770
    (B) 1030
    (C) 1130
    (D) 1320
    (E) 1530

77. Assuming isentropic flow with no separation or shocks, the pressure at point (2) just prior to the exit of the nozzle, expressed in psia, is most nearly

    (A) 1.5
    (B) 4.7
    (C) 7.2
    (D) 14.7
    (E) 26.4

78. The corresponding Mach number at point (2), just prior to the exit of the nozzle, is most nearly

    (A) 0.15
    (B) 1.0
    (C) 2.2
    (D) 2.9
    (E) 3.1

79. If a normal shock should occur at point (2), the pressure measured in psia that would be realized just downstream of the shock would be most nearly

    (A) 2
    (B) 5
    (C) 7
    (D) 13
    (E) 15

80. Assuming the normal shock introduced in problem #79, the exit velocity of the air, measured in feet per second, would be most nearly

    (A) 530
    (B) 1030
    (C) 1130
    (D) 1870
    (E) 2010

Mechanics of Materials

The following problem statement applies to problems #81 through #90, inclusive.

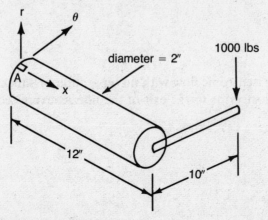

The 2″-diameter shaft illustrated above is rigidly supported at its left end and is subjected to a 1000-pound vertical load as shown, causing a torque and a bending moment. Assume that point A is at the top of the shaft where the horizontal shear stress due to flexure is zero.

81. The bending stress σ_x at A, expressed in pounds/square inch, is most nearly

   (A) 0
   (B) 6370
   (C) 7640
   (D) 12,740
   (E) 15,280

82. The shearing stress, in psi, due to torsion, $\tau_{x\theta}$ at A, is most nearly

   (A) 0
   (B) 6370
   (C) 7640
   (D) 12,740
   (E) 15,280

For problems #83 through #90 inclusive, assume the state of stress at A is given by

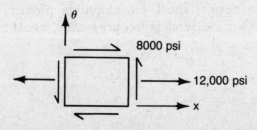

and that E $= 30 \times 10^6$ psi, $\gamma = 0.3$, and G $= 11.5 \times 10^6$ psi

83. The maximum normal stress, in psi, at A is most nearly

    (A) −4000
    (B) 6000
    (C) 10,000
    (D) 12,000
    (E) 16,000

84. The minimum normal stress, in psi, at A is most nearly

    (A) −12,000
    (B) −10,000
    (C) −4000
    (D) 0
    (E) 12,000

85. The maximum shearing stress in the x − θ plane at A, expressed in psi, in most nearly

    (A) −10,000
    (B) 0
    (C) 4000
    (D) 6000
    (E) 10,000

86. The maximum normal stress makes a counterclockwise angle with the x-axis which is most nearly equal to

    (A) 27°
    (B) 53°
    (C) 90°
    (D) 307°
    (E) 333°

87. The strain ε_x is most nearly

    (A) −120μ
    (B) 0μ
    (C) 320μ
    (D) 400μ
    (E) 700μ

88. The strain ε_θ is most nearly

    (A) −120μ
    (B) 0μ

(C) 320μ
(D) 400μ
(E) 700μ

89. The shear strain $\gamma_{x\theta}$ is most nearly

(A) -120μ
(B) 0μ
(C) 320μ
(D) 400μ
(E) 700μ

90. The axial strain ε_r is most nearly

(A) 0

(B) $\dfrac{\sigma_r}{E}$

(C) ε_θ

(D) $+\dfrac{\nu\sigma_x}{E}$

(E) $\sqrt{\left(\dfrac{\varepsilon_x - \varepsilon_\theta}{2}\right)^2 + \dfrac{\gamma_{r\theta}^2}{4}}$

Thermodynamics/Heat Transfer

The following diagram and description apply to problems #91 through #98, inclusive.

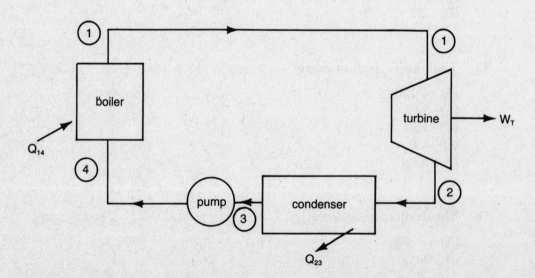

A steam power plant operates using a Rankine cycle with an isentropic pump and turbine. Assume that there are no frictional losses in the pipes, boiler, or condenser (i.e., constant pressure processes). The steam enters the turbine at 300 psia and 800°F and exhausts at one atmosphere. At the exit of the condenser, the quality (x) of the fluid is zero but it is not supercooled.

91. Referring to the steam power plant described, the values of enthalpy and entropy at the turbine inlet are, respectively:

   (A) h = 1202.8 Btu/lb; s = 1.5104 Btu/lb°R
   (B) h = 1202.8 Btu/lb; s = 1.7184 Btu/lb°R
   (C) h = 1416.4 Btu/lb; s = 1.6842 Btu/lb°R
   (D) h = 1420.6 Btu/lb; s = 1.7184 Btu/lb°R
   (E) h = 1424.8 Btu/lb; s = 1.7655 Btu/lb°R

92. Referring to the system described, the quality of the fluid at the inlet to the condenser is most nearly

   (A) 0.83
   (B) 0.91
   (C) 0.97
   (D) 0.99
   (E) 1.0

93. The output of the turbine is most nearly

   (A) 210 HP
   (B) 374 HP
   (C) 296 Btu/lb
   (D) 363 Btu/lb
   (E) 435 Btu/lb

94. How much heat, in Btu/lb, is extracted from the fluid in the condenser?

   (A) 806
   (B) 945
   (C) 960
   (D) 970
   (E) 1240

95. The power required to increase the fluid pressure from 15 psia to 300 psia is most nearly

   (A) 0.9 Btu/lb

(B) 3.8 Btu/lb
(C) 4.8 Btu/lb
(D) 102 Btu/lb
(E) 214 Btu/lb

96. The heat added to the fluid in the boiler, expressed in Btu/pound, is most nearly

(A) 945
(B) 970
(C) 1020
(D) 1240
(E) 1260

97. The cycle efficiency is most nearly

(A) 0.225
(B) 0.240
(C) 0.300
(D) 0.350
(E) 0.440

98. If the pump is driven from the turbine shaft, approximately what water/steam flow rate is required to drive an electric generator requiring 200 horsepower input? (Neglect gear losses.)

(A) 2 cfm
(B) 5 gpm
(C) 15 gpm
(D) 15 lb/min
(E) 29 lb/min

99. Air is cooled in a counterflow heat exchanger from 500°F to 160°F by water entering at 80°F and leaving at 200°F. What is the log mean temperature difference?

(A) 162°F
(B) 166°F
(C) 172°F
(D) 190°F
(E) 230°F

100. Equal quantities of 40°F air at 90% relative humidity and 80°F air at 90% relative humidity are mixed (with no change in pressure and no heat transfer). Which of the following best describes the resulting mixture?

(A) 60°F at 80% R.H.
(B) 60°F at 90% R.H.
(C) 60°F at 100% R.H.
(D) a mixture with a dew point of 58°F
(E) fog

Answer Key
Practice Examination 2—P.M. Part

Engineering Mechanics

1.	B	6.	C	11.	B
2.	D	7.	A	12.	A
3.	E	8.	E	13.	D
4.	C	9.	B	14.	D
5.	E	10.	A	15.	C

Mathematics

16.	A	21.	C	26.	C
17.	B	22.	B	27.	A
18.	D	23.	A	28.	C
19.	E	24.	C	29.	E
20.	D	25.	E	30.	D

Electrical Circuits

31.	E	35.	C	38.	D
32.	A	36.	A	39.	D
33.	E	37.	B	40.	B
34.	B				

Engineering Economics

41.	B	45.	A	48.	C
42.	C	46.	E	49.	A
43.	B	47.	D	50.	D
44.	E				

Computer Programming

51.	C	55.	B	58.	B
52.	B	56.	D	59.	E
53.	D	57.	A	60.	E
54.	D				

Electronics and Electrical Machinery

61.	E	65.	D	68.	C
62.	A	66.	B	69.	C
63.	E	67.	C	70.	D
64.	A				

Fluid Mechanics

71.	D	75.	B	78.	D
72.	E	76.	B	79.	E
73.	C	77.	A	80.	A
74.	C				

Mechanics of Materials

81.	E	85.	E	88.	A
82.	B	86.	A	89.	E
83.	E	87.	D	90.	C
84.	C				

Thermodynamics/Heat Transfer

91.	D	95.	A	98.	E
92.	C	96.	D	99.	B
93.	C	97.	B	100.	E
94.	B				

SOLUTIONS
PRACTICE EXAMINATION 2
P.M. PART

Engineering Mechanics

1. *Answer:* (B)

   Solution: $\bar{x} = \dfrac{\Sigma Ax}{\Sigma A} = \dfrac{4(2) + 8(4.5) + 2(6)}{4 + 8 + 2} = 4.0$ inches

2. *Answer:* (D)

   Solution: $\bar{y} = \dfrac{\Sigma Ay}{\Sigma A} = \dfrac{2(1/2) + 8(4) + 4(7.5)}{4 + 8 + 2} = 4.6$ inches

3. *Answer:* (E)

   Solution: $I = \Sigma I_{cg} + \Sigma Ad^2 = \dfrac{4(1)^3}{12} + \dfrac{1(8)^3}{12} + \dfrac{2(1)^3}{12} + 4(7.5)^2 + 8(4)^2 + 2(1/2)^2$

   $= 397$ in^4

4. *Answer:* (C)

   Solution: $I = \Sigma I_{cg} + \Sigma Ad^2 = \dfrac{1(4)^3}{12} + \dfrac{8(1)^3}{12} + \dfrac{1(2)^3}{12} + 4(2)^2 + 8(4.5)^2 + 2(6)^2$

   $= 257$ in^4

5. *Answer:* (E)

   Solution: $P_{xy} = 4(7.5)(2) + 8(4)(4.5) + 2(6)(1/2) = 210$ in^4

6. *Answer:* (C)

   Solution: $I_{cg} = I_{xx} - Ad^2 = 500 - 14(4.25)^2 = 247$ in^4

7. *Answer:* (A)

   Solution: $I_{xycg} = I_{xy} - Axy = 0 - (14)(4.25)^2 = -253$ in^4

8. *Answer:* (E)

   Solution: The velocity of the vehicle before impact is found from conservation of momentum.

   $$2000v = 12,000(50)$$

   $$v = 300 \text{ ft/sec}$$

   From the principle of impulse and momentum

   $$F_{avg}\Delta t = \frac{2000}{32.2}(300 - 50)$$

   $$F_{avg} = 77,640 \text{ lbs}$$

9. *Answer:* **(B)**

   Solution: From the work-energy principle

   $$1/2mv^2 = Fx + 1/2kx^2$$

   $$\frac{1}{2}\left(\frac{12,000}{32.2}\right)(50)^2 = \frac{1}{2}(10,000)\,(x) + \frac{1}{2}(100,000)\,x^2$$

   $$x^2 + 0.1x - 9.317 = 0$$

   $$x = 3.002 \text{ feet}$$

10. *Answer:* **(A)**

    Solution: v will be maximum when $a = \dfrac{dv}{dt} = 0$

    But $a = \dfrac{F}{m} = \dfrac{5000 - 100,000x}{m}$

    $$x = 0.05 \text{ ft}$$

11. *Answer:* **(B)**

    Solution: $\omega = \sqrt{\dfrac{k}{m}} \qquad T = \dfrac{2\pi}{\omega} = 2\pi\sqrt{\dfrac{m}{k}}$

    $$T = 2\pi\sqrt{\frac{12,000/32.2}{100,000}} = 0.384 \text{ sec}$$

12. *Answer:* **(A)**

    Solution: $\omega = \dfrac{150}{60} \times 2\pi = 15.708 \text{ rad/sec}$

    $$I = 0.50 + \frac{5}{32.2}(1)^2 = 0.6553$$

    $$\text{Power} = \frac{\Delta E}{\Delta t} = \frac{1}{2}\frac{I\omega^2}{\Delta r} = \frac{1}{550} \times \frac{1}{2} \times 0.6553 \times 15.708^2 \times \frac{1}{5}$$

    $$P = 0.0293 \text{ HP}$$

13. *Answer:* **(D)**

    Solution: Before the string breaks

    $$I_1 = 0.50 + \frac{5}{32.2}(1)^2 = 0.6553 \text{ ft-lb/sec}^2$$

    As the collar approaches the stop

    $$I_2 = 0.50 + \frac{5}{32.2}(3)^2 = 1.8975 \text{ ft-lb/sec}^2$$

    From conservation of angular momentum

    $$\omega_2 = \frac{I_1\omega_1}{I_2} = \frac{0.6553}{1.8975} \times 15.708 = 5.425 \text{ rad/sec}$$

From conservation of energy

$$\frac{1}{2}\left(\frac{5}{32.2}\right)(V_r^2) + \frac{1}{2}(1.8975)(5.425)^2 = \frac{1}{2}(0.6553)(15.708)^2$$

$V_r = 26.11$ ft/sec

Note that the contribution of the tangential component to the kinetic energy is included in $\frac{1}{2}I\omega^2$.

14. *Answer:* (D)

   Solution: Since there is no force in the radial direction, the radial acceleration will be zero.

   Therefore, $\dfrac{d^2r}{dt^2} - r\omega^2 = 0$

   $r = C_1\varepsilon^{wt} + C_2\varepsilon^{-wt}$

15. *Answer:* (C)

   Solution: From $k(r - r_0) = mr\omega^2$

   $$r = \frac{kr_0}{k - m\omega^2} = \frac{60(1)}{60 - \dfrac{5}{32.2}(15.708)^2} = 2.766 \text{ ft}$$

   thus $r - r_0 = 2.766 - 1 = 1.766$ feet

Mathematics

16. *Answer:* (A)

   Solution: At center of catenary, $x = 0$, $y = 250 \cosh 0 = 250$ feet
   At support tower, $x = 100$, $y = 250 \cosh(100/250) = 270.3$ feet
   ∴ Total sag in cable = $270.3 - 250 = 20.3$ feet
   ∴ Minimum height of tower = $120 + 20.3 = 140.3$ feet

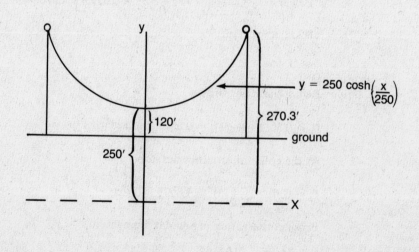

17. *Answer:* **(B)**

    Solution: $x = \tan \theta$

    $$dx = \sec^2 \theta \, d\theta$$

    $$1 + \tan^2 \theta = \sec^2 \theta$$

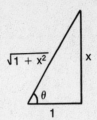

$$\int \left[\frac{x^2}{1 + x^2} \right] dx = \int \left[\frac{\tan^2 \theta}{1 + \tan^2 \theta} \right] \sec^2 \theta \, d\theta = \int \tan^2 \theta \, d\theta$$

$$= \int (\sec^2 \theta - 1) \, d\theta = \tan \theta - \theta + c$$

$$= x - \tan^{-1} x + c$$

18. *Answer:* **(D)**

    Solution: $\dfrac{dy}{dx} + 60y = 120$ with initial conditions $y = 1.2$ at $x = 0$

    $$sY(s) - 1.2 + 60Y(s) = \frac{120}{s}$$

    $$Y(s) = \frac{1.2s + 120}{s(s + 60)} = \frac{A}{s} + \frac{B}{s + 60}$$

    Using partial fraction expansion,

    $$A = \left. \frac{1.2s + 120}{s + 60} \right|_{s=0} = 2$$

    $$B = \left. \frac{1.2s + 120}{s} \right|_{s=-60} = \frac{-72 + 120}{-60} = \frac{-48}{60} = -0.8$$

    $$Y(s) = \frac{2}{s} - \frac{0.8}{s + 60}$$

    $$y = 2 - 0.8\varepsilon^{-60x}$$

    at $x = 0.015$, $\quad y = 2 - 0.8\varepsilon^{-0.9}$

    $$y = 1.67$$

19. *Answer:* **(E)**

    Solution: $V = \displaystyle\int_0^1 \int_0^{2-2x} (4 - 4x^2 - y^2) \, dx \, dy = \int_0^1 \left[4y - 4yx^2 - \frac{y^3}{3} \right]_0^{2-2x} dx$

    $$V = \int_0^1 \left[8 - 8x - 8x^2 + 8x^3 + \frac{1}{3}(2 - 2x)^3 \right] dx$$

    $$V = \left[8x - 4x^2 - \frac{8}{3}x^3 + 2x^4 - \frac{1}{24}(2 - 2x)^4 \right]_0^1$$

    $$V = \left[8 - 4 - \frac{8}{3} + 2 \right] - \left[\frac{-1}{24}(16) \right]$$

    $$V = 6 - \frac{8}{3} + \frac{2}{3} = 4$$

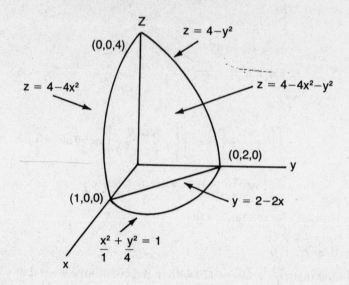

20. *Answer:* (D)

    Solution: Rearranging the terms of the given expression,

    $$4x^2 + 32x - 9y^2 + 36y - 8 = 0$$

    $$4[x^2 + 8x + 16] - 9[y^2 - 4y + 4] = 36$$

    $$\frac{(x + 4)^2}{9} - \frac{(y - 2)^2}{4} = 1$$

    This expression conforms to the classical equation of a hyperbola. Its center is located at $x = -4$ and $y = 2$, and its transverse axis (going through both foci) is horizontal.

21. *Answer:* (C)

    Solution: Refer to solution #20.

22. *Answer:* (B)

    Solution: Based on the parameters of the equation of the hyperbola, and based on the positive polarity of the x-term, the transverse axis is horizontal, passing through the center $(-4, 2)$. Its equation is $y = 2$.

23. *Answer:* (A)

    Solution: The equations for the asymptotes of a hyperbola are obtained by replacing the 1 in the standard form of the equation by zero, and solving for y. Specifically,

    $$\frac{(x + 4)^2}{9} - \frac{(y - 2)^2}{4} = 0$$

    $$\therefore 4(x + 4)^2 - 9(y - 2)^2 = 0$$

    $$(y - 2)^2 = \tfrac{4}{9}(x + 4)^2$$

    $$y - 2 = \pm\tfrac{2}{3}(x + 4)$$

$y - 2 = +\tfrac{2}{3}(x + 4)$	$y - 2 = -\tfrac{2}{3}(x + 4)$
$y = \tfrac{2}{3}x + \tfrac{14}{3}$	$y = -\tfrac{2}{3}x - \tfrac{2}{3}$

24 *Answer:* (C)

Solution: The average amplitude of the sine wave is

$$y_{avg} = \frac{1}{\pi} \int_0^\pi 10 \sin x \, dx = \frac{1}{\pi} (-10) \cos x \Big|_0^\pi$$

$$y_{avg} = -\frac{10}{\pi} [-1 - 1] = \frac{20}{\pi} = 6.366$$

The average amplitude of the triangular wave is

$$y_{avg} = \frac{1}{\pi/2} \int_0^{\pi/2} y \, dx = \frac{2}{\pi} \int_0^{\pi/2} \frac{10}{\pi/2} x \, dx = \frac{40}{\pi^2} \left[\frac{x^2}{2} \right]_0^{\pi/2} = \frac{20}{\pi^2} \left[\frac{\pi}{2} \right]^2 = 5$$

$$\text{Ratio} = \frac{6.366}{5} = 1.27$$

25. *Answer:* (E)

Solution: Using the Initial Value and the Final Value Theorems,

$$\text{Initial Value} = sV(s)|_{s=\infty} = \frac{s(5000)(s+1)}{s(s+51)} \Big|_{s=\infty} = \frac{5000 \left(\frac{s}{s} + \frac{1}{s} \right)}{\frac{s}{s} + \frac{51}{s}} \Bigg|_{s=\infty}$$

$$= \frac{5000}{1} = 5000$$

$$\text{Final Value} = sV(s)|_{s=0} = \frac{s(5000)(s+1)}{s(s+51)} \Big|_{s=0} = \frac{5000(1)}{51} = 98$$

$$\text{Ratio} = 5000:98$$

26. *Answer:* (C)

Solution: Let $u = \log(2x + 1)$

$$du = \left(\frac{1}{2x+1} \right) 2 \, dx$$

when $x = 1$, $u = \log 3$

when $x = 0$, $u = \log 1 = 0$

$$\int_0^1 \frac{\log(2x+1)}{2x+1} \, dx = \int_0^{\log 3} \frac{u \, du}{2} = \frac{1}{2} \left(\frac{u^2}{2} \right)_0^{\log 3}$$

$$= \frac{1}{4} [(\log 3)^2 - 0] = 0.25(\log 3)^2$$

27. *Answer:* (A)

Solution: The repeating decimal may be considered to be a geometric series consisting of

$$0.273(1) + 0.273(10)^{-3} + 0.273(10)^{-6} + \cdots$$

in which $a = 0.273$ and $r = 0.001$.
The sum of a geometric series is

$$S = \frac{a}{1-r} = \frac{0.273}{0.999} = \frac{91}{333}$$

$$N + D = 91 + 333 = 424$$

28. *Answer:* (C)

    Solution: Side of cube = 5 feet

    Diagonal across face of cube = $5\sqrt{2}$ feet

    Diagonal through center of cube = $(5\sqrt{2})\sqrt{2} = 10$ feet

    $\therefore$ Inner diameter of sphere = 10 feet

    Volume of sphere: $V_s = \frac{4}{3}\pi R^3 = \frac{4}{3}\pi(5)^3 = 523.6$ cubic feet

    Volume of cube: $V_c = (5)^3 = 125$ cubic feet

    Difference: $V_s - V_c = 523.6 - 125 = 398.6$ cubic feet

29. *Answer:* (E)

    Solution: $\dfrac{1 + \cos x}{\sin x} + \dfrac{\sin x}{1 + \cos x} = \dfrac{(1 + \cos x)^2 + \sin^2 x}{\sin x(1 + \cos x)}$

    $$= \frac{1 + 2\cos x + \cos^2 x + \sin^2 x}{\sin x(1 + \cos x)}$$

    $$= \frac{2 + 2\cos x}{\sin x(1 + \cos x)}$$

    $$= \frac{2}{\sin x} = 2\csc x$$

30. *Answer:* (D)

    Solution: (A) $\sin\dfrac{\pi}{4} = \dfrac{\pi}{4} - \dfrac{\left(\frac{\pi}{4}\right)^3}{3(2)} = 0.70465$, accuracy = 0.35%

    (B) $\cos\dfrac{\pi}{4} = 1 - \dfrac{\left(\frac{\pi}{4}\right)^2}{2} = 0.691575$, accuracy = 2.2%

    (C) $\varepsilon^{0.5} = 1 + 0.5 = 1.5$, accuracy = 9.0%

    (D) $\ln 1.1 = 0.1 - \dfrac{(0.1)^2}{2} = 0.095$, accuracy = 0.33%

    accuracy $= \dfrac{0.00031079}{0.09531079} \times 100 = 0.326\%$

    E. $\sinh 1.5 = 1.5 + \dfrac{(1.5)^3}{3(2)} = 2.0625$, accuracy = 3.1%

Electrical Circuits

31. *Answer:* (E)

    Solution: $I_{TOT} = I_1 + I_2 + I_3 = \dfrac{V}{Z_1} + \dfrac{V}{Z_2} + \dfrac{V}{Z_3}$

    $Z_1 = R_1 = 20\Omega$

    $Z_2 = R_2 + jX_{L2} = 1 + j7.54 = 7.606 \;\underline{|82.45°}$

    $Z_3 = R_3 + jX_{L3} - jX_{C3} = 10 + j7.54 - j13.26 = 11.52 \;\underline{|-29.77°}$

$$I_1 = \frac{120}{20} = 6 \; \underline{|0°}$$

$$I_2 = \frac{120 \; \underline{|0°}}{7.606 \; \underline{|82.45°}} = 15.78 \; \underline{|-82.45°} = 2.074 - j15.64$$

$$I_3 = \frac{120 \; \underline{|0°}}{11.52 \; \underline{|-29.77°}} = 10.42 \; \underline{|29.77°} = 9.042 + j5.172$$

$$I_{TOT} = 6 + 2.074 - j15.64 + 9.042 + j5.172$$

$$I_{TOT} = 17.12 - j10.47$$

$$I_{TOT} = 20.07 \; \underline{|-31.45°}$$

32. *Answer:* (A)
    Solution: Contained in the solution for problem #31.

33. *Answer:* (E)
    Solution: $V_c = i_3 X_c = 10.42(13.26) = 138.2$ volts
    Note that the partial resonance in branch #3 causes the voltage across the reactive elements to exceed the applied voltage.

34. *Answer:* (B)
    Solution: From solution #31,

    $$i_{TOT} = 17.12 - j10.47$$

    $$\cos \theta = 0.95, \theta = 18.195°$$

    $$\tan \theta = 0.3287 = \frac{a}{17.12}$$

    $$a = 5.627$$

    $$b = i_c = 10.47 - 5.63 = 4.84 \text{ amps}$$

    $$X_c = \frac{120 \text{ volts}}{j4.84} = 24.79\Omega$$

    $$C = \frac{1}{2\pi f X_c} = \frac{1}{2\pi(60)(24.79)} = 107\mu F$$

35. *Answer:* (C)
    Solution: The reactive current required = j10.47 amperes
    $$\therefore \text{ vars} = 120(10.47) = 1256 \text{ vars}$$

36. *Answer:* (A)
    Solution: From solution #31, the total current in the original circuit is:
    $$i_T = 20.07 \; \underline{|-31.45°} = 17.12 - j10.47$$
    Since the capacitive current will be equal and opposite to the $-j10.47$ term, the resultant i_T will be 17.12 amperes.

37. *Answer:* (B)

   Solution: The vector diagram of the total current is:

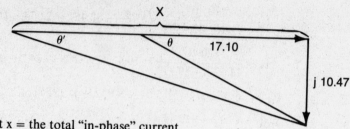

   Let x = the total "in-phase" current

   $$\theta' = \cos^{-1} 0.91 = 24.49°$$

   $$\tan \theta' = 0.4556 = \frac{10.47}{x}$$

   $$\therefore x = 22.98$$

   $$22.98 - 17.10 = 5.88 \text{ amperes}$$

   $$\therefore 6 \text{ bulbs required}$$

38. *Answer:* (D)

   Solution: The voltage at secondary #1 is $\frac{400}{200} \times 120$ volts = 240 volts

   The voltage at secondary #2 is $\frac{300}{200} \times 120$ volts = 180 volts

   The power into the primary is 120 volts × 20 amps = 2400 watts
   The total power transferred to the secondaries is 75% × 2400 watts
   = 1800 watts
   Since $P_{s1} + P_{s2} = 1800$,

   $$\frac{(240)^2}{R} + \frac{(180)^2}{R/2} = 1800$$

   $$\frac{R}{2} = 34 \text{ ohms}$$

39. *Answer:* (D)

   Solution: i_L at time = 0^- is + 20 amps

   i_L at time = 0^+ is + 20 amps

   i_L at time = ∞ is 0 amps

   $$i = 20\varepsilon^{-\frac{R_{eq}t}{L}}, \; 2 = 20\varepsilon^{-\frac{R_{eq}(0.5)}{2}}, \; R_{eq} = 9.210 \text{ ohms}$$

   R_{eq} is the parallel combination of R and 25Ω, as seen by the inductor.

   $$\therefore \frac{25R}{25 + R} = 9.210$$

   $$\therefore R = 14.6 \text{ ohms}$$

40. *Answer:* (B)

   Solution: The exponential factor $\varepsilon^{-\frac{t}{\tau}} = \varepsilon^{-\frac{Rt}{L}} = \varepsilon^{-\frac{t}{L/R}}$

$$\therefore \tau = \frac{L}{R} = \frac{2}{9.2} = 0.22 \text{ seconds}$$

Note that the 9.2 ohm resistance, as derived in problem #39, is the parallel combination of 25 ohms and the 14.6 ohm resistor which bypasses the inductor.

Engineering Economics

41. *Answer:* (B)

    Solution: Model A: $A_p = \$30,000(A/P, 10\%, 10)$
                        $A_p = 30,000(0.1627) = \$4881.$
              Model B: $A_p = \$32,000(A/P, 10\%, 12)$
                        $A_p = 32,000(0.1468) = \$4557.$
              Model C: $A_p = \$35,000(A/P, 10\%, 14)$
                        $A_p = 35,000(0.1357) = \$4750.$
              Model D: $A_p = \$38,000(A/P, 10\%, 16)$
                        $A_p = 38,000(0.1278) = \$4856.$
              Model E: $A_p = \$40,000(A/P, 10\%, 18)$
                        $A_p = 40,000(0.1219) = \$4876.$

42. *Answer:* (C)

    Solution: Model A: $A_s = \$2000(A/F, 10\%, 10)$
                        $A_s = 2000(0.0627) = \$125.40.$
              Model B: $A_s = \$3000(A/F, 10\%, 12)$
                        $A_s = 3000(0.0468) = \$140.40.$
              Model C: $A_s = \$4000(A/F, 10\%, 14)$
                        $A_s = 4000(0.0357) = \$142.80.$
              Model D: $A_s = \$5000(A/F, 10\%, 16)$
                        $A_s = 5000(0.0278) = \$139.00.$
              Model E: $A_s = \$6000(A/F, 10\%, 18)$
                        $A_s = 6000(0.0219) = \$131.40.$

43. *Answer:* (B)

    Solution: $A_{TOT} = A_p - A_s$, as calculated in the solutions to problems #41 and #42.
              Model A: $\$4881 - \$125 = \$4756.$
              Model B: $\$4698 - \$140 = \$4558.$
               Model C: $\$4750 - \$143 = \$4607.$
               Model D: $\$4856 - \$139 = \$4717.$
               Model E: $\$4876 - \$131 = \$4745.$

44. *Answer:* (E)

    Solution: Using the equivalent annual costs from the solution to problem #43,
              Model A: $\$4756 \div 10,200$ units/year = 46.6¢ per unit
              Model B: $\$4558 \div 10,400$ units/year = 43.8¢ per unit
              Model C: $\$4607 \div 10,600$ units/year = 43.5¢ per unit
              Model D: $\$4717 \div 10,800$ units/year = 43.7¢ per unit
              Model E: $\$4745 \div 11,000$ units/year = 43.1¢ per unit

45. *Answer:* (A)
  Solution: Model A: [\$4756 + 4000 + 4000(0.80) + 1400 + 0.30(10,200)]
          ÷ 10,200
          \$16,416 ÷ 10,200 = \$1.61
      Model B: [\$4558 + 4000(1.8) + 1300 + 0.30(10,400)] ÷ 10,400
          \$16,178 ÷ 10,400 = \$1.56
      Model C: [\$4607 + 4000(1.8) + 1200 + 0.30(10,600)] ÷ 10,600
          \$16,187 ÷ 10,600 = \$1.53
      Model D: [\$4717 + 4000(1.8) + 1100 + 0.30(10,800)] ÷ 10,800
          \$16,257 ÷ 10,800 = \$1.51
      Model E: [\$4745 + 4000(1.8) + 1000 + 0.30(11,000)] ÷ 11,000
          \$16,245 ÷ 11,000 = \$1.48

46. *Answer:* (E)
  Solution: Model E. Refer to the analysis in the solution of problem #45.

47. *Answer:* (D)
  Solution: Sum of digits $= \dfrac{N}{2}(A + L) = \dfrac{18}{2}(1 + 18) = 171$

  $$\text{Depreciation} = \frac{18 + 17 + 16 + 15 + 14}{171}[40,000 - 6000]$$

  $$= \frac{80}{171}[34,000] = \$15,906$$

48. *Answer:* (C)
  Solution: Annual depreciation $= \frac{1}{12}(32,000 - 3000) = \$2416.67$

      Book Value $= 32,000 - 3(2416.67) = \$24,750$

49. *Answer:* (A)
  Solution: S.F. $= (38,000 - 5000)(A/F, 10\%, 16)$
      S.F. $= (33,000)(0.0278) = \$918$

50. *Answer:* (D)
  Solution: Compounded annually, $A = 33,000\dfrac{0.1}{(1.1)^{16} - 1} = \$917.95$

  Compounded continuously, $A = 33,000\dfrac{\varepsilon^{0.1} - 1}{\varepsilon^{0.1(16)} - 1} = \$877.97$

  $$\text{Decrease} = \frac{917.95 - 877.97}{917.95} = 4.36\%$$

Computer Programming

51. *Answer:* (C)
  Solution: The ON ERROR statement in line 80 causes the program to branch to line 350 when an error (such as end-of-file) occurs. The error value for

end-of-file (in this system) is 8, and it therefore allows the program to fall through to line 360, which causes resumption of processing to take place at line 160.

52. *Answer:* (B)
    Solution: In line 120, the value of CM is zero (by default) when the program begins. Each time a line is read from the input file its length (LEN(I$)) is compared with CM (in line 120) and the length value is assigned to CM if it is larger than the "old" value of CM.

53. *Answer:* (D)
    Solution: The two-dimensional array is defined in line 70 as having EL elements in the first dimension and L elements in the second. The total number of elements is the product EL * L.

54. *Answer:* (D)
    Solution: Line 110 lies within two nested FOR loops beginning at line 90 and ending at line 150. The inner loop (lines 100 to 140) calls for execution of line 110 "L" times. The outer loop (lines 90 and 150) calls for execution of the inner loop "EL" times. The total number of executions of line 110 is therefore the product L * EL.

55. *Answer:* (B)
    Solution: Whatever the nature of a line read from the input file and assigned to the variable I$ (in line 110), line 130 assigns this value (null for a blank line) to the element of array E$ identified by the values of X and Y at the time of execution.

56. *Answer:* (D)
    Solution: The three lines 170 to 190 cause execution of line 180 "EL" times. The STR$ function in line 180 converts the numeric value of "(CM + SP) * I" to a string value for concatenation with the previous value of the string T$. Because CM, SP, and I are all positive whole numbers, the "numbers" concatenated with T$ must be related by some integer multiplier, as in answer (D).

57. *Answer:* (A)
    Solution: The variables X and Y serve as indices for two nested FOR loops and as subscripts for the array E$ in line 290. These two loops therefore treat every element of the array (of L by EL elements).
    The first element of the X (or EL) dimension is skipped by line 270. But from that point on, the program assigns a "&" character to the string L$, then concatenates with it all the elements from array E$ having the same Y (or L) subscript.

58. *Answer:* (B)
    Solution: Lines 200 through 230 are executed to print the character string shown on each line (200–230) before any other printout begins.

59. *Answer:* (E)
    Solution: The program expects enough data to fill the "EL" by "L" array. If less data is received, the program functions properly because of the ON ERROR statement in line 80, which causes program resumption at

line 160. If too much data is available, the excess is not read in, and the program continues at line 160 after filling the array via lines 90 through 150.

60. *Answer:* (E)
   Solution: (A) This program is missing the DIM statement.
   (B) In this program, x is not initialized to "1". Also, statements 30, 40, and 50 form an endless loop.
   (C) This program fails at line 30, when first element is set equal to 2. Every subsequent element is in excess by one.
   (D) This program skips the first element, and sets every succeeding element equal to the value of the first element.

Electronics and Electrical Machinery

61. *Answer:* (E)
   Solution: The circuit shown is actually that of a voltage doubler, as redrawn below, in which the voltage developed across each capacitor is added. Each capacitor charges to a peak voltage approximately equal to:

$$V_c \approx 120(\tfrac{1}{2})\sqrt{2} - 0.7 = 84.1 \text{ volts}$$

$$2V_c \approx 84.1(2) = 168.2 \text{ volts}$$

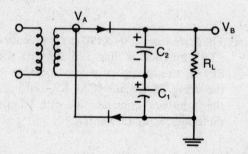

62. *Answer:* (A)
   Solution: Since C_1 and C_2 are in series, the net capacitance C_{TOT} equals

$$\frac{C_1 C_2}{C_1 + C_2} = 50 \text{ microfarads}$$

$$\therefore RC = 1000(50)(10)^{-6} = 0.05 \text{ seconds}$$

63. *Answer:* (E)
   Solution:
$$V_{C_1} = V_{MAX}\varepsilon^{-\frac{t}{RC}}$$

$$V_{C_1} = 84.1\varepsilon^{-\frac{1/60}{(1000)(50)(10)^{-6}}}$$

$$V_{C_1} = 84.1(0.7165) = 60.26 \text{ volts}$$

$$V_{ripple\ p-p} = 84.1 - 60.3 = 23.8 \text{ volts}$$

64. *Answer:* (A)

    Solution: Since the voltage regulator unit establishes 20 volts between V_0 and A, point A is 4 volts above ground. The current i_1 in resistor R_1 is normally $i_1 = \dfrac{20v}{500} = 40$ milliamperes.

    Since i_q is nominally 10 milliamperes, the current i_2 through resistor R_2 is $i_2 = i_1 + i_q = 40 + 10 = 50$ milliamperes

    $$\therefore R_2 = \frac{4v}{50ma} = 80\Omega$$

    For $\Delta i_q = 20\%$, $i_q = \pm 2$ milliamperes

    $$\therefore \Delta V_0 = \Delta i_q R_2 = (0.002)(80) = 0.16 \text{ volts}$$

    $$\% \text{ error} = \frac{0.16}{24} = 0.67\%$$

65. *Answer:* (D)

    Solution: $V_0 = -V_{IN} \left[\dfrac{R_F}{R_i + \dfrac{1}{A}(R_F + R_i)} \right] = +6 \left[\dfrac{20K}{10K + \dfrac{1}{100}(30K)} \right]$

    $V_0 = 11.65$ volts

    $$\frac{12 - 11.65}{12} = 2.9\%$$

66. *Answer:* (B)

    Solution: $V_0 = 11 = 0.5 \left[\dfrac{240K}{10K + \dfrac{1}{A}(250K)} \right] = \dfrac{120}{10 + \dfrac{250}{A}}$

    Solving, $A = 275$

    $dB = 20 \log 275 = 48.79$ dB

    $dB \text{ loss} = 80 \text{ dB} - 48.79 \text{ dB} = 31.21 \text{ dB}$

67. *Answer:* (C)

    Solution: Normally, in a closed delta, $I_L = I_\phi \sqrt{3}$. In an open delta, however, I_L is reduced, since I_L equals I_ϕ. The rated secondary current per transformer is $\dfrac{10 \text{ KVA}}{440 \text{ volts}} = 22.73$ amperes. Since the line current is limited to this value, the total KVA is not $3_{V_L} I_\phi$, but rather:

    Total KVA $= \sqrt{3} V_L I_L = \sqrt{3}(440)(22.73) = 17.32$ KVA,

    which is equal to 57.7% of the original capability.

68. *Answer:* (C)

    Solution: $P_{IN} = \dfrac{P_{OUT}}{0.85} = \dfrac{5(746)}{0.85} = 4388 \text{ watts}$

    $I_{TOT} = \dfrac{4388}{220} = 19.95 \text{ amperes}$

$$I_A \text{ at full load} = I_{TOT} - I_f = 19.95 - \frac{220}{100} = 17.75 \text{ amperes}$$

$$175\% \, I_A \approx 31.06 \text{ amperes}$$

$$R_{TOT} = \frac{220v}{31.06} = 7.083\Omega$$

$$\therefore R_{EXT} = R_{TOT} - R_A - R_i = 7.083 - 0.64 - 0.35 = 6.09\Omega$$

69. *Answer:* (C)
    Solution: Back EMF $= V - I_A(R_A + R_s + R_{EXT})$

$$= 220 - 17.75(0.64 + 0.35 + 6.09) = 125.7 \text{ volts}$$

$$\frac{(220 - 125.7) \text{ volts}}{31.06 \text{ amps}} = 3.036\Omega - 0.99\Omega = 2.046\Omega$$

$$\text{Back EMF} = 220 - 17.75(3.036) = 166.1 \text{ volts}$$

$$\frac{(220 - 166.1) \text{ volts}}{31.06 \text{ amps}} = 1.73\Omega - 0.99\Omega = 0.74\Omega$$

$$\text{Back EMF} = 220 - 17.75(1.73) = 189.3 \text{ volts}$$

$$\frac{(220 - 189.3) \text{ volts}}{31.06 \text{ amps}} = 0.99\Omega - 0.99\Omega = 0\Omega$$

NOTE: See solution to problem #68 for calculation of $R_{EXT} = 6.09\Omega$

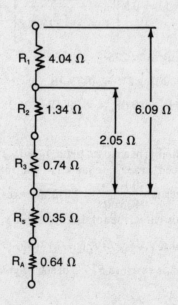

70. *Answer:* (D)
    Solution: Counter EMF $=$ Applied voltage $- I_A(R_A + R_s)$

$$\text{CEMF} = 220 - 17.75(0.64 + 0.35) = 202 \text{ volts}$$

Fluid Mechanics

71. *Answer:* (D)

Solution: $HP = \dfrac{Q\Delta P}{550} = \dfrac{Q[\rho h + \rho V^2]}{550}$

$$V = \frac{Q}{A} = \frac{10 \text{ cfs}}{0.196 \text{ ft}^2} = 50.93 \text{ fps}$$

$$1/2\rho V^2 = \frac{62.4(50.93)^2}{2(32.2)} = 2510 \text{ psf}$$

$$\rho h = 62.4(800) = 49,920 \text{ psf}$$

$$HP = \frac{(10)(49,920 + 2510)}{550} = 953$$

72. *Answer:* (E)

Solution: $P_s = \rho h - \dfrac{1}{2}\rho V^2$

$$= \frac{(62.4)(10)}{144} - \frac{(62.4)(50.9)^2}{2(32.2)144}$$

$$= 4.33 - 17.45$$

$$P_s = -13.1 \text{ psig}$$

73. *Answer:* (C)

Solution: $V = \dfrac{Q}{A} = \dfrac{10 \text{ cfs}}{\pi(\frac{1}{2})^2 \text{ ft}^2} = 12.73 \text{ ft/sec}$

$$\frac{e}{d} = \frac{0.01 \text{ inches}}{12 \text{ inches}} = 0.000833$$

$$N_R = \frac{\rho d V}{\mu} = \frac{(62.4 \text{ lb/ft}^3)(1.0 \text{ ft})(12.73 \text{ ft/sec})}{(32.2 \text{ ft/sec}^2)(2.359 \times 10^{-5} \text{ lb-sec/ft})}$$

$$N_R = 1.046(10)^6$$

From graphs of friction factor vs Reynolds Number, for varying roughness factors (e/d),

$$f = 0.019$$

74. *Answer:* (C)

Solution: For the 12-inch pipe,

$$\frac{1}{2}\rho V^2 = \frac{1}{2}\left(\frac{62.4}{32.2}\right)(12.73)^2 = 157.0 \text{ lbs/sq. ft.}$$

$$\Delta P = \left[\frac{fl}{d}\right]\left[\frac{1}{2}\rho V^2\right] = \left[\frac{0.019(1000)}{1.0}\right][157.0] = 2983 \text{ psf}$$

75. *Answer:* **(B)**

    Solution: The increase in horsepower is

    $$\Delta HP = \frac{Q\Delta P}{550} = \frac{(10 \text{ cfs})(2983 \text{ psf})}{550}$$

    $$\Delta HP = 54 \text{ HP}$$

76. *Answer:* **(B)**

    Solution: $T_1 = \dfrac{T_0}{1 + \left(\dfrac{k-1}{2}\right)M^2} = \dfrac{530}{1 + \left(\dfrac{1.4-1}{2}\right)(1)^2} = 441.7°R$

    $$V_1 = \sqrt{kgRT} = \sqrt{(1.4)(32.2)(53.35)(441.7)}$$

    $$V_1 = 1031 \text{ fps}$$

77. *Answer:* **(A)**

    Solution: The desired pressure may be determined directly from a table of "Flow Parameters versus Mach Number for Supersonic Flow." Alternatively, it may also be determined analytically from the equation

    $$\frac{A_1}{A_2} = \frac{\left[1 - \left(\dfrac{p}{p_0}\right)^{\frac{\gamma-1}{\gamma}}\right]^{1/2}\left(\dfrac{p}{p_0}\right)^{1/\gamma}}{\left(\dfrac{\gamma-1}{2}\right)^{1/2}\left(\dfrac{2}{\gamma+1}\right)^{\frac{\gamma+1}{2(\gamma-1)}}}$$

    $$\frac{1}{4} = \frac{\left[1 - \left(\dfrac{p}{p_0}\right)^{\frac{1.4-1}{1.4}}\right]^{1/2}\left(\dfrac{p}{p_0}\right)^{1/1.4}}{\left(\dfrac{1.4-1}{2}\right)^{1/2}\left(\dfrac{2}{1.4+1}\right)^{\frac{1.4+1}{2(1.4-1)}}}$$

    $$\frac{p}{p_0} = 0.02980, \quad p = 1.49 \text{ psia}$$

78. *Answer:* **(D)**

    Solution: The desired Mach number may be determined directly from a table of "Flow Parameters versus Mach Number for Supersonic Flow," Table III. It may also be determined analytically from the equation

    $$\left(\frac{A_2}{A_1}\right)^2 = \frac{1}{M^2}\left[\left(\frac{2}{\gamma+1}\right)\left(1 + \frac{\gamma-1}{2}M^2\right)\right]^{\frac{\gamma+1}{\gamma-1}}$$

    With $A_2 = 4A_1$, and with $\gamma = 1.4$, solving for M yields M = 2.94

79. *Answer:* **(E)**

    Solution: The desired pressure may be determined directly from tables of "Parameters for Shock Flow." Alternatively, it may be derived analytically from the following equation, in which the subscripts a and b refer to locations just upstream and just downstream from the shock at point 2, respectively.

$$\frac{p_{2b}}{p_{2a}} = 1 + \frac{2\gamma}{\gamma + 1}(M_{2a}{}^2 - 1)$$

At $M = 2.94$ and $\gamma = 1.4$, $p_{2b}/p_{2a} = 9.918$, and $p_{2b} = 1.49(9.918) = 14.8$ psia

80. *Answer:* (A)

Solution: From the table used in solution #78, at $M = 2.94$,

$T/T_0 = 0.3665$ and $T = 194.2°R$

From the table used in solution #79, at $M = 2.94$, the temperature ratio across a normal shock is 2.609, and therefore

$T = (194.2°R)(2.609) = 506.8°R$

The resulting Mach number is 0.4788.

$V = M\sqrt{kgRT} = 0.4788\sqrt{(1.4)(32.2)(53.35)(506.8)}$
$V = 528.6$ feet/second

Mechanics of Materials

81. *Answer:* (E)

Solution: $\sigma_x = \dfrac{Mc}{I} = \dfrac{1000 \times 12 \times 1}{\dfrac{\pi(1)^4}{4}} = 15{,}280$ psi

82. *Answer:* (B)

Solution: $\tau_{x\theta} = \dfrac{Tr}{J} = \dfrac{1000 \times 10 \times 1}{\dfrac{\pi(1)^4}{2}} = 6370$ psi

83. *Answer:* (E)

Solution: $\sigma_{max} = \dfrac{\sigma_x + \sigma_y}{2} + \sqrt{\left(\dfrac{\sigma_x - \sigma_y}{2}\right)^2 + \tau_{xy}{}^2}$

$= 6000 + \sqrt{(6000)^2 + (8000)^2}$

$\sigma_{max} = 6000 + 10{,}000 = 16{,}000$ psi

84. *Answer:* (C)

Solution: $\sigma_{min} = \dfrac{\sigma_x + \sigma_y}{2} - \sqrt{\left(\dfrac{\sigma_x - \sigma_y{}^2}{2}\right) + \tau_{xy}{}^2} = 6000 - \sqrt{(6000)^2 + (8000)^2}$

$\sigma_{min} = 6000 - 10{,}000 = -4000$ psi

85. *Answer:* (E)

Solution: $\tau_{max} = \sqrt{\left(\dfrac{\sigma_x - \sigma_y{}^2}{2}\right) + \tau_{xy}{}^2} = \sqrt{(6000)^2 + (8000)^2} = 10{,}000$ psi

86. *Answer:* (A)

    Solution: $\tan 2\theta_p = \dfrac{2\tau_{xy}}{\sigma_x - \sigma_y} = \dfrac{2(8000)}{6000}$

    $2\theta_p = 53.1°$

    $\theta_p = 26.6°$

87. *Answer:* (D)

    Solution: $\varepsilon_x = \dfrac{\sigma_x}{E} - \dfrac{v\sigma_y}{E} = \dfrac{12{,}000}{30 \times 10^6} = 400 \times 10^{-6} \text{ in/in} = 400\mu$

88. *Answer:* (A)

    Solution: $\varepsilon_\theta = \dfrac{-v\sigma_x}{E} = \dfrac{-0.3(12{,}000)}{30 \times 10^6} = -120 \times 10^{-6} \text{ in/in} = -120\mu$

89. *Answer:* (E)

    Solution: $\gamma_{x\theta} = \dfrac{\tau_{x\theta}}{G} = \dfrac{8000}{11.5 \times 10^6} = 696 \times 10^{-6} = 696\mu$

90. *Answer:* (C)

    Solution: $\varepsilon_r = -\dfrac{v\sigma_x}{E} = \varepsilon_\theta$

Thermodynamics/Heat Transfer

91. *Answer:* (D)

    Solution: From "Thermodynamic Properties of Steam" Keenan and Keyes (Properties of Superheated Steam) at 800°F and 300 psia

    h = 1420.6 Btu/lb

    s = 1.7184 Btu/lb°R

92. *Answer:* (C)

    Solution: Based on an isentropic expansion through the turbine, the pressure out of the turbine is 14.7 psia and the entropy is 1.7184 Btu/lb°R. From the "Dry Saturated Steam: Pressure Table" at a pressure of 14.7 psia, the saturated liquid entropy is 0.312 and the $\Delta S_{fg} = 1.4446$.

    Quality $(X_2) = \dfrac{1.7184 - 0.3120}{1.4446} = 0.9736$

93. *Answer:* (C)

    Solution: From the same table used in the solution to problem #92, the enthalpy out of the turbine is:

    $h_2 = h_f + x(\Delta h_{fg})$ at 14.7 psia

    $h_2 = 180.07 + 0.9736(970.3)$

    $h_2 = 1124.7$ Btu/lb

The change in enthalpy equals the work for adiabatic conditions:

$W_T = h_1 - h_2 = 1420.6 - 1124.7 = 295.9$ Btu/lb

where $h_1 = 1420.6$ Btu/lb from problem #91.

94. *Answer:* (B)

   Solution: From the steam table used in problem #92, the enthalpy out of the condenser (at 14.7 psia and saturated liquid, x = 0) is:

   $h_3 = 180.07$ Btu/lb

   $Q_{23} = h_2 - h_3 = 1124.7 - 180.07$

   $Q_{23} = 944.63$ Btu/lb

95. *Answer:* (A)

   Solution: For a reversible process: $T\,ds = dh$
   and since the pump is isentropic: $dh = v\,dp$
   For a liquid v = constant and from the steam table at 14.7 psia,
   $v_p = 0.01672$

   $\Delta h = v(p_4 - p_3)$

   $\Delta h = 0.01672\, \dfrac{\text{ft}^3}{\text{lb}}\, (300 - 14.7)\, \text{psia} \times 144\, \dfrac{\text{psfa}}{\text{psia}} \times \dfrac{1\ \text{Btu}}{778\ \text{ft-lb}}$

   $\Delta h = 0.8829$ Btu/lb

96. *Answer:* (D)

   Solution: The enthalpy out of the pump from problem #95 is:

   $h_4 = h_3 + \Delta h_{3-4}$

   $h_4 = 180.07 + 0.88 = 180.95$ Btu/lb

   The change in enthalpy from 4 to 1 is the heat required from the boiler:

   $h_1 = 1420.6$ Btu/lb

   $Q_{14} = 1420.6 - 180.95 = 1239.65$ Btu/lb

97. *Answer:* (B)

   Solution: The cycle efficiency is equal to the net work output divided by the heat input:

   $$\eta = \frac{W_T - W_P}{Q_{14}}$$

   From the solutions to previous problems, $W_T = 295.9$ Btu/lb, $W_p = 0.88$ Btu/lb, and $Q_{14} = 1239.65$ Btu/lb

   $$\therefore \eta = \frac{295.9 - 0.88}{1239.65} = 0.238$$

98. *Answer:* (E)

   Solution: The net power output is $W_T - W_P$
   As in the solution to problem #97,

   $W_T - W_P = 295.9 - 0.88 = 295.02$ Btu/lb

$$HP = \frac{\dot{W}(\text{lb/min})W_{NET}(\text{Btu/lb})}{33,000 \text{ ft-lb/min/HP}} \times \frac{778 \text{ ft-lb}}{\text{Btu}}$$

$$\dot{W} = \frac{(33,000)(200)}{(295.02)(778)}$$

$$\dot{W} = 28.75 \text{ lb/min}$$

99. *Answer:* (B)

   Solution: The log mean temperature difference (Δt) is defined as:

$$\Delta t_m = \frac{\Delta t_a - \Delta t_b}{\ln \Delta t_a / \Delta t_b}$$

where Δt_a is the inlet Δt ($500°F - 200°F = 300°F$)
and Δt_b is the exit Δt ($160°F - 80°F = 80°F$)

$$\Delta t_m = \frac{300 - 80}{\ln 300/80} = 166°F$$

100. *Answer:* (E)

   Solution: The simplest solution is to draw a straight line between the 40°F and 80°F conditions on a psychrometric chart. The midpoint of this line (equal quantities) is to the left of the saturation line, hence liquid water will condense (fog). Alternatively, from the psychrometric chart:

   At 40°F & 90% RH, w_s = 0.0047 lb water/lb dry air
   h = 14.7 Btu/lb

   At 80°F & 90% RH, w_s = 0.020 lb water/lb dry air
   h = 41.14 Btu/lb

   This mixture consists of: w_s = 0.01235 lb H_2O/lb air
   h = 27.92 Btu/lb

   The saturated temperature (wet bulb) corresponding to 0.01235 lb H_2O/lb air is 63°F with h = 28.6 Btu/lb. Since the enthalpy of the mixture is less than the saturated value, some of the water vapor will condense, resulting in a fog condition.